David George Ritchie

Natural rights

A criticism of some political and ethical conceptions

David George Ritchie

Natural rights
A criticism of some political and ethical conceptions

ISBN/EAN: 9783337134617

Printed in Europe, USA, Canada, Australia, Japan

Cover: Foto ©Suzi / pixelio.de

More available books at **www.hansebooks.com**

THE LIBRARY OF PHILOSOPHY.

THE LIBRARY OF PHILOSOPHY is in the first instance a contribution to the History of Thought. While
much has been done in England in tracing the course of evolution in nature, history, religion, and morality, comparatively
little has been done in tracing the development of Thought
upon these and kindred subjects, and yet "the evolution of
opinion is part of the whole evolution."

This Library will deal mainly with Modern Philosophy,
partly because Ancient Philosophy has already had a fair
share of attention in this country through the labours of Grote,
Ferrier, and others, and more recently through translations
from Zeller ; partly because the Library does not profess to
give a complete history of thought.

By the co-operation of different writers in carrying out this
plan, it is hoped that a completeness and thoroughness of treatment otherwise unattainable will be secured. It is believed,
also, that from writers mainly English and American fuller
consideration of English Philosophy than it has hitherto received from the great German Histories of Philosophy may
be looked for. In the departments of Ethics, Economics, and
Politics, for instance, the contributions of English writers to
the common stock of theoretic discussion have been especially
valuable, and these subjects will accordingly have special prominence in this undertaking.

Another feature in the plan of the Library is its arrangement according to subjects rather than authors and dates,
enabling the writers to follow out and exhibit in a way
hitherto unattempted the results of the logical development of
particular lines of thought.

The historical portion of the Library is divided into two
sections, of which the first contains works upon the development of particular schools of Philosophy, while the second ex-
hibits the history of theory in particular departments. The
third series contains original contributions to Philosophy, and
the fourth translations of valuable foreign works.

To these has been added, by way of Introduction to the
whole Library, an English translation of Erdmann's " History
of Philosophy," long since recognised in Germany as the
best.

J. H. MUIRHEAD,

General Editor.

ALREADY PUBLISHED.

THE HISTORY OF PHILOSOPHY. By DR. JOHANN EDUARD ERDMANN.
English Translation. Edited by WILLISTON S. HOUGH, M.Ph., Professor of
Mental and Moral Philosophy and Logic in the University of Minnesota.
In 3 vols., medium 8vo, cloth.

    Vol. I. Ancient and Mediæval Philosophy, 15s. .   .   . *Third Edition.*
    Vol. II. Modern Philosophy, 15s. .   .   .   .   . *Third Edition.*
    Vol. III. Modern Philosophy since Hegel, 12s. .   .   . *Third Edition.*

THE HISTORY OF ÆSTHETIC. By BERNARD BOSANQUET, M.A., LL.D., late Fellow of
University College, Oxford.   [SECOND SERIES.
THE DEVELOPMENT OF RATIONAL THEOLOGY since Kant. By PROFESSOR OTTO
PFLEIDERER, of Berlin.   [SECOND SERIES. *Second Edition.*
PHILOSOPHY AND POLITICAL ECONOMY IN SOME OF THEIR HISTORICAL RELATIONS.
By JAMES BONAR, M.A., LL.D.   [SECOND SERIES.
APPEARANCE AND REALITY. By F. H. BRADLEY, M.A., Fellow of Merton College,
Oxford.
NATURAL RIGHTS. By DAVID G. RITCHIE, Professor of Logic and Metaphysics in the
University of St. Andrews.   [THIRD SERIES.
SIGWART'S LOGIC. Translated by HELEN DENDY. 2 vols.   [FOURTH SERIES.

LIST OF WORKS IN PREPARATION.

FIRST SERIES.

EARLY IDEALISM : Descartes to Leibnitz. By W. L. COURTNEY, M.A., LL.D. (St.
Andrews), Fellow of New College, Oxford.
GERMAN IDEALISTS : Kant to Hegel. By WM. WALLACE, M.A., Whyte Professor of
Moral Philosophy, University of Oxford.
MODERN REALISTS : Leibnitz, Herbart, Lotze. By ANDREW SETH, M.A., Professor of
Logic and English Literature, University of Edinburgh.
SENSATIONALISTS : Locke to Mill. By W. S. HOUGH, M.Ph., Professor of Mental and
Moral Philosophy, University of Minnesota, U.S.A.
THE UTILITARIANS : Hume to Contemporary Writers. By W. R. SORLEY, M.A., Fellow
of Trinity College, Cambridge, and Professor of Philosophy in University College, Cardiff.
PRINCIPLE OF EVOLUTION IN ITS SCIENTIFIC AND PHILOSOPHICAL ASPECTS. By JOHN
WATSON, LL.D., Professor of Moral Philosophy, University of Queen's College,
Kingston, Canada.

SECOND SERIES.

THE HISTORY OF PSYCHOLOGY : Empirical and Rational. By ROBERT ADAMSON, M.A.,
LL.D., Professor of Logic, University of Aberdeen.
THE HISTORY OF POLITICAL PHILOSOPHY. By D. G. RITCHIE, M.A., Professor of
Logic and Metaphysics in the University of St. Andrews, and J. H. MUIRHEAD,
M.A., Lecturer in Philosophy, Royal Holloway College, Egham, and Bedford College,
London.
THE HISTORY OF THE PHILOSOPHICAL TENDENCIES OF THE NINETEENTH CENTURY.
By JOSIAH ROYCE, Professor of Philosophy, Harvard University.

THIRD SERIES.

FIRST PRINCIPLES OF PHILOSOPHY. By JOHN STUART MACKENZIE, M.A., Fellow of
Trinity College, Cambridge.
THE THEORY OF ETHICS. By EDWARD CAIRD, LL.D., Master of Balliol College,
Oxford.
EPISTEMOLOGY ; OR, THE THEORY OF KNOWLEDGE. By JAMES WARD, D.Sc., LL.D.,
Fellow and Lecturer of Trinity College, Cambridge.
PRINCIPLES OF PSYCHOLOGY. By G. F. STOUT, M.A., Fellow of St. John's College,
Cambridge.   [Shortly.
PRINCIPLES OF INSTRUMENTAL LOGIC. By JOHN DEWEY, Ph.D., Professor of Philo-
sophy, University of Michigan.

SWAN SONNENSCHEIN & Co., LONDON.
MACMILLAN & Co., NEW YORK.

iii

NATURAL RIGHTS

A CRITICISM OF SOME POLITICAL AND ETHICAL CONCEPTIONS

BY

DAVID G. RITCHIE M.A.

Professor of Logic and Metaphysics in the University of St. Andrews
Late Fellow and Tutor of Jesus College, Oxford; Author of "Darwin and Hegel," etc.

London
SWAN SONNENSCHEIN & CO
NEW YORK: MACMILLAN & CO
1895

Butler & Tanner,
The Selwood Printing Works,
Frome, and London.

To
E. S. H. R.

PREFACE

When I began, some three years ago, to write a paper on "Natural Rights," which has grown by degrees into the present volume, I had a certain fear that in criticising that famous theory I might be occupied in slaying the already slain. Recent experience has, however, convinced me that the theory is still, in a sense, alive, or at least capable of mischief. Though disclaimed by almost all our more careful writers on politics and ethics, it yet remains a commonplace of the newspaper and the platform, not only in the United States of America, where the theory may be said to form part of the national creed, but in this country, where it was assailed a century ago by both Burke and Bentham. If it be suggested that an exposure of fallacies, which have survived the attack of two critics so great and of such diverse genius, is either futile or superfluous, I should answer that I hope I have approached the theory in a spirit more appreciative and sympathetic than was possible to the eloquent passion of Burke, or to the keen, cold, abstractly logical analysis of Bentham. At least, I have endeavoured to regard the theory in the light of its historical significance; for it is never sufficient to argue that a widely held opinion is erroneous without trying to show how and why it came to be widely held. What I have attempted is simply a contribution to an historical and critical analysis of a set of conceptions which have had, for good and evil, an enormous influence in the region of practical politics and legislation. The study is but a fragment of political philosophy; and even in itself it is inevitably incomplete. Illustrations and applications might have been multiplied indefinitely; and any selection must always seem arbitrary to some readers. The subject of "liberty of thought" has been discussed at what may seem disproportionate length; but it appeared to me one of the most suitable for the sake of illustration, and the treatment accorded to it is, after all, not very lengthy. Chapter VIII. will serve its purpose best, if it should help to provoke some competent historical student to undertake an history of the practice and of the *idea* of toleration, on which I have only given a few jottings.

In writing on any political subject, however scientific and academic

PREFACE

When I began, some three years ago, to write a paper on "Natural Rights," which has grown by degrees into the present volume, I had a certain fear that in criticising that famous theory I might be occupied in slaying the already slain. Recent experience has, however, convinced me that the theory is still, in a sense, alive, or at least capable of mischief. Though disclaimed by almost all our more careful writers on politics and ethics, it yet remains a commonplace of the newspaper and the platform, not only in the United States of America, where the theory may be said to form part of the national creed, but in this country, where it was assailed a century ago by both Burke and Bentham. If it be suggested that an exposure of fallacies, which have survived the attack of two critics so great and of such diverse genius, is either futile or superfluous, I should answer that I hope I have approached the theory in a spirit more appreciative and sympathetic than was possible to the eloquent passion of Burke, or to the keen, cold, abstractly logical analysis of Bentham. At least, I have endeavoured to regard the theory in the light of its historical significance; for it is never sufficient to argue that a widely held opinion is erroneous without trying to show how and why it came to be widely held. What I have attempted is simply a contribution to an historical and critical analysis of a set of conceptions which have had, for good and evil, an enormous influence in the region of practical politics and legislation. The study is but a fragment of political philosophy; and even in itself it is inevitably incomplete. Illustrations and applications might have been multiplied indefinitely; and any selection must always seem arbitrary to some readers. The subject of "liberty of thought" has been discussed at what may seem disproportionate length; but it appeared to me one of the most suitable for the sake of illustration, and the treatment accorded to it is, after all, not very lengthy. Chapter VIII. will serve its purpose best, if it should help to provoke some competent historical student to undertake an history of the practice and of the *idea* of toleration, on which I have only given a few jottings.

In writing on any political subject, however scientific and academic one may seek to be, it is impossible to avoid matters of practical controversy or to escape all suspicion of partisanship. I would only ask fair-minded readers to take no one passage as conveying my opinions apart from qualifications expressed or implied in what is said elsewhere in the volume. Conservative, Liberal, Radical, Socialist, may each, amid much to dissent from, find something with which he may agree; and I think this ought to be so, for each of them represents some aspect of political truth neglected by the others. The only political theorists whom I expect to dissent from everything I have written are Anarchists, whether calling themselves such, or by one of the other four names. Anarchism is the creed of unreason in politics, and is a political philosophy only in the sense in which absolute scepticism may be called a metaphysical system.

For much of the historical material that I have used in this book I am indebted, directly or indirectly, to the kind help of special students of history, whom I have the good fortune to count among my friends. Of these I ought particularly to name Mr. Charles H. Firth. For many valuable suggestions I have to thank my friend Mr. J. H. Muirhead, who, as editor of this Series, has read the book through, both in MS. and in proof. And in every stage of the work I owe more than I can fittingly express here to the advice, encouragement and criticisms of my wife. But for all errors and shortcomings I must myself accept the full responsibility. The book has been written at intervals, and amid many interruptions and much pressure of other work. Yet I trust that it may be of some interest to the general reader, as well as of some use to the special student of ethics and politics. None of it has appeared in print before, except the short chapter on " The Rights of Property," which was published, in an Italian translation, in *La Riforma Sociale* of May, 1894. The appendix is given for the convenience of the student. It contains the two oldest of the American Declarations of Natural Rights, and all the French Declarations, as the latter are not very easily accessible in this country. The translation of the Declaration of 1789, which appears in Paine's *Rights of Man*, is inserted, as possessing an historical interest on its own account.

ST. ANDREWS,
    October, 1894.

CONTENTS

APPENDIX.

PART I

THE THEORY OF NATURAL RIGHTS

" THE principles of 1789 " were embodied in the Declaration
of the Rights of Man, which was prefixed to the Constitution
promulgated in 1791. They are often spoken of, by those
who admire and by those who reject them, as if they were
the distinctive and peculiar creed of the French Revolution.
But France deserves neither the credit nor the blame of
endeavouring to express for the first time, and for all time,
in a few abstract phrases the political and social faith on
which her institutions were to be founded and built up.
France has suffered more than any nation because of this creed
of liberty and equality that she proclaimed in the face of the
world; but her critics, among whom may now be found many
Frenchmen as well as Englishmen and Germans, are guilty
of historical inaccuracy, if, on the evidence of this creed, they
contrast the foolish abstractions of the Gallic spirit with the
prudent positivism of those whom they are pleased to call
" Anglo-Saxons." If the French may be blamed at all in the
matter, there is more ground for alleging that they simply
plagiarised " Anglo-Saxon " formulas. Every article in the
French revolutionary creed had been already formulated—and
often (as will be shown in detail) in less carefully guarded
phraseology—by the emancipated " Anglo-Saxons " on the other
side of the Atlantic. When Lafayette sent the key of the
destroyed Bastille by Thomas Paine to George Washington, he
was, in a picturesque symbol, confessing the debt of France to
America.[1] It is true that neither the " Articles of Confederation " of 1777, nor the " Constitution of the United States," as
originally proposed (1787) and ratified, contained any " Bill," or
" Declaration of Rights "; it is true, also, that the first ten
" Amendments," which were added in 1789, were regarded by
Jefferson as a somewhat inadequate substitute for the Declaration of Rights which he desired.[2] But it should not be for-

---

[1] See Moncure Conway, *Life of Thomas Paine*, I. pp. 272-275.
[2] See his letters to Madison quoted by Janet, *Hist. de la Science
Politique* (Ed. 3). I., Introd., pp. xxix.-xxxi.

gotten. *first*, that the Declaration of Independence (1776) had already named the natural and "unalienable rights," in virtue of which the American colonists justified their rebellion against the British Government and their existence as a group of leagued but independent States : and *second*, that the Constitution of the United States—even that of 1787—was regarded as only drawing closer the bonds of alliance between States which were still supposed to retain, in many respects, their sovereign rights. The Constitution of the Union only contains the terms of the federal compact.[1] It declares the rights of the *States* as against the Federal Government. The appropriate place for the declaration of the rights of the individual citizen is not in the federal constitution, but in the constitutions of the several States.[2] And in most of the Constitutions which originated after 1776 (some of the States retaining for a considerable period—Rhode Island as late as 1842—their old colonial charters), there is a Declaration, or Bill of Rights, exactly analogous to the French declaration. The "Bill of Rights" of Virginia (June 12th, 1776) may be taken as typical : it has served as the model for many similar declarations, adopted after American independence had been secured. "Other colonies," says Bancroft, "had framed bills of rights in reference to their relations with Britain: Virginia moved from charters and customs to primal principles; from a narrow altercation about facts to the contemplation of immutable truth. She summoned the eternal laws of man's being to protest against all tyranny."[3] These words are worth pondering, and also the words of the "Bill of Rights" itself. They may serve as a wholesome warning against the habit of explaining political institutions and political ideas by facile theories of race-difference.

As M. Paul Janet has well said, "If the French Revolution has lasted longer and been more violent than the English

---

[1] See below, pp. 241, 242.

[2] Franklin had the American State Constitutions translated into French, and presented them to Louis XVI. Cf. Moncure Conway, *Life of Paine*, I. p. 290.

[3] *History of the United States* (ed. 5), VIII. p. 383. In M. Paul Janet's "Introduction" to the 3rd edition of his *Histoire de la Science Politique*, the contrast drawn by M. Boutmy between the French and American Constitutions in this matter of natural rights, seems to me very effectively criticised.

Revolution, it is because it has taken place a century later." [1]
The English parliamentarian was able to appeal, with more
or less accuracy, to "historical rights"—not in a forgotten, ·
but in a recent past. The advocate of constitutional government in the France of 1789 could not appeal to any "historical
rights" that were known to any one but antiquarians. Apart
from the longer postponement of the crisis, the remedy was
more difficult to find in France than in England, secured
against continental complications by her insular position, or
than in America, separated by the ocean from the government
she was shaking off, and either receiving the sympathy, or
free from the interference of distant European powers. The
principles of the French Revolution were phrased in "metaphysical" language. This was not due to a special defect in
the French mind, but to the spirit of the eighteenth century.
The English revolutionists of 1640 to 1660 spoke in theological
language; it was the fashion of their time. The inheritors
of English traditions in America talk the same "metaphysical
jargon" which the French were to repeat in the next decade.
The Virginians declare—

"That all men are by nature equally free and independent, and have
certain inherent rights, of which, when they enter into a state of society,
they cannot by any compact deprive or divest their posterity; namely,
the enjoyment of life and liberty, with the means of acquiring and possessing property, and pursuing and obtaining happiness and safety.

"That all power is vested in, and consequently derived from, the
people; that magistrates are their trustees and servants, and at all times
amenable to them.

"That government is, or ought to be, instituted for the common
benefit, protection and security of the people, nation or community; of
all the various modes and forms of government, that is best which is capable of producing the greatest degree of happiness and safety, and is most
effectually secured against the danger of maladministration; and that
when a government shall be found inadequate or contrary to these purposes, a majority of the community hath an indubitable, unalienable and
indefeasible right to reform, alter or abolish it, in such manner as shall
be judged most conducive to the public weal."

Is there anything more extreme in the French declarations
of 1791 and 1793? And is there one word of Burke's eloquent
denunciation of "metaphysic rights" which would not be
equally applicable to this Virginian declaration of 1776? And
the Americans should, in his eyes, have had the less excuse

[1] *Hist. de la Sc. Pol.* (ed. 3), p. lxi.

for their metaphysics, because they might have continued to appeal, as they already had appealed, to the inheritance of English liberties.

We must not suppose that this appeal to natural rights was due solely to the influence of Rousseau, or that save for French " metaphysics " such ideas would never have found a home in the minds of men of English race and English speech. "Men being by nature all free, equal and independent, no one can be put out of this estate and subjected to the political power of another without his own consent." These are the words of the sober Englishman, John Locke ;[1] and in his *Treatise of Civil Government*, the great intellectual vindication of the principles of the Whig revolution of 1688,[2] will be found every one of the three principles which Burke condemns, and which he doubtless did not find expressly formulated in the Act of the 1st of William and Mary, sess. 2, ch. 2, which is known as the "Declaration of Right." The principles of the revolution of 1688, according to Dr. Richard Price, were these :— that we have a right (1) " To choose our own governors ; " (2) " To cashier them for misconduct ; " (3) " To frame a government for ourselves."[3] The doctrines of the American Declaration of Independence resemble far more closely the views of Locke than those of Rousseau. None at least of those theories in respect of which Rousseau differs from Locke are to be found in the American Declaration. And one passage in the American Declaration echoes not merely the ideas, but the very phraseology of Locke's Treatise.[4]

But the theory of natural rights was not Locke's invention. Neither he nor Jean Jacques can claim the credit of having " discovered the lost title-deeds of the human race." The theory of natural rights is simply the logical outgrowth of the Protestant revolt against the authority of tradition, the logical outgrowth of the Protestant appeal to private judgment, *i.e.* to the reason and conscience of the individual. Speaking

---

[1] *Treatise of Civil Government*, II. § 95.

[2] It was published in 1690, though the greater part of it may have been written before 1688. See Fox Bourne, *Life of Locke*, II. pp. 165, 166.

[3] *Discourse on the Love of our Country, delivered on Nov. 4th, 1789.* Cf. Burke, *Reflections on the Revolution in France*, near the beginning.

[4] Compare with the Declaration (see Appendix) Locke's *Treatise of Civil Government*, II. § 225, especially the words, "But if a long train of abuses," etc.

generally, we may say that throughout all the struggles of
the Middle Ages, it was not "liberty" for which men fought,
but "liberties." Privileges were claimed because of some
real or fancied authority in the past. A town, a district, a
corporation, or a social class alleged on its own behalf immemorial custom or some definite royal, imperial, or papal
grant or charter. The political theories of the Middle Ages
were mostly the theories of men living in the cloister, or
trained under monastic influences. They implied the acceptance of three great authorities, which might be interpreted
or applied, but were not to be questioned—the authority of
the Bible, of Aristotle, and of Justinian. Now, as we shall
see, each of these authorities contributed something (Aristotle
least of all) to that idea of a Law of Nature which, in the
eighteenth century, became the basis of the revolutionary
creed. But, while the intellect of Europe still lived under the
abiding shadow of the Holy Roman Empire and the Holy
Roman Church, man did not think of himself except as the
member of a particular nation, and, still more even, as the member of a definite social class or caste. The Aristotelian doctrine
that "man is by nature a political animal" had acquired the
sanctity of a dogma, and kept the mediæval thinker from
imagining man's rights in abstraction from any particular
political society. Still, even in the Middle Ages among the
unlettered multitudes, with whom Aristotle and Justinian
counted for nothing, but the dimly known Hebrew Scriptures
for a great deal, we find the first germs of an appeal to something beyond all charters and all customs and usages of
which lawyers knew. Wycliffe's startling thesis that "every
one in a state of grace has real lordship over the whole universe,"[1] from which he deduces his ideal of community of
property, can hardly be cited as a mediæval example of the
natural rights theory, because it is not man as man, but
only the saints that are in this fashion to inherit the earth.
The man who is in mortal sin cannot hold *dominion* or lordship at all. Nevertheless, it is easy to see what might become
of such interpretations of the Bible when they made their
way into the minds of the poor parish priests, or of oppressed

[1] See Wycliffe, *De Civili Dominio*, edited by R. L. Poole. Pref., pp.
xxii.-xxiv.

peasants, who found in some scriptural phrase a voice for
their sufferings and for their claims.

> " When Adam dalf and Evè span,
> Who was then the gentleman ? "

In these words, which fixed in the popular mind the teachings of the "mad" Wycliffite, John Ball, we have a genuine
appeal to the *natural* equality of mankind. The Bible, which
Wycliffe had tried to open to his countrymen, admitted, indeed, of diverse interpretations. Adam's dominion over the
creatures was appealed to by Sir Robert Filmer[1] in the seventeenth century as a ground for the divine right of kings to
rule despotically ; but an English peasant of the fourteenth
century, or of the seventeenth, was likely to find a different
lesson in the story of the "grand old gardener and his wife."
If all mankind were the sons of Adam, and if all might become by adoption the sons of God, distinctions of birth, and
wealth, and power seemed a mere human invention, a consequence (but why an inevitable consequence ?) of sin and the
corruption of human nature. Under the reign of the saints
might we not get rid of these inequalities ? The doctrine of
the "Levellers" may not be the doctrine of the most learned,
nor of the most orthodox, theologians, but it represents the
ideal which the exercise of private judgment in the study of
the Bible had kindled in the minds of the disinherited and
the oppressed.

I have already referred incidentally to the historical or
quasi-historical character of the rights claimed by the English
parliamentarians in the seventeenth century. The more
advanced sections of the anti-royalist party find themselves
driven farther and farther back in their claims. " To recover
our birthrights and privileges as Englishmen," " to purchase
our inheritances which have been lost," are alleged by some
of Cromwell's soldiers as the reason why they had taken up
arms.[2] They are not content with Lancastrian precedents :
they profess to seek to undo the mischief of "Normanism."
The times before the Norman Conquest are imagined as a
golden age when Englishmen had their rights. According to

---

[1] In his *Patriarcha*, published 1680 (Filmer died 1653). It is against
this book that Locke wrote his first *Treatise of Civil Government.*

[2] See *The Clarke Papers* [debates in the Parliamentary army, 1647],
edited by C. H. Firth, Vol. I. pp. 235, 322.

some of the "Levellers," the law and the constitution alike were part of the Norman yoke.[1] "The greatest mischief of all, and the oppressing bondage of England ever since the Norman yoke," says Lilburn, "is a law called the common law. . . . The laws of this nation are unworthy a free people, and deserve from first to last to be considered and seriously debated, and reduced to an agreement with common equity and right reason, which ought to be the form and life of every government. Magna Charta itself, being but a beggarly thing, containing many marks of intolerable bondage, and the laws that have been made since by Parliaments have in very many particulars made our government much more oppressive and intolerable."[2]

Thomas Edwards, the "shallow Edwards" of Milton's sonnet, a Presbyterian and constitutionalist, complains of the "sectaries" in his *Gangræna*:—"As they do in matters of religion and conscience fly from the Scriptures, and from supernatural truths revealed there, that a man may not be questioned for going against them, but only for errors against the light of nature and right reason ; so they do also in civil government and things of this world, they go from the laws and constitution of kingdoms, and will be governed by rules according to nature and right reason ; and though the laws and customs of a kingdom be never so plain and clear against their ways, yet they will not submit, but cry out for natural rights derived from Adam and right reason."[3]

Elsewhere the same writer explains what these sectaries meant by natural rights. "All men [according to them] are by nature the sons of Adam, and from him have legitimately derived a natural propriety [*i.e.* property], right and freedom. . . . By natural birth all men are equally and alike born to like propriety, liberty, and freedom ; and as we are delivered of God by the hand of nature into this world, every one with a natural innate freedom and propriety, even so we are to live, every one equally and alike, to enjoy his birthright and privilege."[4]

---

[1] *The Clarke Papers*, Pref., p. lxi.

[2] Quoted from Lilburn's *Just Man's Justification*, pp. 11–15, by Mr. C. H. Firth, in his Pref. to the *Clarke Papers*, I. p. lxi.

[3] *Gangræna*, pt. iii. p. 20, quoted likewise by Mr. Firth, p. lx. (I have modernised the spelling.)

[4] *Ib.*, pt. iii. p. 16, quoted by Mr. Firth, p. lxii.

Thus already in the Puritan revolution of the seventeenth century the appeal to historic right was replaced by an appeal to natural rights. The struggle for parliamentary liberties led some men to go behind parliaments and charters, just as the independent study of the Bible led some men to go behind the authority of Bible and to rely on the authority of " the inner light " alone. This is the logical outcome of Protestantism, however unacceptable to the majority of those calling themselves Protestants, however unsatisfactory and dangerous in the eyes of those who were more influenced by the historic spirit and who realised in more or less intelligent fashion the necessity of social cohesion and continuity. When compared with the " Levellers "—those Puritan precursors of Robespierre and St. Just—Cromwell and Ireton show their intellectual affinity with Burke, or even with Dr. Johnson. " We are very apt, all of us, to call that faith which perhaps may be but carnal imagination." [1] In these words Cromwell pours cold water on the fire of the mystical enthusiasts, who abounded in the parliamentary army. Cromwell objects to the " Agreement of the People " that it contained too great alterations in the government of the country. [2] Ireton abhors arguments about abstract justice, and scents danger in the appeal to natural rights. " When I do hear men speak of laying aside all engagements to consider only that wild or vast notion of what in every man's conception is just or unjust, I am afraid and do tremble at the boundless and endless consequences of it. . . . If you do paramount to all constitutions hold up this law of nature, I would fain have any man shew me where you will end." [3]

Puritan England had produced the theory of natural rights; but the conditions were not yet favourable for its abundant growth. The American colonists a century later appealed at first to the customary and traditional rights of all British subjects. The Convention at New York, in October, 1765, while protesting loyalty to His Majesty King George, declared " That it is inseparably essential to the freedom of a people, and the undoubted right of Englishmen, that no taxes be imposed on them but with their own consent, given person-

[1] *Clarke Papers*, I. p. 258.
[2] *Ibid.*, p. 256.
[3] *Ibid.*, pp. lxix., 261, 307.

ally or by their representatives. . . . That trial by jury
is the inherent and invaluable right of every British subject
in these colonies," and so on, entirely in the spirit of the
English Bill of Rights of 1689. But in the Declaration of
Rights of the Philadelphia Congress of 1774 appeal is made
not only to "the principles of the English constitution
and the several charters or compacts," but to "the immutable laws of nature"; and first among the rights claimed
comes the right "to life, liberty, and property."[1] In the
Declaration of Independence of July 4th, 1776, no more is
said about the rights of British subjects. The thirteen united
States of America base their claim to independence on "certain unalienable rights," which come to man direct from his
Creator. The French Declarations of 1791 and 1793 are proclaimed "in the presence of the Supreme Being," but the
"imprescriptible rights" are said to come to man simply by
nature or by birth. Thus the theory of natural rights appears
full grown, detached from history, and freed from the Biblical
or theological wrappings which at first in part concealed its
metaphysical nakedness.

The tendency is, however, always strong to translate logical
or metaphysical theories into the easier language of imagined
history. The ordinary mind thinks in pictures: and even
those who are counted among philosophers fall a prey to the
habit. Thus, while Hobbes does not seem to ascribe any historical character to the social contract, which is at the basis
of all political society, and while Rousseau expressly disclaims
the attempt to offer an historical explanation[2] of how governments came into existence, Locke seeks to give historical
proofs of the origin of political society by means of contract,
referring to the cases of Rome and Venice,[3] and speaks of
the state of nature as a golden age in the past.

---

[1] These declarations will be found in *Documents Illustrative of American History with Introductions and References*, edited by Howard W.
Preston. 2nd edit. New York, 1891.

[2] Cf. *Contrat Social*, l. c. i.: "L'homme est né libre, et partout il est
dans les fers. . . . Comment ce changement s'est-il fait? Je l'ignore.
Qu'est-ce qui peut la rendre légitime? Je crois pouvoir résoudre cette
question." It is thus no refutation of Rousseau to say that Jean
Jacques has not fixed the date of the social contract.

[3] *Treatise of Civil Government*, II. § 102. In an early essay, "Reflections
upon the Roman Commonwealth," written probably about 1660, parts of

THE PRINCIPLES OF '89 [CH. I

Similarly we find that Thomas Paine, in the passionate rhetoric of his reply to Burke, defends the doctrine of the rights of man, not as one might expect, by turning away from the dust of parchments to the eternal laws of nature, but by appealing from antiquity to an antiquity still more venerable. "The error of those who reason by precedents drawn from antiquity, respecting the rights of man, is that they do not go far enough into antiquity. . . . Portions of antiquity, by proving everything, establish nothing. It is authority against authority all the way, till we come to the divine origin of the rights of man at the creation. Here our enquiries find a resting place and our reason finds a home." [1]

As a rhetorical argument, this of course is quite justifiable.[2] When charters, precedents, and title-deeds are quoted to stop the mouth of the reformer, it is quite legitimate in the court of public opinion, though not in the law-courts, to appeal to the title-deeds of the human race; and against opponents who have tried to silence one by the authority of Scripture to appeal to our common descent from Adam. At all times it has been customary to represent reform as the return to some earlier and better condition of affairs. The very word " reform " suggests this. The " Levellers," and the champions of the natural rights of man, might very well think of themselves as only extending farther the principle of appealing to the past, which more moderate or more timid reformers, ecclesiastical and political, expressly adopted. It was especially easy to do this in an age when, even among professed historians, the sense of historical perspective was very weak, when the theory of evolution had not yet been proclaimed from the house-tops, when people were still influenced in their practical thinking by the classical dream of a golden

which are printed in Mr. Fox Bourne's *Life*, I. pp. 148 *seq.*, Locke speaks of the " colony " which founded Rome as being "in the original state of nature, free, and independent of any dominion whatsoever," and at liberty to choose their own form of government.

[1] *Rights of Man*, p. 18. (Freethought Publishing Company's edition. London, 1885.)

[2] It should be noted, moreover, that Paine expressly avoids the appearance of appealing merely to the origin of mankind. " Every child," he says, " born into the world must be considered as deriving its existence from God. The world is as new to him as it was to the first man that existed, and his natural right in it is of the same kind." Generation is regarded as the mode by which creation is continually repeated.

age, and by the Hebrew legend of Paradise ; and when it
was possible, before the birth of anthropological science,
and at a safe distance from savage races, to idealise the
noble inhabitant of the woods. Even now, as I shall have
occasion to point out later on—even now, with the phraseology
of evolution in everybody's mouth, it is remarkable how per-
sistent is the belief in those ever-receding " good old days " ;
and stray attempts are sometimes made, where we should least
expect them, to rehabilitate the Golden Age.

The real significance of the theory of natural rights is, however, entirely independent of any historical, or quasi-historical,
setting that may be given to it. The real significance of the
theory is not to be determined by reference to remote ages, or
to rude peoples ; as with all political theories, and as with all
philosophical theories which are a genuine expression of the
thought and feeling of the period in which they prevail, its
meaning is only understood aright if we consider it in relation
to the circumstances of the very time in which it was maintained. The real significance of the appeal to nature is, in the
first place, the *negative* element in the appeal ; it is an appeal
against authorities that had lost their sacredness, against institutions that had outlived their usefulness; against artificiality
in art, in literature, in manners, in dress—against wigs and
hair-powder.

Secondly, as we have already seen, the theory of natural
rights is Protestantism transferred to the region of worldly
affairs, and stripped of the traditionalism against which at
first it did not " protest "—the paramount authority of a book,
accepted on the guarantee of the " Church " whose authority
was rejected, and interpreted on certain traditional assumptions. Mediæval doctors accepted the authority of the Church,
of the Bible, and of the Law of Nature interpreted by reason,
but under a general guidance from the other two authorities.
The earlier Protestants, protesting against the corruptions in
the Church, were not careful to lay down the precise relationship between the other two authorities. When Protestantism
had in its turn crystallised into a traditional system, the intellectual descendants of the first Protestants appeared as the
Deists and Rationalists of the eighteenth century. Calvin's
Geneva in due time brought forth Rousseau; and English
Puritanism on American soil produced the Declaration of

Independence.[1] All other authorities are thrown aside or are ranked as subordinate. Nature interpreted by Reason, and by Reason not embodied in any society, but existing in the individual mind, becomes the ultimate court of appeal. That is to say, the assertion of natural rights implies not merely a protest against the authority of customs and institutions, but an appeal from this authority to the judgment of every individual simply as such. The individualism of the theory may indeed not seem as conspicuous as its negative character, because in appealing to Reason people have generally assumed that Reason will give the same judgments in different minds. The appeal to *common* sense (alike in the colloquial and in the more philosophical use of that term) involves an assumption of an objective or universal aspect of human reason, an assumption which has restrained the theory of natural rights within what have seemed "reasonable" limits, but only at the cost of inconsistency with the assumed antagonism between reason and convention. But to this logical defect in the theory I shall have to return later on. The ambiguities in its application can be shown at once by an illustration. "Negativity" and "individualism" both imply *abstractness, i.e.* want of close relationship or organic connection with the concrete facts of social life and history. And all abstract theories about human society admit of divergent and conflicting application. Thus the theory of social contract is used by Hobbes to condemn rebellion, and by Locke to justify it. The conception of social organism is used by Plato to justify the extremest interference with individual liberty, and by Mr. Herbert Spencer to condemn a very moderate amount of State control. And so the theory of natural rights is used by Anarchists to condemn the existing inequalities of social conditions, and by Conservatives to check attempts on the part of govern-

---

[1] John Wyse published in 1717, " A Vindication of the Government of New England Churches, Drawn from Antiquity, the Light of Nature, Holy Scripture, its Noble Nature, and from the Dignity Divine Providence has put upon it," 1717. It was twice reprinted in 1772. Some sentences quoted from this book by Mr. Charles Borgeaud in his *Établissement et Révision des Constitutions en Amérique et en Europe*, p. 17, express the social contract theory in the form in which it is held by Locke and by Rousseau. (There is no copy of the book in the Bodleian Library.) Wyse may be regarded as helping the transition from the seventeenth-century Puritan to the eighteenth-century revolutionist.

ments to remedy these inequalities. The first of these modes
of application may seem indeed the more logical outcome of a
theory whose essence lies in protest and negation; but the
second is, at the present day, quite as common. Protestant-
isms crystallise into dogmatisms; and the theory of the revolutionist becomes the watchword of the Conservative and of the
reactionary. The English revolution of 1688 and the American revolution of 1776 were carried out in defence of the
rights of "liberty and property."[1] The "Liberty and Property Defence League" of our own days regards itself as
a bulwark against revolutionary legislation. Mr. Herbert
Spencer, in sad isolation, defends "natural rights" against the
logical consequences of the evolutionist philosophy with
which he has familiarised his contemporaries.[2] It is difficult
to know whether Mr. Auberon Herbert is to be classed among
the Anarchists or among the reactionaries. Perhaps his case
proves that there is more affinity between these apparent
extremes than appears at first sight. People are in the habit
of building the sepulchres of the prophets their fathers stoned,
and although, so far as I know, Tom Paine has not yet been
made a saint by the Knights and Dames of the Primrose
League, the spirit of the "rebellious stay-maker," if it ever
frequents the meetings of that highly respectable organisation, may have felt a grim delight in hearing the "Rights of
man" preached by a Tory Lord Chancellor. At a Primrose
League meeting in the town of Dingwall, August, 1891 (I
quote from a newspaper report),[3] Lord Halsbury, in opposition
to the subversive proposals of Radicals, declared that "one of
the things which the British people most cherished was their
own freedom of action, the right to do as they willed with
their own, whether it was their labour, their property, or their
skill." These are just the rights which figure in the American and the French Declarations. Paine or Robespierre would

[1] Janet, in his *Hist. de la Science Politique* (ed. 3, II. p. 202, quotes
Voltaire as saying: "*Liberty and property* voilà la devise des Anglais;
elle vaut bien: Montjoye et Saint Denis." In saying "property," it
should perhaps be noted, Voltaire has *not* the British matron in his
mind's eye.

[2] See *The Man versus the State*, pp. 87, *seq.* The conception of society
as essentially organic or super-organic, if it be once really accepted, is
incompatible with the individualism of the "natural rights" theory.

[3] *Bradford Observer*, Aug. 19th, 1891.

doubtless have asked for some definition of the right of property; but as to the right of labour it was only the *droit du travail* and not yet the *droit au travail* ("the right to do work" —not "the right to get work") which formed one of the principles of 1789.

The change which has taken place in English political thought with regard to the American constitution is another illustration of the way in which the Conservatives of one generation may take up the ideas of a past generation of Radicals. The supremacy of parliament and its competency to reform itself were attacked by Paine as aristocratic and despotic elements in the British Constitution. Now the demand for a rigid Constitution on the American plan, exempting certain rights from the control of the legislature, comes not from the Radical but from the Conservative side. " Americanise our institutions," is a cry which has passed from the mouth of Paine to the mouth of Maine.[1]

It argues an imperfect knowledge of the history of human thought if we are astonished at this apparent shifting of sides in the controversy. The very fact that some formula served to express the special needs of a particular age might lead us to expect that it would not adequately express the special needs of a later age, in which the course of events had brought new problems to the surface. And thus the very watchwords of the reformer of one generation may be repeated most fervently by the opponents of reform in another. This need not make us sceptical about the possibility of mankind knowing anything that is true, or holding any belief that is worth holding; the very reverse, if we read the facts rightly. If we would avoid such scepticism about humanity as would paralyse all serious effort, and make us hesitate to call anything right or wrong, we must admit the fundamental rationality of all institutions or practical beliefs that have been able to hold their ground for some considerable time, and to afford shelter and supply cohesion to considerable numbers of human beings. They must in some way have been advantageous to the society in which they prevailed, else—on the principle of natural selection—they could not have prevailed; they would have been crushed out along with a society which fed on poisonous stuff. The evolution theory compels

[1] See his *Popular Government*, Essay IV. (orig. publ. in *Quarterly Review*).

those who accept it to regard social cohesion and durability as the proof of some degree at least of ethical value and truth. It is a shallow wisdom which can see nothing but falsehood and nothing but evil in widely diffused creeds and long enduring institutions; and the dogmatic despiser of the past does not observe that, while he is challenging the bitter antagonism of those who, by blind sentiment or reasonable conviction, cling to whatever they find of seeming stability around them, he is losing the argumentative advantage which comes from an appeal to the spirit of the initiators of bygone days against the mere repetition of the letter of their teaching by those who profess to be their followers. Paine makes a most effective point against Burke, when he shows the inconsistency of accepting the results of the revolution of 1688 as necessarily and for ever prohibiting any further change in the constitution. The example of the men of 1688 is more significant than their illogical and impossible attempt to bind all future generations. Let us admit that in practical affairs, in the complex material of human society, we never get complete truth or perfect institutions. Progress is only from one partial and one-sided expression of the whole truth which hovers before us as an ideal to another expression of it which may be equally, and sometimes even more, partial and one-sided, and which at the best is only less inadequate than that which it replaces. In this long controversy, this dialectic of the human spirit, the earlier and cruder stages are certainly more apt to take the form of mere antagonism and mutual negation; in the higher stages only does the new conception appear as simply the fuller development of that which it replaces. In political controversy, however, this " higher stage " is, as yet, more an ideal possibility than a fact.

But, while admitting that durable institutions and widely diffused practical beliefs must have had in them some element of truth and value for the very reason that they flourished, we are the more justified in considering whether they still retain a greater element of truth and value for our age than others which have risen to compete with them. Institutions and beliefs are apt to outlive their utility, and to prove in the long run destructive to the well-being, if not to the very existence, of the society which clings to them amid changed surroundings. The reformer who proposes a change is not contradicting the

teachings of evolutionary science: he is obeying them, by
seeking to save his society from suffering unnecessarily through
the operation of natural selection.

Looking back calmly at the history of Europe from mediæval
times down to the French Revolution, we can see certain
obvious merits in the structure of mediæval society which it
was impossible for the representative spirits of the Reformation
period or of eighteenth-century Rationalism to appreciate
aright. We can see that the principle of Authority, the
principle that the life and thought of the individual man are
dependent on something greater and wider and more enduring
than himself,—we can see that this principle was true, although
mediæval institutions realised it only in an external fashion,
in the Church as a visible, outward organisation, and in the
fixed castes of civil society. The revolt of the individual
against this external organisation was inevitable and necessary,
if mankind was to advance to new conquests over nature and
over itself; and yet this revolt, when carried out logically, took
the form of making one man's private judgment (however
foolish and however prejudiced, *i.e.* however little it might in
reality be either "judgment" or "private") count for as much
as another's, and of substituting the mere temporary "cash-
nexus" between individual and individual for the older bond
of permanent mutual obligation. And so this principle of
individualism tends in its turn, because only a partial truth
(true as against what the old society had come to be), to prove
itself false and mischievous. Those, therefore, who repeat the
formulas of the individualist negation and revolt, where and so
far as the circumstances which gave them a meaning have
passed away, are repeating what once was truth, but has now
become false, because meaningless.

An illustration from a different but kindred case may make
my argument clearer. People have sometimes wondered how
the Calvinistic doctrine of Election, which, looked at logically,
seems much the same as Fatalism,[1] could have been held by
men of the most vigorous character, and should have been the

---

[1] The notion of Predestination only seems identical with Fatalism,
because people are apt to think "abstractly," *i.e.* to take some one part
of the whole process and isolate it from the series to which it belongs.
The *eternal* decrees of God are pictured as if they were arbitrary intrusions into a process of cause and effect, which, apart from such intrusions,
goes on of itself.

religious stimulus and education of the very nations which
struggled most stubbornly and most successfully for civil
liberty. Consider to what the doctrine was opposed, and the
mystery is explained; the salvation of the individual depends
solely on the eternal and unalterable decree of God—that is
to say, it depends not at all on the will or act of any ecclesiastical authority, of any human authority whatever. The
doctrine of Election robs the priest of his power; it is the
appeal from man to God. And thus, in its negative aspect, it
was a liberating creed, training up stern, independent men
who feared God and feared none beside. The creed becomes
something very different when it stiffens into a traditional
dogma, isolated from any relation to the opinions to which it
was opposed, and pictured with all the crude materialism of
popular thought. It tends to become a dreary, other-worldly
individualism. Having helped men to shake off tyrants, it
turns a too abstract conception of God into a frightful picture
of a tyrant worse than any of them. It is the same with this
theory of natural rights. At first it represents the revolt
against external authority, against the traditional maintenance of the *status quo*. When in its turn it is handed down as
a traditional dogma out of relation to the particular circumstances which gave it its value, it comes to be used as a
support of what is now the established economic and social
order, save where some of its phraseology passes into the
mouths of fanatical Anarchists, who carry out the principles
of individualism to their logical conclusion—the destruction
of all orderly society whatever.

It is my purpose in the following chapters to examine the
conception of natural rights, the history of which has been
here briefly sketched. I shall first take the idea of "*Nature*,"
considering it from the point of view both of history and of
philosophical analysis. I shall then consider the conception of
"*rights*" generally, and shall afterwards take the most conspicuous of the alleged "natural rights" in detail. I trust
that I shall be found, consistently with what has just been
said, while exposing ambiguities and criticising what seem to
me false applications of the conception, to do full justice to its
relative truth and its historic value.

CHAPTER II

ON THE HISTORY OF THE IDEA OF "NATURE" IN LAW AND POLITICS [1]

THE words "nature" and "natural" are constantly bandied about in controversy as if they settled quarrels, whereas they only provoke them by their ambiguity. Slavery has been condemned as an "unnatural" institution; and has been defended on the ground of the "natural" inferiority of some races to others. The equality of the sexes is asserted and denied on the ground of "nature." The "natural" goodness and the "natural" badness of mankind have been maintained with like earnestness and sincerity. "To live according to Nature" was the Stoic formula for the good life; those Christian theologians, who have in some ways most intellectual and moral affinity with the Stoics, have been those who have spoken most strongly about the corruption of "the natural man." "Natural religion" means something very different from "Nature-worship." "A natural child" means a child born out of wedlock; but "an unnatural child" is not necessarily legitimate. "A state of nature" may mean the absence of clothing; but such absence is not considered essential to the possession of "a natural manner" in society. To the sentiment that "Nature is a holy thing" may always be opposed the proposition that "Nature is a rum 'un," and, in view of the ambiguity of the term, the theory of Mr. Squeers is perhaps the more easily defensible of the two.

In no case can we understand what is meant by "Nature" or "natural" unless we know *to* what the speaker is opposing the term. As has already been pointed out, the special characteristic of the appeal to Nature is negation, antagonism; it is an appeal from what exists or from what is proposed,

[1] It is a pity that the English language does not allow one any short equivalent for the convenient German phrase "*Zur Geschichte*, etc." "Contributions to," is cumbrous.

and has therefore at all times been a convenient form of criticism, rather than a good basis for construction.

We have seen that, though not originating in the eighteenth century, it is specially characteristic of that period—a period of criticism and individualism, a period of awakening and enlightenment. If we go back to an older period, which in many ways presents similar characteristics, we shall find this use of "nature" as the antithesis to convention and definite institutions anticipated in the ancient world. The age of the Sophists is the ancient equivalent of the age of the Encyclopædists; in the phraseology of German historians of philosophy, it is the Greek "Illumination" (*Aufklärung*). Both periods represent a rationalistic revolt against traditional beliefs; both prepare the way for a profounder philosophical study, especially of social institutions, than would have been possible without the intellectual revolution produced by the exercise of critical and sceptical reflection. In speaking of the Sophists, we must of course clear our minds completely of the misleading associations which have accumulated round that word. We must remember that our ideas of them are derived mostly from the caricatures of Aristophanes and from the adverse criticisms of Plato. What fair-minded historian, with a sense of humour, would be content to take history from the cartoons of a partisan comic paper, or to accept as true whatever an orthodox writer has said about the opinions of a heretic? Besides, even Aristophanes and Plato may be summoned as witnesses against German or English writers who have libelled the Sophists as the corrupters of Hellas. Aristophanes hated the Sophists as an old Tory (or an old Whig—for that matter) hated the French Revolution and Tom Paine; but Aristophanes selects Socrates as the typical example of the class. Plato is respectful to Protagoras and Gorgias; and Plato has expressly answered the charge of corruption, "It is not the individual Sophists, but that great Sophist, the public, that has a bad effect on our young men." [1]

Grote has conclusively proved—strange, that proof should have been needed—that "Sophist" is not the name of a sect, but the name of a profession, a profession called into existence by the demand for "higher education." There was a mental exhilaration produced in the Hellenic world, and especially in

[1] Plato, *Republic*, VI. 492.

Athens, by the defeat of the Persian invasions [1]—the most striking, and in its consequences the most significant of the many examples in history of the intellectual stimulus which follows the shock of a successful war of liberation.   This mental exhilaration and the growth of democracy, itself in part due to the same cause, created a demand among the ambitious youth for something more than the old education of reading, writing, music, and reciting passages from the great poets, who took the place of a "Bible" to the Greeks—an education like that given in Mohammedan countries at the present day, or, in its essential elements and defects, like that which till lately was among ourselves the usual education of young women of the middle and upper classes—an education which gave no scope whatever to the reasoning and critical faculties, but which produced, and was defended as producing, a contented acquiescence in traditional beliefs.   The young Athenian of the new generation that grew up after Salamis wished for something more; and the class of Sophists—professed "wise men"—arose to supply the demand.   They were, in fact, an itinerant University—University Extension lecturers, before the days of settled and endowed institutions for the promotion of learning and the higher education.   They came from various parts of the Hellenic world, they had themselves been trained in various schools of the older philosophers, who had speculated about nature, but had, on the whole, left ethics and politics alone.   They taught with a directly practical object, to fit men for a successful career in public life; they taught their pupils *how* to speak, and were the first of a long line of teachers of rhetoric (" the art of persuasion"); they taught, or professed to teach, also *what* to speak about— the subject-matter of ethics and politics.   What is justice? What are laws?   What is the State?   The man who speaks in the law-courts or political assemblies speaks as if he knew what these terms meant.   The Sophists made him think whether the terms as ordinarily used had any definite meaning at all.

[1] Cf. Arist. *Pol.* VIII. 6, § 11: " When their wealth gave them greater leisure, and they had loftier notions of excellence, being also elated (φρονηματισθέντες) with their success both before and after the Persian war, with more zeal than discernment they pursued every kind of knowledge."   Cf. also II. 12, § 5.

Such questions may well have seemed scandalous to old-fashioned people who had never reflected about the basis of social life and conduct; and doubtless, then as now, such questions were often rudely asked and crudely answered. The clever lad has always felt a certain pleasure in shocking his elderly relatives. The shock, as a rule, does no good to the elderly relatives; and when the youth is a little more mature in mind, he may think with hardly less audacity, but with a juster sense of the proportion of things. These popular teachers of public speaking, of the art of reasoning, of miscellaneous useful knowledge, of literary criticism, of the way to succeed in private or political life, were the beginners of all *humanist* studies—I mean, of all studies which concern not the nature of the material universe, and the problems it suggests, but the work of the spirit of man himself in his efforts to know himself, his relations to nature and to the social world into which he is born. Religion, art, laws, institutions, were now claimed as proper subjects for thought and science. The first effort to think out anything implies a certain antagonism to the subject thought about. We must get out from among the trees to look at the wood, we must stand at some distance from a building to get a full view of it. And so the first attempts at a philosophical understanding of religion, of morality, of art, seem to take the form of revolts against religion, morality, and art; and very often they are in reality revolts. It was inevitable, therefore, that the Sophists should give offence to those who remained too completely under the shelter of old institutions to allow that their value might be questioned and disputed. It was inevitable also that this first attempt at reflection on what had previously been accepted on authority should seem crude and one-sided to those who, having been themselves trained in the new learning, were able in their turn to see the defects of it. Grote is right in denying that there is any common " Sophistic " doctrine ; but he fails to recognise that the Sophists represent a common tendency—a tendency not, of course, limited to these professional teachers for pay. Xenophanes in his attacks on the anthropomorphic polytheism of the traditional Greek religion, and Plato in his attacks on both religion and art, are in the same stage of thought as the Sophists, who seemed to be attacking the foundations of society by their revolutionary theories—theories not more revolutionary, however, in some respects than those of Plato himself. Aristotle, coming after all this ferment of speculation, is able to think more calmly and more objectively, to avoid a quarrel with the popular religion, while putting his own metaphysical interpretation on religious phraseology, to construct a philosophical defence of poetry, to see the rationality, not merely of an ideal state, but of ordinary Hellenic society, and to appreciate the ethical significance of institutions, such as the family and private property, which Plato had attacked.

Now one main characteristic of the "Sophistic" way of thinking—and it is a characteristic that always repeats itself in similar stages of thought, whether in the development of the individual mind or in the development of the general intelligence of the community—is the habit of falling into Antithesis. To split the confused intricate mass of the universe, or whatever part of it one is studying, into two sharply divided sections, by the use of an "either . . . or," seems always an immense gain in the early stages of reflection. Only get hold of some fundamental conception, and with the help of a sufficiently crude and narrow logic, you can easily construct a philosophy of everything. Divide all human instincts into egoistic and altruistic, distinguish all human co-operation as voluntary and compulsory, recognise two types of society, the militant and the industrial, above all distinguish the natural from the artificial, and you are able to make the most striking generalisations, and to reduce all the complex " facts " into neat bundles—except that the facts, even when they have been picked out in the light of the theory, are apt to prove a little awkward now and then. You never need to move out of the easy category of quantity. " More " or "less" will represent the finest shades of distinction you need to recognise. If government is gaining in power, the individual must be losing in liberty ; if more laws are passed by parliament, we are reverting to the militant stage ; and so on, and so on. In alluding to Mr. Spencer's political writings as examples of "Sophistic," I am, of course, not using the word in any except a technical sense ; and I ought to add that Mr. Spencer himself, by preaching and advertising "Evolution," has done more than any other English philosopher to get people beyond the Sophistic stage of thought. Hobbes, Locke,

and Rousseau are modern representatives of the Sophistic
stage, and the greatness of these names may help to make us
appreciate the intellectual debt that we owe to the much-
abused Sophists of Greece. Glaucon, in the second book of
Plato's *Republic*, propounds a theory of social contract which
is clearly due to some Sophist's speculation; and this theory
is identical with that of Hobbes, Locke, and Rousseau.[1] "Justice," he says, "is a contract neither to do nor to suffer
wrong." Thrasymachus, the rhetorical Sophist, in the first
book of the *Republic*, propounds a theory of justice, which is a
crude version of Hobbes' doctrine of law and sovereignty—the
theory which Hobbes handed on to Bentham and Austin, and
which is still prevalent among English jurists. "Right is that
which the government, being the stronger part of the political
society, commands." Lycophron the Sophist is quoted by
Aristotle[2] as maintaining that law depends upon a contract,
and that the end of law is the security of individual rights,
and that the State has no moral function—the very theory,
familiar to us in many modern writers, which Professor
Huxley has named "Administrative Nihilism." This same
Lycophron is said to have held that the difference between
noble and base-born was a difference in men's opinions merely
and not in reality.[3] There can be little doubt that the attack
on the rightness of slavery, with which Aristotle deals in his
Politics,[4] was made by some Sophist. A certain rhetorician,
Alcidamas, is reported to have said, "God made all men free;
nature made none a slave."[5] Aristotle's argument is directed
alike against those who justified all slavery simply because it
was an existing fact, or because it was due to the right of the
stronger, and against those who condemned all slavery as
dependent merely on human institution and not on nature.

These illustrations may suffice to show the similarity in
manner of thinking between the Greek Sophists—it might be
safer to say, between *some* Greek Sophists of the fifth century
B.C.—and the advocates of liberal ideas in the seventeenth and
eighteenth centuries. In the eyes of the modern student the

---

[1] I only refer to the element which is common to the three.

[2] *Pol.*, III. 9, § 8.

[3] Quoted by Stobæus, *Flor.* 86, 24 (Meineke's edit., Vol. III. p. 158),
from Aristotle's dialogue, "On Nobility of Birth" (Arist., *Fragm.* 82).

[4] I. c. 4-7.

[5] Scholiast on Arist. *Rhet*. I. 13.

attack on slavery alone should serve to clear up the nature of
much of their teaching, which found its way into literature
through "Euripides the human," through the poets of the New
Comedy, and, in naïve combination with pious credulity, in
the *History* of Herodotus. At the same time an attack on the
very basis of ancient society helps one to understand the un-
popularity of these old-world freethinkers. They seem to have
maintained a good many social heresies which have succeeded
better in our time than in theirs; but there is no evidence
that they based any of their theories or their paradoxes on
anything but a somewhat superficial reasoning. "Fire burns
both in Hellas and in Persia; but men's ideas of right and
wrong vary from place to place."[1] The enlightened man who
has travelled about and shaken off local prejudices soon notes
this, and with his good-humoured scepticism cannot understand why a Persian king should despise the Egyptian animal-
worship. "Custom is lord of all."[2] This disinterested attitude
towards human conduct and beliefs is a necessary step towards
a true understanding of them. But it is only the first step.
When we have once contrasted the uniformity of "natural"
processes with the diversity of human observance, we are only
then face to face with the problems of ethics and politics.
"Every one according to his taste" is a shallow maxim in art-
criticism; but such "impressionism" is still less in place in

[1] Arist., *Eth. Nic.*, V. 7, § 2.
It does not affect my argument, if it could be proved that Aristotle is
here alluding, not to the Sophists, or to any Sophists, but to the Cynics.
The contrast between nature and convention is a typical example of that
"reflection" which is characteristic of the whole stage of mental development that produced the Sophists and the one-sided Socratics and the
cynical worldly wisdom of a Callicles. Just so in modern times, one
may find the same type of thinking in Locke, in Pope, in Voltaire, in
Rousseau, despite their enormous differences from one another.
The antithesis between nature and convention has been sometimes
associated with the Democritean physics, according to which in reality
there exist only atoms and the void, everything else—all the world that
appears to the senses—being due simply to arrangements among the
atoms. Democritus was probably twenty years younger than his fellow-
townsman Protagoras, and can hardly therefore have been his teacher
(see Zeller, *Pre-Socratic Philosophy* [tr.], II. pp. 210, 411, 412). But the
atomist philosophy probably contributed to the popularity of the antithesis between convention and nature, appearance and reality.

[2] Herodotus, III. 27-38; the story of how the "mad" Cambyses killed
the calf-god, and the reflections of Herodotus thereon.

regard to matters of right and wrong.   If applied in practice it means anarchy, or, quite as often, a cynical acquiescence in successful tyranny or in irrational and indefensible custom. In practice these extremes are always near to one another. The Greek Sophists were not the cause, but were only a symptom of the dissolution of the fabric of Greek society into selfish individualism; and we know that some of them were expressly accused of being the apologists of tyranny.   A general irreverence towards constitutions and towards institutions paves the way for some "people's friend" who will make himself tyrant, and, everything else being open to doubt, will fall back on the two undeniable facts of superior force and superior fraud.   Rationalism, scepticism, pessimism, blind submission, is a too familiar cycle in the history of political and of religious beliefs.   Is there any escape from it?   Only by a rationalism which is true to itself, and which is prepared to find reason not merely in the mind of the individual, but in the concrete works of the human spirit, in the very institutions, ethical, political, religious, which rationalism began by classifying as "not natural."   They are not "natural" in the sense in which "nature" means the blind forces of nature, working only in one direction; but they are the outcome of the highest things we know in "nature" as the whole universe, namely, the thought and will of man.   The very fact that they are not according to mere nature proves them higher in kind; the very errors in human beliefs and institutions are evidence of the reason which is struggling for expression in them.   We must get rid of the mere antithesis between "nature" and "convention," of the illogical combination of too great trust in the reason that criticises and condemns institutions as bad, with too little faith in the reason that once created these institutions themselves and embodied itself in them, however imperfectly.

Aristotle's famous sentence, "Man is by nature a *political animal*," shows the gap between his view of "nature" and that of the Sophists.   This sentence is often quoted as if Aristotle only meant that man was a gregarious animal.   He meant very much more.   At the lowest man is gregarious— that he has in common with many other animals.   But man does not attain to the possibilities open to him, save as the member of a city-state.   The true "nature" of a thing is to

be found not in its rudest, lowest, or most elementary stage,
but in the very highest development of it; and to Aristotle
the Greek city, with its vigorous political life, its opportunities
for friendly intercourse, its art, its philosophy, was the highest
social organisation.   Thus, if it be asked whether there is
anything right by nature, Aristotle's answer is : that is right
by nature which is right, not apart from political institutions
(for that has no meaning to him), but according to the institutions of the best or ideal state.   As with Plato, to find what
justice really is, we look to an ideal society, which is justice
" writ large."

Aristotle's use of the term " nature " does indeed vary, but
the sense of the term which pervades his ethical and political
philosophy is that just noticed.   Nature means to him also the
whole universe, organic and inorganic ; [1] but, by preference, he
uses it for the organic, in which " necessity " does not rule,
but freedom or rationality (the potentiality of opposites), showing itself most clearly in man.   There is never any real
ambiguity in his application of the conception in ethics or
politics.   There are only two important uses of the term
" Nature " in his ethical and political writings : (1) that in
which he uses " natural " for " original," e.g. when he speaks
of man having certain natural (i.e. innate, inherited) impulses
prior to training ; and (2) that in which he uses " nature " for
the ideal.   In the former sense he says that the family is " by
nature " prior to the state (Eth. Nic., VIII. 12, § 7), in the
latter that the state is " by nature " prior to the family and to
the individual (Pol., I. 2, § 12).   As a rule these two senses are
sharply and clearly distinguished.   But even Aristotle seems
to be led away by the fatal and ever-recurring confusion
between the two senses, when (in Pol., I. cc. 8–11) he condemns
those forms of the art of wealth, which he has proved to be less
" natural " only in the sense that they belong to a more complicated stage of human society ; though, in judging of his
opinions on economic matters, one must remember that he has in
his mind an ideal of what the life of the citizen of the good state
ought to be—an ideal which excludes the money-making life.[2]

[1] For Aristotle's distinction between the Nature which works " by
necessity " (= the inorganic), and the Nature which works towards an
end (= the organic), see Mr. Stewart's Notes on Nic. Eth., I. pp. 256–258.

[2] On the subject of Aristotle's economic ideas I may refer to Mr.

There are indeed two phrases in Aristotle's writings, in both of which he seems to be referring to older theories; both of which have, however, led to the belief that Aristotle held a conception of the Law of Nature, substantially identical with that of later times. These two phrases are: (1) the "natural justice" (τὸ φυσικὸν δίκαιον) of the fifth book of the Ethics; and (2) the "universal law" (ὁ κοινὸς νόμος) of the Rhetoric.

1) In discussing Justice, Aristotle has before him the "Sophistic"[1] assertion that there is no natural justice, because the natural must be everywhere the same, whereas men's ideas about what is just and right vary in different places.[2] Accepting the fact of the actual diversity of moral ideas, he still contends that there is an element of unity underlying all this diversity. The existence of left-handed persons does not prevent our saying that "by nature" the right hand is better than the left; it is so on the whole, as a rule. Natural justice is an ideal towards which human justice tends. Natural justice may be found "among the gods"[3]—a phrase that must not be taken literally, for in Eth. Nic., X. 8, § 7, Aristotle ridicules the ascription of justice or any moral excellence to the divine being, which consists in pure intelligence, unmixed with the element of desire from which action springs. "Among the gods" is only a way of saying that perfect justice is for men an ideal only.[4]

In the Sophistici Elenchi (c. 12, 173, a. 7) Aristotle refers to the antithesis between nature and convention as simply a sophistic method, employed e.g. by Callicles in Plato's Gorgias, as a way of reducing an opponent to silence.[5] The essence of the Sophistic argument lies in the antithesis being absolute. Aristotle

Bonar's Philosophy and Political Economy, Bk. I. ch. ii., and to a short article on "Aristotle" contributed by me to Mr. Inglis Palgrave's Dictionary of Political Economy. Those who are not interested in Aristotelian questions may be recommended to omit the next 4 pages. The habitual appeal to Aristotle as sanctioning the idea of a Law of Nature is my reason for entering on the discussion here.

[1] See above, p. 26, note 1.   [2] Eth. Nic., V. 7. §§ 1, 2.   [3] Ibid., § 3.

[4] In Eth. Nic., V. 9, § 12, τὸ πρῶτον δίκαιον is equivalent to τὸ φυσικὸν δίκαιον. So in Pol., IV. 8, § 9, ἡ ἀληθινὴ καὶ πρώτη ἀριστοκρατία means the ideal state. τὸ φυσικὸν δίκαιον would be more correctly translated "jus naturale."

[5] Callicles's "natural justice," or rather "natural right" (τὸ τῆς φύσεως δίκαιον) is might, as opposed to the conventions that the weak set up for their protection (Gorg., 484).

does not hold that there is any absolute antithesis between
nature and convention. This is clear from his discussion of
slavery in the first book of the *Politics*. Nature and convention (positive institutions) do not always coincide—unfortunately; but there is no necessary inconsistency between them.
And similarly, in the fifth book of the *Ethics*, political justice,
or, more correctly, *jus civile* (τὸ πολιτικὸν δίκαιον) is said to be
in part natural and in part conventional (V. 7. § 1), *i.e.* in part
merely conventional. There are some things which before
they are definitely instituted are not obligatory, but become
so by being instituted. I think Aristotle's meaning would be
correctly expressed in the following illustration: it is a
general political duty everywhere for the citizen to pay legally
imposed taxes; but whether it is his duty to pay sixpence or
eightpence in the pound Income-tax depends on the Budget of
the year.

(2) In the *Rhetoric* Aristotle only treats of ethical questions
on the level of ordinary Greek thought, so that when he refers
to the universal law, the unwritten law which is admitted
by all mankind (*Rhet.*, I. 10, 1368, *b.* 7), nay even when he
identifies this universal law with the law according to nature
(13, 1373, *b.* 6), he must not be understood as necessarily accepting the theory in the form in which people in general accepted
it. He is referring to a commonplace of orators.[1] His attitude
towards this commonplace may be learnt from a subsequent
passage, where he gives advice about the use that can be made
of it. "When you have no case according to the law of the
land, appeal to the law of nature and quote the Antigone of
Sophocles.[2] Argue that an unjust law is not a law, etc." (15,

---

[1] Demosthenes (*adv. Aristocr.*, p. 639, 22. Reiske) speaks of the "universal law of all mankind" as something over and above the "written
law." It may be noted that Aristotle, in *Rhet.*, I. 13, 1373, *b.* 18, quotes
Alcidamas, as well as Sophocles and Empedocles, as evidence of the general
belief in this universal law of nature. Now what Alcidamas said was,
if the Scholiast may be believed, that "God made all men free; Nature
has made none a slave" (cf. p. 25 above, *note* 5)—an opinion which Aristotle certainly did not hold (see *Pol.*, I. 4–7). Thus his language in this
passage of the *Rhetoric* is no evidence of his own opinion as a philosopher, but only of a current opinion among his contemporaries.

[2] This stock quotation (*Ant.*, 456) of writers about the law of nature
really means that Antigone is more moved by custom and traditional
religious belief about the duty of burying relatives than by fear of a
tyrant's prohibition. It is no appeal away from *all* institutions.

1375, a. 27 seq.). Athenian courts, it should be noted, had no trained professional judges to check rhetorical vagaries. But if the written law is in your favour, Aristotle is equally ready with suggestions. You must warn the jury against the danger of trying to be wiser than the law: a professional physician may make mistakes, but it does not pay to be cleverer than the doctor: all the best codes forbid the attempt to go behind the law, etc. (1375, b. 16 seq.). In the *Ethics* and *Politics* Aristotle never makes any reference to this "universal law" of the *Rhetoric*; and his feeling about the scientific value of the conception may be fairly inferred from the discussion in the *Politics* (III. 16) of the question whether it is better that an individual or the law should be supreme. He decides, unless under quite exceptional circumstances, in favour of the rule of law, which is "reason without passion." Under law Aristotle explains that he understands customary ($\kappa\alpha\tau\grave{\alpha}$ $\tau\grave{\alpha}$ $\check{\epsilon}\theta\eta$) as well as written law;[1] but customary law is law which admits of proof by means of precedents; it is not a law of nature to be interpreted only by the arbitrary decisions of an absolute monarch. And, when one turns from this discussion to the passage in the *Rhetoric*, one might almost imagine Aristotle looking forward with prophetic vision on the vast turgid river of rhetoric flowing through long ages from its source in the upspringing protest against the rocky barrier of mere external authority—a river destined to sweep away in its course some things that were evil and some things that were good. But Aristotle treats the whole question with scientific impartiality, just as in the *Politics* he sees no inconsistency between sketching an ideal state on the one hand and on the other laying down prescriptions for preserving a tyranny with a cold-blooded calmness which anticipates and explains Machiavelli.[2] "No case: talk about the law of nature," is a more lofty suggestion than "No case: abuse plaintiff's attorney," but is equally a *rhetorical* device. Such a suggestion is hardly sufficient evidence that Aristotle believed in

[1] In *Rhet.*, I. 13, 1373, b. 5, the ἴδιος νόμος (*jus civile*) is divided into written and unwritten. All unwritten law is not κοινὸς νόμος (*jus gentium?*), as might seem to be suggested by 10, 1368, b. 8 standing alone.

[2] *Pol.*, V. c. 11, which should be compared with *The Prince*. The *Prince* has too often been read apart from the *Discourses on Livy*, and has been misunderstood as Aristotle has never been in this matter. Cannot people see that even in the worst state there is a better and worse?

the law of nature in the sense in which its modern advocates
have appealed to it as settling what is right and wrong, apart
from any reference to either statutory or customary law.
Throughout the whole of his *Ethics* and *Politics*, he seems to
hold that in practical matters we can be more certain of
particular judgments as to right and wrong than of general
principles. General principles we must have for the sake of
legislation; but they can only be valid " for the most part," and
may need correction on the grounds of equity by an adminis-
trator, who from his experience has acquired an " eye " (*Eth.
Nic.*, VI. 11, § 6, that will enable him to see rightly in particulars. He does not speak of equity—" the correction of
legal right " (*ibid.*, V. 10, § 3), as the introduction of the law
of nature to correct human law, but as a correction in some
particular instance " of such a kind as the legislator himself
would make, were he present " (*ibid.*, § 5).

If further proof were needed of Aristotle's attitude to the
idea of the law of nature, I might refer to an example which
he gives in the *Topics* (VI. 2, 140, *a*. 6) of a bad definition :
" Law is the measure or image of natural rights " (ὁ νόμος
μέτρον¹ ἢ εἰκὼν τῶν φύσει δικαίων). " Such phrases," he says,
" are *worse than metaphors*: an image arises through imitation, and this is not the case with law." Now to call law an
image is, so far as I can see, very like the notion of positive
human law being a copy or reflection of the Law of Nature.
But we must leave Aristotle for less exact thinkers, on whose
minds these rhetorical phrases took a stronger and firmer hold,
and whom modern defenders of Natural Rights can quote as
authorities with better justification than that with which
they can appeal to " the philosopher."

A set of men, more grimly in earnest with life than the
majority at least of the fashionable Sophists, took this antithesis of nature and convention, not merely as a weapon for
attacking existing institutions with clever dialectic, but as a
guide in conduct. One of the Socratic circle was Antisthenes,
who is said to have previously been a pupil of the Sophist
Gorgias. Antisthenes taught " that the wise man is self-

---

¹ What is meant by this is left obscure—Aristotle does not discuss this
alternative—probably that law *determines* what is otherwise vague, just
as in Aristotle's own theory of exchange (*Eth. Nic.*, V. 5) money " measures " values.

sufficient ; and that virtue does not need learning nor arguments, but deeds only. The wise man will live not according
to the established laws, but according to the law of virtue."
The pupil of Antisthenes, Diogenes, is better known than his
master, because of the gossip about him which has come down
to us through that editor of philosophical " Tit Bits," his
namesake, Diogenes Laertius.[1] Diogenes became the typical
cynic. He represents a revolt against convention, not in
words only, but in life. He disowns the state ; he is a " citizen
of the world." He scoffs at Plato's philosophy ; he appeals
from fine arguments to the coarser evidence of his senses. " I
see a table and a cup ; but I see no tableness or cupness." He
scoffs at Plato's elegant carpet, trampling on it, as on Plato's
pride, " with pride of his own," as Plato retorted. He lives in
a tub instead of in a house. He sees a child drinking out of his
hands, and thereupon throws away his drinking cup, saying,
" The child has beaten me in the simplification of life." In all
things he will follow nature rather than convention. He prefers liberty before everything. There is to be no property.
He argues (in a way that anticipates Wycliffe, *mutatis mutan-
dis*) that as everything belongs to the gods, and the gods are
the friends of the wise, therefore everything belongs to the wise.
There should be no marriage; women and children should be in
common. There is no impiety even in tasting human flesh. It
is said that once he attempted to eat raw meat, but could not
digest it. Of the Cynics generally we are told that they wished
to abolish the whole system of logic and natural philosophy, and
to give up literature, science, and art. They taught that men
should live very simply, using only just as much food as is
sufficient, and wearing only one garment, despising riches and
glory and nobleness of birth. Some of them fed on nothing but
herbs and drank only cold water, living in any chance shelter
they could find. Diogenes used to say that the gods are in
want of nothing, and that therefore, when a man wished for
nothing, he was likest to the gods.[2]

Here we have the " return to nature," the protest against
convention, in its most extreme form. It is a protest which finds
many echoes at various periods, and even in our own day. It

---

[1] " A learned man, in the worst sense of the term," as the late Professor Jowett once described him.

[2] See Diogenes Laertius, Lib. VI., esp. §§ 105–105.

is the Hellenic anticipation of Rousseauism. In the history of thought it is most significant as the starting-point of Stoicism. In Stoicism the Cynic maxims are toned down so as to make them compatible with a fulfilment of the ordinary duties of an honest citizen's life. The self-sufficingness of the Cynic is still professedly held up as an ideal; but his savage individualism gives way before a more social creed, and " Nature " means something more than a mere absence of all that separates man from the beasts. It seems that in the Stoic maxim "to live in harmony with Nature," the words "with Nature " are an addition to the original formula, which meant therefore " to live in a way that is self-consistent." [1] Absence of contradiction in the maxim of conduct reminds one at once of Kant, whose affinity with the Stoics has been frequently noted. Thus reason is the ultimate judge of right conduct ; but reason to the Stoic is not the mere arbitrary whim of the individual. It is something whose decisions admit of argument and discussion. The Stoics, far from despising logic, cultivated it more than any other post-Aristotelian sect. But all theoretical philosophy was in their view subordinate to the practical guidance of life. "Nature " to the Stoics is not the mere chaos of sensible things *minus* whatever results from man's rational efforts. It is objective reason ; it is, as with Aristotle, the divine element in the Universe. The reason of the individual man is only a partial manifestation of it : his reason is a divine element in him, and it is in virtue of this divine element in him that man can understand the reason that is in the Universe and can live the life according to Nature. Thus reason is not something that separates the judgment of one man from that of another. The appeal to reason is an appeal to the common reason of mankind. Human laws and institutions, therefore, are no longer despised as merely conventional. They are a realisation, however imperfect, of the law of Nature which is behind and above them. Even the popular religion is not to be despised as merely false ; it is an imperfect recognition of the deity that pervades the Universe. And the Stoic philosopher may with a good conscience take part in the national worship. Thus Stoicism touches the practical spirit of the legally-minded and conservative Roman on one side, whilst it passes over into Eastern or Neo-Platonic mysticism on the other. Stoicism,

[1] Stobaeus, *Ecl.*, II. c. 6, § 6 (132).

developed among the Greeks when the decaying Greek city-state could no longer provide a basis for the moral life of the individual, developed possibly under Semitic influence, found its truest disciples among the Romans.[1] To some of the noblest souls of the ancient world it became a religion. And it was a religion before which outward distinctions counted for nothing; it was equally the creed of the lame slave Epictetus and of the Emperor Marcus Aurelius.

Cynicism had merely offered a protest against a civilisation in which luxury was beginning to sap the vigour of the race. Stoicism was likewise a creed of political despair; it had no belief in social progress. Nevertheless, by placing its practical ideal, not in the isolation of the individual human being, but in his union with the great whole of nature and humanity— an abstract universal, instead of an abstract particular—it favoured the very social progress which it seemed to deny. It was the fitting creed of the best citizens of a universal empire; it gave an intellectual justification for the breaking down of the barriers of race and caste. Earlier than Christianity it proclaimed that all men were brothers, and that all might be by adoption the sons of God. In its contempt for "things external" as things indifferent, like Christianity, it escaped the need of directly facing many social problems; but it introduced a cosmopolitan and humanising spirit into the minds of practical citizens, who were engaged in the work of administering and interpreting the law of the Roman world.

Cicero is not now considered a great name in the history of philosophy; but he is a very important person in the history of human thought in general. He had no genuine speculative interest in philosophical problems; he is mildly sceptical of all solutions, but kindly disposed to all Schools. Yet in ethics he can be dogmatic enough, and has most affinity with the Stoics, tempering the harshness of their doctrines with elements borrowed from Plato and Aristotle and with the sane, practical judgment of the Roman spirit softened by Greek culture. For the very reasons which make his writings unsatisfactory to the special student of philosophy, they were admirably fitted to

---

[1] It must not indeed be forgotten that the practical character of later Stoicism and its fitness to influence legal reformers was greatly due to the fact of its being adopted by practical and politically-minded Romans. Cf. Zeller. *Eclecticism* (tr.). pp. 11–16.

influence the average educated man. And it is through Cicero's graceful Latin, more than through any other single channel, that so large a portion of Greek, and above all of Stoic ethics, has become the common heritage of the civilised world.

The customary appeal, away from the disputes of the philosophers, to the feelings implanted by God and Nature in the heart of every man, to the common sense or the universal opinion of mankind—this commonplace of popular philosophy is the very essence of Cicero's ethical teaching. And here we find the first distinct formulation of the idea of the law of nature, in that very form of it which survives in modern thought. "In every matter the consent of all peoples is to be considered as the law of nature." "Universal consent is the voice of nature."[1] Not only the fundamental principles of morality, but the existence of God and the immortality of the soul are revealed to us by "that voice of nature" which speaks through the general consent of mankind. This innate consciousness of what is right and true may indeed be obscured and depraved by evil habits, but it is there nevertheless, and it appears clearly in the opinions of the best men, and in the uncorrupted minds of the young, "in whom as in a mirror nature is seen."[2] Is not this just the "Common Sense" or "Intuitionist" philosophy to which so many moderns have resorted as the safest, and undoubtedly the easiest, defence against Scepticism?

It is in this Ciceronian and popular form that Stoic philosophy found its way into Roman law. I do not mean to suggest that the later jurists were conscious of borrowing the idea of the law of nature directly from Cicero, or from any Greek or Roman Stoic philosopher; but that Cicero's use and interpretation of the idea of nature sufficiently explains the introduction of that idea as an equivalent or as a basis for the *jus gentium.* The phrase *jus gentium* was, in the seventeenth century, by a mistranslation taken to mean "the law of nations," what we now call "international law." The mis-

---

[1] "Omni autem in re consensio omnium gentium lex naturae putanda est" (*Tusc.*, I. 13, § 30). "Omnium consensus naturae vox est" (*Ibid.*, 15, § 35).

[2] *De Fin.*, II. 14, § 45; V. 22, § 61. "Indicant pueri, in quibus ut in speculis natura cernitur."

translation was a fortunate one, because it allowed Grotius, and
others, to introduce the humane conceptions of the Roman
" law of nature " into the theory of the right relations between
independent political societies. Nevertheless, it was a mistranslation. *Jus gentium* was the term used to describe those
principles on which Roman magistrates decided cases in which
the parties were not both Roman citizens, and in which,
therefore, the *jus civile* was regarded as inapplicable. *Jus
gentium* meant simply "the principles generally accepted
among mankind," the common law of the world.[1]   In practice
this meant the generally recognised principles of right among
those peoples with whom the Romans came most in contact,
primarily, of course, the other Italian races who were more or
less akin to the Romans in blood, in language, and in social
usages. This *jus gentium*, however, could never be anything
so fixed and definite as the *jus civile* of any particular State.
Hence it left much more scope for the exercise of his own
judgment of what was right or wrong on the part of the
prætor, tempered by that respect for precedent in which the
Romans resemble the English—a respect for precedent which
has contributed so largely to the stability and quiet growth
of legal and social institutions among both peoples. It is
obvious how easily this idea of *jus gentium* or " equity " would
coalesce with that of the law of nature, when the latter conception found its way from Greek philosophy into the minds
of Roman jurists. The law of nature was regarded as something permanently existing behind the particular law of this
or that State; and it came to serve as an ideal of excellence
towards which the civil law should, when possible, be made to
approximate. It served as a standard of simplicity and of
perfection, and, as Sir Henry Maine has suggested, is probably
the chief reason for the progressive character of Roman legal
conceptions.[2]

---

[1] See art. on *Jus Gentium*, by the late Prof. Henry Nettleship in
Journal of Philology. Vol. XIII. p. 169 *seq.*

[2] *Ancient Law*, p. 78. Muirhead (*Roman Law*, p. 304) quotes a remark
of Voigt's " that the risk which arose from the setting up of the precepts
of a speculative *jus naturale*, as derogating from the rules of the *jus
civile*, was greatly diminished through the position held by the jurists
of the early empire. Their *jus respondendi* made them legislative organs
of the State; so that in introducing principles of the *jus naturale* or of
æquum et bonum, they at the same moment positivised them, and gave

One great jurist, Ulpian, drew a peculiar distinction between the *jus naturale* and the *jus gentium* ; according to his view, which is embodied in Justinian's *Institutes*, I. Tit. 2, the law of nature applies not only to men, but to all animals. " It is that which nature has taught to all animals." The union of male and female, which we call marriage, and the rearing of children are in this sense said to belong to the law of nature. Ulpian apparently did not know, or did not take account of the fact, that among some of the lower animals reproduction may occur without sex, and that, except among the higher animals, the young are left to shift for themselves. This distinction, however, allows Ulpian to utter a sentence which was to awaken far-reaching echoes when, after long centuries, it passed out of the region of theoretical jurisprudence into the region of practical politics. Slavery exists *jure gentium*, undoubtedly; *i.e.* all civilised peoples known to the Romans recognised this institution: ancient political society was based on it. But " by the law of nature all men at the first were born free." The appeal to the common usage of all animals would hardly have served Ulpian here, had he known of the slave-holding communities of ants. In using these words, he probably only meant that apart from definite human institution the status of slave did not exist. It might be added, neither did that of the free citizen—the free man in the full sense of the term.

As Maine has pointed out,[1] the chief intellectual discipline of the Western mind, of all that part of the empire whose culture came to it in the Latin and not in the Greek tongue, for nearly three centuries was the study of Roman law.[2] When the first revival of learning began in the twelfth century, it was Roman law which divided with Aristotle the

them the force of law" (Voigt, *Das Jus Naturale, etc., der Römer*, Vol. I. p. 341.)

[1] *Ancient Law*, ch. ix.

[2] It was undoubtedly from the Roman lawyers that " the natural freedom of all mankind " found its way into the Ordinance of Louis X. (Louis Hutin) of France (1315), which was intended to induce serfs to purchase their freedom (as a means of bringing money into the royal treasury). "Comme selon le droit de nature chacun doit naistre franc" is the preamble of the ordinance. The attempt to raise money, says Michelet, was ineffectual; but a king's proclamation of the natural liberty of mankind was not forgotten. (*Histoire de France*, III. p. 198.)

interests of students. And, finally, when the Reformation displaced scholastic Aristotelianism or weakened its authority in Protestant Universities, it was once again Roman law and that Augustinian theology, which was based so largely on legal conceptions, that dominated the thought of most of the nations of Northern Europe. The famous treatise of Grotius, *De Jure Belli et Pacis*, was a principal medium through which the Roman conception of a law of nature came to influence ethical and political speculation. The idea of a law of nature, which forms the background of Locke's political theories, and which from Locke passed on to Rousseau, and to the fathers of the American Republic, comes to Locke mainly from Grotius and from Pufendorf. The other writer who influences Locke, and the writer whom he mostly quotes, is Hooker; and Hooker is the medium through whom the ethical and political philosophy of Thomas Aquinas finds its way into English popular thought. Now the conception of Nature in Thomas Aquinas is derived from Aristotle; but he adds to it the Ciceronian conception of a law of nature, and the law of nature he understands in a far more definite manner as a code of rules which can be ascertained and fully formulated by the use of reason. The ancient conception is generally that of *jus naturale*, though, as we have seen, Cicero already speaks of *lex naturæ*. But in the middle ages the influence of the Hebrew idea of a divinely given code, and the influence of Roman law, no longer as something living and growing, but as finally summed up in a venerable code, tend to give a quasi-legal character to ethics, which has left deep traces on modern thought and made it difficult for us to appreciate the Greek point of view.[1] "Moral law" is the most familiar of modern ethical terms; it is not to be found in Aristotle at all.[2]

Thomas Aquinas makes a very important distinction among the precepts of the law of nature. "First of all there is in man an inclination to that natural good which he shares along with all *substances*, inasmuch as every substance seeks the preservation of its own being, according to its nature. In virtue of this inclination there belongs to the natural law the taking of those means whereby the life of man is preserved,

---

[1] Cf. Sidgwick, *History of Ethics*, pp. 108–110, 112.

[2] As to the κοινὸς νόμος of the *Rhetoric*, see above, pp. 30–32.

and things contrary thereto are kept off. Secondly, there is
in man an inclination to things more specially belonging to
him, in virtue of the nature which he shares with other
animals. In this respect those things are said to be of the
natural law, which nature has taught to all animals, as the
intercourse of the sexes, the education of offspring, and the
like. [With this compare Ulpian, quoted above.] In a third
way there is in man an inclination to good, according to the
rational nature which is proper to him; as man has a natural
inclination to know the truth about God, and to live in society.
In this respect there belong to natural law such natural inclinations as to avoid ignorance, to shun offending other men,
and the like." [*Summa*, 1a 2ae, qu. 94, art. 2. I quote from
Father Rickaby's very convenient translation, *Aquinas Ethi-
cus*, I. p. 282.] Here we have a careful distinction between
natural tendencies and the precepts of reason, which it would
be well if all those who have talked about nature and the
law of nature had always observed. In discussing particular
natural rights, I shall have again to refer to some of the
opinions of the Angelic Doctor and of his followers.

The general conception of natural law in Aquinas corresponds with that of the Stoics: "Natural law is nothing else
than the participation in the eternal law of the mind of a
rational creature" (1a 2ae, qu. 91, art. 2), *i.e.* man partaking
partly in the divine reason can thereby know in some reflection
of it the eternal law, which can be fully known by none save
God Himself and the blessed who see God in His essence (1a
2ae, qu. 93, art. 2). Human law, *i.e.* the positive laws of particular states, is derived from the law of nature, and is only
true so far as it partakes of the law of nature, or is not in conflict with it. By positive divine law Aquinas means the
eternal law as expressly revealed. That of course has no
connection with Greek or Roman ideas, and does not here
concern us.

Now it is to be noted that the Roman conception of a law of
nature, although it did good service in leading to the progressive reform and humanisation of the civil law, did not imply
any direct conflict with positive human law: it was, except on
Ulpian's theory, nearly, if not altogether, identical with the
common element in the customary law of various communities.[1]

---

[1] According to the late Professor Muirhead (*Roman Law*, pp. 298, 299),

And Ulpian's law of nature only differed by including the lower animals. But when the codification of Roman law by Justinian—which we might call in a certain sense the last act of the ancient world—had given it a character of finality, the conception of the law of nature was received by the mediæval world as the conception of something not merely more perfect than any positive human laws, but as something distinct from them. It came to be thought of as an ideal code, not merely as the common or universal element amid the varieties of human usage, but distinct from positive human laws, which might very often conflict with this code. This reverence for the law of nature did good service in helping to bring some degree of order and system into the chaos of French law. As Maine says, "the admission of its dignity and claims was the one tenet which all French practitioners (whether of the *pays de droit écrit*, or of the *pays de droit coutumier*) alike subscribed to."[1]

To the service rendered by the idea of a law of nature in the formation of the modern conception of a law of nations I have already referred. But the influence of the idea on the simplification of French law, and its utility in supplying a set of legal conceptions for the relations of independent political societies, were both only extensions of that power which it had already exercised among the later Roman jurists. In the application of the idea by Thomas Aquinas and his followers we have the germ of something new,[2] of the use of nature as a court of appeal by those whose consciences or whose political aspirations were offended by the positive law of their country.

the notion of a *jus naturale* as distinct from the *jus gentium* was not peculiar to Ulpian. A *jus naturæ* common to man and the lower animals is indeed a law of nature of which we find no other jurist taking account. "But many of them refer again and again to the *jus naturale*; and Gaius is the only one (Justinian following him) that occasionally makes it synonymous with the *jus gentium*." This is a controversy which I must leave to competent students of the Civil Law. The opinion of Muirhead and of Voigt, whom he follows in this matter, brings the Roman *jus naturale* a little nearer to the mediæval conception of it than the opinion of those (*e.g.* Dr. Moyle in his edition of Justinian's *Institutes*, Vol. I. p. 92), who say that Ulpian is the only leading jurist who makes anything of the distinction.

[1] *Ancient Law*, p. 85.

[2] Though, from another point of view, only a return to the idea of the Greek Sophists and Cynics.

Lex injusta non est lex, says Suarez (*De Legibus*, III. c. 19): not merely is an unjust law not to be obeyed, but it is not to be regarded as a law at all. Was it the assurance of a Divine revelation and of an infallible guide in the authority of the Church which made Scholastic ethics so ready to sanction the rejection of the authority of human law? When the authority of the Church was shaken, the way was cleared for revolution in the name of Nature.

But in the writers of the seventeenth century we hear not only of the law, but of the state of nature. For Hobbes the state of nature is simply what would remain if all human institutions were taken away; and this state of nature, he holds, would be a state of war of all against all. In modern phrase we should call it "the struggle for existence," unmitigated by any associations—not even by that of the family; for Hobbes does not appear to take note of the fact that even among the animals, who have never entered into a social contract, there is in some cases a certain limit, temporary at least, imposed on the state of war by the relation subsisting between mates, and still more by that between parent and offspring. Hobbes's argument is that rebellion against the existing government means a return to the "state of nature." Locke, who wishes to justify revolution in certain cases, is therefore concerned to maintain that this state of nature is not a state of mere anarchy, but has a law to govern it; and whereas Hobbes makes the laws of nature all simply consequences of the natural instinct of self-preservation, Locke, thinking of his state of nature as a social state, although not yet a political state, includes in his conception of law of nature very much what Thomas Aquinas includes in it. Locke's "state of nature" is thought of by him as a fairly happy condition, the only drawback to which was that every one had to be judge in his own cause. Locke, moreover, has an idea of "a golden age" existing even after government has come into existence —a time when people did not need "to examine the original and rights of government."[1] A little confusion on the part of his readers (perhaps in his own mind) makes it possible to regard the state of nature as itself the golden age, and the way is prepared for the favourite theory of the eighteenth century :—

[1] *Civil Government*. II. § 111.

> " Nor think in nature's state they blindly trod ;
> The state of nature was the reign of God :
> Self-love and social at her birth began.
> Union the bond of all things and of man.
> Pride then was not, nor arts that pride to aid ;
> Man walk'd with beast. joint tenant of the shade :
> The same his table, and the same his bed ;
> No murder cloath'd him, and no murder fed." [1]

In these lines of Pope's the state of nature is identified with the golden age of the Greek and Latin poets ; and " the reign of God " is an equivalent for Locke's words " has a law of nature to govern it." [2]

Now to think of the law of nature not simply as an ideal which the reason of man may discover behind or above all actual positive laws, but as a law which has in some past age, however dimly conceived, really prevailed, makes a very considerable difference in the way in which the idea of that law affects the conduct of mankind. It becomes something more vivid for the imagination, and the feeling is pretty sure to suggest itself that what once has been may be restored again, if only we can get rid of the evil institutions that have interfered with this blessed state of nature. It is a small step from these lines of Pope's to the passionate invective of Rousseau against civilisation. To the Thomist the law of nature is an ideal *for* human law ; to the Rousseanist it is an ideal to be reached by getting rid of human law altogether.

In explaining the rise of this new conception of the law of nature as the law of a pre-political stage, we must take into account firstly the diminished respect for Aristotle, due to the Reformation and to the Renaissance—to the revolt against the Church, and to the revolt against Scholasticism ; and secondly, the diminished respect for theology and for the authority of the Bible. The Protestantism of the sixteenth century has passed into the rationalistic Deism of the eighteenth. Thus the Scriptural story of Adam in Paradise fades away into the Greek myth of a Golden Age. We must remember, too, that although the Aristotelianism of Thomas Aquinas leads him to regard political institutions as natural to man,[3] yet many Christian theologians had held that government had only come into existence as a consequence of sin. Cain and Nim-

---

[1] *Essay on Man.* III. 147 *seq.*   [2] *Civil Government.* II. § 6.
[3] *De Reg. Princ..* I. 1.

rod[1] were its founders. This is the theological equivalent of
William Godwin's view that "Law is an institution of the
most pernicious tendency." Suarez has to introduce a distinction between the "directive" and "coercive" powers of
government in order to conceal the discrepancy between the
views of St. Thomas and St. Gregory; even if man had not
fallen from the state of innocence, Suarez holds it "probable"
that the directive power of government would have been
necessary, "for even among the angels there is order and lordship *(ordo et principatus)*." The coercive power of government
presupposes some deterioration, so that in respect of it government may be said to have been introduced because of sin.[2]
Thus the heresy of Rousseauism might in this matter claim a
certain degree of ecclesiastical sanction.

The mention of Rousseau suggests another element in the
conception of nature, which came into prominence in the
eighteenth century, and towards the close of it effected the
great revolution in literature and art and manners of which
Rousseau was the earliest conspicuous prophet. The love of
natural scenery, the interest in country life, the preference for
what appeals directly to sentiment over what appeals to the
intellect, form part of the new reverence for Nature as opposed
to human institutions. Rousseau's attack upon literature and
art ended by giving an enormous stimulus to the production
of new forms of them. Pope was little conscious that in those
lines I have quoted he was preparing the way for a reaction
against the whole style of literature and of thought, of which
he was one of the most famous representatives. It is Classicism itself preparing the way for Romanticism and "Natu-
ralism." But the significance of Rousseau in respect of this
idea of Nature is so important, and has been so often misre-
presented, that I must reserve it for separate discussion.

The rationalistic Deism of the eighteenth century affects
the conception of Nature in a further way. "Natural
Theology" gains in importance with the decay of general
belief in ecclesiastical or scriptural authority: when first the

---

[1] Cf. Milton, *Paradise Lost*, XII. 24, for the idea that Nimrod invented
the dominion of man over man, which is contrary to the law of nature.
On the words in *Gen.* x. 9, "a mighty hunter before the Lord," Milton
gives the gloss, "Hunting (and men, not beasts, shall be his game)," etc.

[2] *De Legibus*, III. 1.

Church and then the Bible begin to be doubted, there remains
Reason, and Natural Theology is common ground to the
theologian who acknowledges "Reason, unaided by Revelation" as one of the sources of knowledge about the ultimate
meaning of the universe, and to the "Deist," who considers it
the only source.[1] Adam Smith's course of lectures on moral
philosophy, out of part of which grew his *Wealth of Nations*,
began with Natural Theology.[2] In the conception of nature
which is implied in his advocacy of "the system of natural
liberty," is presupposed the idea of "that great, benevolent,
and all-wise Being, who directs all the movements of nature,
and who is determined to maintain in it at all times the
greatest possible quantity of happiness." This optimistic
Deism, which is common to Pope and Bolingbroke, to Jefferson
and Robespierre, is presupposed alike in the theory of natural
rights of the American declarations and in the theory of
natural liberty of the *laissez faire* economists, though in both
cases doubtless the idea of Nature would not have been applied
in this special way, had it not been for the recognition of evils
caused by oppressive or foolish governments. The theory of
the "Physiocrats,"[3] that man ought to study natural law and
not to disturb its action, assumes that nature is operating in
a way that is beneficial to man.

Finally we must take into account the idea of natural laws
as that is held by the students of natural science, for it affects
not only the conception of economic laws but also the theory
of natural rights as maintained in our own time by Mr.
Herbert Spencer. When the phenomena of human society
come to be brought under conceptions and studied by methods
similar to those used in the study of the phenomena of
vegetable and animal life, the notion of causality is introduced
into ethics and politics and economics which now become
branches of sociology. "Laws of nature" in this sense have,
however, no direct connection with the Law of Nature (*jus
naturale*) of Roman jurists, mediaeval theologians and intui-

[1] The optimism of the Deists is, in one aspect of it, a reaction and a
protest against the gloom of the popular theology.

[2] Cf. T. E. Cliffe Leslie, *Essays in Political and Moral Philosophy*,
p. 150; Bonar, *Philosophy and Political Economy*, p. 148.

[3] Mr. Bonar in his *Philosophy and Political Economy*, p. 96, points
out how the idea of the law of nature had carried Locke in the direction
of what was afterwards known as Physiocracy.

tional moralists. Only in the *lex æterna* of Aquinas and his followers do we find any meeting-point between them; but there is this important difference, that whereas natural laws in the sense of causal sequences or uniformities among phenomena are, if correctly stated, incapable of being broken by man (I say nothing of the controversy about the relation of God to the *lex æterna*, as it is irrelevant here), laws of nature in the ethical sense, like political laws, are statements of what man "ought" to do and are therefore capable of being broken. When we speak of violating a law of physiology, we are using inaccurate language; we mean violating a maxim of health based on, or supposed to be based on, a knowledge of physiology. So far as economic laws are statements of what under certain conditions does happen, they are "natural laws" and cannot be violated. Mr. Herbert Spencer is making use of a mere ambiguity of language when he speaks of the folly of our legislators in trying "to repeal by Act of Parliament a law of Nature."[1] No Act of Parliament can affect what is really a law of nature; and Mr. Spencer need not be afraid of the folly of our legislators, if it only leads them to attempt the genuinely impossible. Mr. Spencer has drawn his own practical maxims from his own conclusions about nature; and some Acts of Parliament run counter to these—that is all.

Mr. Spencer seeks to justify his defence of natural rights by appealing to the actual customs of various savage and barbarian peoples.[2] This may seem to be the appeal to the *consensus humani generis*, except that savages seem to be preferred to civilised races in the appeal, so that we have here rather the Rousseauist than the Roman or Thomist conception of nature; but there are, I think, also present certain associations derived from the modern scientific conception of nature, in the sense of the system of permanent relations subsisting between phenomena. Sociological *facts* are brought forward to settle what is really a practical controversy about what *ought* to be done.

Natural rights have been explained as "biological rights," by which, I understand, is meant that there are certain *natural instincts* or tendencies in human nature which must be re-

---

[1] *Ethics* Part III.), p. 546.
[2] *Man versus State*, pp. 90 *seq.*

spected by legislation. This is obviously very much less than
is meant by " rights " under the law of nature in its old sense.
It is simply an appeal to fact ; and I do not see that it settles
for us which instincts deserve our respect and which do not,
and that is just the important matter in practice. To this
subject I must return.

CHAPTER III

"This transition from the state of nature to the civil state produces a very remarkable change in man, by substituting in his conduct justice for instinct and giving to his actions the morality which they previously lacked. It is then alone that, the voice of duty taking the place of physical impulse, and right taking the place of appetite, man, who hitherto has considered no one but himself, sees himself forced to act on different principles and to consult his reason before listening to his inclinations. Although he deprives himself in the civil state of several advantages which nature gives him, he gains such great advantages in their stead, his capacities are exercised and developed, his ideas are enlarged, his sentiments are ennobled, his whole soul is elevated to such a degree that if the abuses of this new condition did not degrade him often below the level of that from which he has come, he ought to bless without ceasing the happy instant which took him from it for ever, and which of an animal stupid and limited made him an intelligent being and a man."

This passage from Rousseau's *Contrat Social* (I. c. 8) might almost serve as a commentary on Aristotle's doctrine that " man is by nature a political animal," save that Rousseau uses the term "nature" only in a negative sense, for the non-civil state. The qualification which is added to the praise of the civil state also finds its counterpart in Aristotle :—

" A social instinct is implanted in all men by nature, and yet he who first founded the state was the greatest of benefactors. For man when perfected is the best of animals, but when separated from law and justice he is the worst of all; since armed injustice is the more dangerous, and he is equipped at birth with the arms of intelligence and with moral qualities which he may use for the worst ends.[1] Wherefore, if he have

[1] Mr. Welldon translates, " Nature has endowed man with arms which

not virtue, he is the most unholy and the most savage of
animals, and the most full of lust and gluttony." [1]

The civilised man can sink himself lower, but he can also
rise higher than the beast or the savage. The savage is incapable of some civilised vices, but he is also incapable of most
civilised virtues.

The passage I have quoted from Rousseau does not contain
what is usually supposed to be Rousseau's view of civilised
society. The evils incident to the civil state are admitted,
but that only in the civil state can man rise above the animal
is recognised by Rousseau as fully as by Aristotle. No great
writer perhaps has suffered more than Rousseau from having
his views judged by his weakest writings. The *Contrat
Social* is a book much more talked about than read, and the
prevalent opinion about Rousseau's social theories is derived
from the paradoxes of his early prize essays, the *Discourse on
the Sciences and Arts* (1750), which gained a prize, and the
Discourse on the Origin of Inequality among Men (1753, publ.
1754), which did not. It is there he maintains that "our souls
have been corrupted in the proportion in which our sciences
and arts have advanced to perfection"; that "the man who
thinks is an animal spoilt"; that "iron and corn have civilised
men and have destroyed the human race." But even in the
Discourse on Inequality he recognises that the state of nature
"has perhaps never existed, and probably will never exist," and
that when he speaks of it he is using a hypothetical argument
and not attempting to describe the actual, original state of
mankind. Though in the sequel he does refer to a primitive
state, he does not make that his ideal, but considers the
happiest period of human existence to be "that of the development of the human faculties, occupying a golden mean between the indolence of the primitive state and the petulant
activity of our self-love." Savages, he holds, are mostly in
this stage, "the true youth of the world"; and all further
progress has been, in appearance, so many steps towards the
perfection of the individual, and, in effect, towards the de-

are intended to subserve the purposes of prudence and virtue, but are
capable of being wholly turned to contrary ends." This gives a much
better sense, but it seems to require a conjectural emendation of the text,
such as that which Mr. Welldon adopts.

[1] Arist., *Pol.*, I. 2, §§ 15, 16 (Jowett's Translation).

crepitude of the species." Nevertheless, in spite of this
glorification of the savage, he acknowledges that along with
a multitude of bad things in civilisation there are a small
number of good.[1]

In the *Contrat Social*, as we have seen, the proportions of
good and evil are reversed. The whole treatise is singularly
free from the faults that are usually ascribed to Rousseau.
The most conspicuous defect in it is that he does not properly
appreciate representative government (III. 15) — a defect
which he shares with many persons at the present day who
have not his excuse. He had not, like Montesquieu, seen the
English government from a favourable (perhaps too favourable)
point of view. His political ideas had been formed by the
reading of Greek and Latin authors, whose only notion of free
government was that of small city states; and he himself was
born a citizen of Geneva, a republic in many ways analogous
to one of these ancient states, owing its political independence
and its special character in a great degree to its Lycurgus, Calvin.[2] The neighbouring Swiss cantons, with which Geneva
was allied, were direct democracies of the antique type, or
else close oligarchies. Was it strange, then, that Rousseau
should accept the generalisation that only small states were
fitted for democracy, that moderate-sized states might be aristocracies, but that large states (unless by the device of confederation") must be monarchies? But this very opinion of
his should save him from the abuse commonly bestowed on
him, as if he had been a doctrinaire democrat, and were personally responsible for all the errors of the French Revolution.
He fully appreciated the "relativity of politics"; he predicted,
we may almost say, the part which federal government was to
play in the solution of political problems, and of complete
democracy he expressly says, "A government so perfect is not
suited to men."[4] His views about the sovereignty of the
people and about the justification of revolution are identical

---

[1] In the *Lettre à M. Philopolis* he says, "According to me, society is
natural to the human species as decrepitude to the individual; arts, laws,
governments are necessary for peoples, as crutches are for old men."

[2] Cf. *Contr. Soc.*, II. 7 ("Of the Legislator"). In a *note* he says: "Those
who only think of Calvin as a theologian know little of the extent of his
genius."

[3] *Contr. Soc.*, III. 15.

[4] *Ib.*, III. 4.

with those of Locke, expressed indeed in more telling language, and addressed to an audience that was suffering graver and older evils than those which had induced the English Whigs of 1688 to change the government of their country. Rousseau's distinction of "the general will" from "the will of all," and his seemingly mystical idea of the common self (moi commun), are anticipations of the political theories of the great German idealists. Kant, Fichte, and Hegel are disciples of Rousseau in a truer sense than those Jacobin Puritans, Robespierre and St. Just, by whom Rousseau has too frequently been judged.[1]

I do not mean to deny the large part which the idea of "Nature" as the antithesis of civilisation, occupies in Rousseau's thinking. I only wish to insist that it cannot be said to have vitiated the great political treatise of his most mature and soundest period any more than it vitiated the political theories of Locke. That period, however, produced also Émile and La Nouvelle Héloïse; and it is with good ground that theory, "Return to Nature," and the exaltation of sentiment above reason are associated in a special manner with Rousseau, and may be described as "Rousseanism." Rousseau sent his children to the foundling hospital, and could not afterwards trace them. His spiritual children can be found more easily. If one considers the most characteristic features of a great part of European thought since Rousseau's time—the literature of sentiment, the genuine or affected love for natural scenery, the reaction against rationalism and against classicism, even the pessimism of the nineteenth century, along with its deeper sense of sympathy (often more sentimental than rational) with the poor, one might say that, in some degree, we are all Rousseau's children,—at least there are a good many of them at the present time who do not know their spiritual father.

If words always meant what their etymology would suggest, if terms of controversy were always selected on strictly logical principles, the opposition between Socialism and Individualism would not lead one to expect that assertors of "natural rights"

---

[1] On Rousseau's influence on German thought, cf. R. Fester, Rousseau und die deutsche Geschichtsphilosophie (Stuttgart, 1890). On the difference between Rousseau's thought at different periods of his life, cf. Charles Borgeaud, J.-J. Rousseau's Religionsphilosophie (Geneva and Leipzig, 1883), esp. pp. 11 seq.

and worshippers of Nature—as the " not due to human reason "
—were to be found among those calling themselves Socialists.
But the fact is, that a great many of those who most loudly
profess themselves Socialists are amongst those who have shown
least faith in the rationality of human society. To the great
confusion of logical terminology, a great many professing
"Socialists" are at heart "Individualists" and "Anarchists."
In defiance of scientific anthropological science and of history,
they seem to believe that individual freedom has decreased
with the growth of civilisation,[1] and that the return to a state
of nature is the ideal of human progress. The name "Socialist" may indeed reasonably be assumed by those who are
appealing from existing social arrangements to what they
conceive to be better social arrangements, not yet anywhere
realised, who are dissatisfied with existing society because it
is still so largely untrue to its ideal, so largely not social, not
organised, but inorganic and anarchical. But this dissatisfaction frequently takes the form of a repudiation not merely of
this or that form of political organisation, but of all institutions
as such, with the exception, perhaps, of the institution of " the
dear love of comrades "[2]—an exception which is no exception ;
for love or comradeship is a personal relationship springing up
spontaneously between two or more human beings. It may and
does give rise to institutions ; in fact, all institutions may be
said to have grown out of it. But of itself it is no institution,

[1] Cf. Rousseau, who says in the *Discourse on Inequality* that "the
savage lives in himself ; whilst a man in the social state is always outside himself, and can only live in the opinion of others."

[2] Walt Whitman, whose phrase is here quoted, defies classification and
argument as much as he defies everything else. He is the absolute extreme of Protestant individualism, an incarnate "natural rights of man";
in him infinite self-assertion is combined with infinite recognition of the
equal rights of others, and both liberty and equality are merged in a
fraternity so wide and all-inclusive that all distinctions of good and bad,
right and wrong, are lost in a general blaze and blare of democratic enthusiasm. With a noble personality and the capacity of a certain poetic
grandeur, he has become a prophet and teacher in the eyes of a good
many in England who are dissatisfied with the existing chaos and un-
reality of our social structure. But it is awkward to use Walt Whitman
as a guide of conscience. His appreciations are so universal. If he can
hardly be likened to " the darkness in which all cows are black," he might
be described as a blaze of exuberant shadowless sunlight, in which all
geese are swans. On Walt Whitman one English author at least has
been able to write with judgment and sobriety—Mr. William Clarke.

such as can form a relatively permanent clothing or shelter which will outlast the individuals who wear or inhabit it ; it is no institution which can take new members into itself to supplement the living or replace the dead, and which remains as a social inheritance for those who are not yet born.

It is this creation of institutions round him which most of all distinguishes man from the lower animals: the more highly developed forms of it are summed up in the word "civilisation." The higher animals below man have already the germ of social inheritance. Thus, while the insect owes everything, or nearly everything, to inherited instincts, the bird learns by imitation how to build its nest and how to rear its young. Pigeons, unless they have an experienced couple among them, will generally fail to bring up a family. But even the most intelligent of birds or mammalia have only the rudiments of such social inheritance when compared with man ; and for this reason they remain stationary, while man progresses. "The owl," says Edgar Quinet, "has outlived Pallas Athene ; the eagle has outlived Jupiter ; they have not lost a feather in the fall of the gods."[1] "They have not lost a feather" ; but neither have they learnt a note of music, nor improved their style of domestic architecture.

Civilisation is a vague term, and to different persons it suggests different ideas. To some people it suggests railways and telegraphs ; to some it suggests bustling streets, showy shop-windows, boulevards, cafés, theatres ; to some it suggests chimney-pot hats and black coats ; to some it means Christian churches, parliaments and policemen ;[2] to some it means mainly art, science, and literature ; to our modern Cynics or Rousseauists, to those whose prophets are Thoreau and Walt Whitman, it is a disease which needs to be cured by "a return to nature."[3]

To analyse civilisation adequately would mean to write a

[1] *L'Esprit Nouveau*, p. 25.

[2] There is a well-known story of an Irishman, shipwrecked in an unknown land ; when he saw a man hanging on a gallows, he exclaimed, "Arrah, but this is a civilised country !" When, soon after, he saw a man lying drunk in a ditch, he cried out in grateful recognition, "Begorrah, but this is a Christian country !"

[3] At the close of his eloquent essay, which bears the significant title, *Civilisation : its Cause and its Cure*, Mr. Edward Carpenter says:

"The present competitive society is more and more rapidly becoming

complete treatise on sociology. At present let me attempt to
distinguish its principal elements or constituents, using the
term to mean what distinguishes man from the animals and
what (to adopt a phrase I have suggested elsewhere [1]) enables
mankind to progress independently of heredity and of mere
natural selection.

(1) First of all, civilisation implies control over the forces of
nature; and greater civilisation implies that such control is
greater. From the discovery of how to make fire by rubbing
sticks together on to the inventions of the telegraph and the
telephone, man has been learning how to use nature as his
servant. Man, it has been suggested, might be defined as a
tool-making animal. (2) Secondly, language makes it possible
to transmit experience; and when to language are added the
inventions of writing and printing, this power of bequeathing
ideas is immensely increased. A greater power of expressing
and of diffusing ideas is thus one mark of a higher degree of
civilisation. Man is a speaking animal; and because a speaking
animal, he is also a rational or thinking animal, for language
makes possible the psychological advance from particular images
or representations to general concepts or ideas. Reflection,
moreover, though it may among the great mass of human
beings be mainly occupied with matters of direct practical
necessity, can be employed also about everything in the
universe, and about man himself, though such reflection may
have only an indirect practical value or apparently none at all.
Thus science, philosophy, history are among the marks which
distinguish a civilised from an uncivilised people. The tales
and myths of primitive races are the germs from which they
spring. (3) Thirdly, man has a delight in doing or making
things which are of no practical utility, for the sheer delight of
doing or making them. This " play," or free purposeless use of

a mere dead formula and husk, within which the outlines of the new and
human society are already discernible. Simultaneously, and as if to
match this growth, a move towards Nature and Savagery is for the first
time taking place from within, instead of being forced upon society from
without." The words " for the first time " show a curious oblivion of
Rousseau, and of the Cynics.
[1] *Darwinism and Politics*, Ed. 2, p. 101. Cf. Weismann *Essays upon
Heredity* (Engl. tr.). Vol. II. p. 51, where the editor of the translation,
Prof. E. B. Poulton, cites my definition, of which he approved when I
first hit upon it.

control over the body and over surrounding objects, exists in
germ among the lower animals, though with them, except among
the very young, it is mostly connected with sexual selection.
Among human beings it is the source of art. From the wild
dances and songs of the savage grow up music, poetry, the
drama; from his attempts to adorn his person, his weapons, his
hut, or to represent the beasts he has seen or the gods he
believes in, are developed architecture, sculpture, painting.
Man is more than a mere imitative animal; he is a creator, so
far as he is able. Art, then, is another mark of civilisation.
(4) Fourthly, men come to use their thinking and their making
powers to regulate their relations with one another; *i.e.* their
social structure comes to depend not merely on natural selection
operating among competing tribes or communities, but to
result in part from conscious attempts at organisation. In other
words, civilised man formulates definitely and becomes fully
conscious of the laws and institutions which have grown up in
his community, and thereby on the one hand deliberately
adopts habits of reverence for law, and on the other hand becomes capable of carrying out political, social, ethical, religious
reforms (or, at least, changes) in a way impossible to him at a
ruder stage of existence. Man is a political animal; and the
use of written laws, which all may (potentially) come to know,
and the possibility of carrying out peacefully constitutional
changes, are marks of civilisation. The habit of " free government," *i.e.* of living under institutions which are not looked on
as some alien authority imposed from without, or existing
merely because they have existed in the past, but which in
some considerable degree correspond to the saner and soberer
sentiments of the more socially minded and orderly members
of the community, is a mark of civilisation, not perhaps the
most obvious; for people governing themselves have often been
behind those more despotically governed in some, if not all, of
the other characteristics of civilisation : but it is a mark which
is directly connected with the original meaning of the term.
To be a *civis* is to be the citizen of a self-governing political
society, the highest form of which known to the ancients was
the city republic of the Hellenic world. Starting from a
similar self-governing town, the Romans first conquered and
then Romanised and civilised the less advanced races of the
Mediterranean world, whilst they themselves assimilated a

great part of that Hellenic culture which had originated in the
cities of Ionia, and had reached its perfection in the city of
Athens, and which was kept alive and spread to east and west
from the cosmopolitan city of Alexandria. And when the incursion of the northern barbarians broke down the fabric of
ancient civilisation, it was in Roman cities above all that some
fragments of it were sheltered, and it was in the self-governing
city republics of Italy and in the "free towns" of the German
empire, that art and the peaceful pursuits of secular life first
revived and flourished. Even the Church, which through
many dark centuries represented the only force in Western
Europe making for peace and order and the intellectual goods
of mankind, was the Roman Church, carrying on in a new
form the discipline and the organisation which had originated
in the Imperial City. Rousseau himself dedicates his second
indictment of civilisation—*The Discourse on Inequality*—to the
Republic of Geneva, of which he was proud to count himself
a citizen. Even Walt Whitman, with his love of fresh air
and with all the prairies of America before him, seems to turn
affectionately to the "populous pavements" of the close-packed
city that covers the island of Manhattan.

It is this connection of civilisation with city life that more
than anything else has caused the revolt against it. The
massing together of human beings makes some good things
possible, but makes the evils of human society more conspicuous.[1] It has been noticed, moreover, by several students
of art and literature, that the love of the sights and sounds,
the quiet and peace of the country, does not enter prominently
into poetry and painting except after the rise of great cities.
Still more is this true with regard to the sentiment for the
wilder and more terrible aspects of nature. "The love of
Nature," it has been said by a subtle critic of Roman literature,
" is not, as we might naturally expect it to be, a feeling much
experienced by those who live in constant contact and conflict
with its sterner forces, as by husbandmen, herdsmen, and
hunters; nor is it developed consciously in primitive times or
unsophisticated races; but it is the accompaniment of leisure,

---

[1] Cf. Plato, *Laws*, III.678: "How can we possibly suppose that those
who know nothing of all the good and evil of cities could have attained
their full development, whether of virtue or of vice?"

culture, and refinement of life." [1] Like many strong feelings. it is due to reaction.

Undoubtedly some races are more susceptible to the beauty or impressiveness of natural scenery than others, the Celts perhaps more than the Saxons, the Italians more than the Greeks. Occupation, however, has probably in all cases more to do with the matter than race : a people of herdsmen or hunters are more likely to develop some taste for scenery than a people engaged in agriculture. But the cultured lover of nature is very apt to mistake the home-sickness of the mountaineer or of the fisherman, for a purely æsthetic appreciation of mountain and sea. Custom strongly affects the feelings even of the most reflective and the most logical minds : with simple and unsophisticated persons who have gone through few changes in their surroundings, custom is all-powerful. It is said that a Shetlander, finding himself for the first time in a beautiful woodland district, was filled with a feeling of terrified oppression : he seemed unable to breathe, and was afraid the trees would fall on him. His longing for the sea and for his bare rocky islands was of the same kind as the longing of many a city-bred person for the smooth pavement and the smell of asphalt. There is probably also in most cases a physical basis in the longing for sea and mountain—a longing which many even of those who have lived chiefly in midland plains can understand. Lungs accustomed to a fresher air seem stifled amid leafy lanes and green meadows as well as amid brick walls. When such physical feelings and the associations derived from habit are left out of account, it will be found that the genuinely æsthetic love of the country is in the main a product of city life.

All the fine arts, indeed, require the existence of city life for their rise and growth. The landscape painter, when landscape painting has once become an established form of art, may work in the country, and may work best in the country, but his pictures are painted for the town : and it is to the landscape painter that we owe a great deal of our admiration of natural scenery.[2] Prof. Weismann has pointed out that "nearly all

<hr/>

[1] Sellar, *Virgil*, p. 47. On p. 46, *note*, Mr. Sellar refers to two German writers, Woermann and Helbig.

[2] "Even such an analysis of natural beauty in the light of physical fact as has been attempted by Ruskin in the *Modern Painters* is chiefly

the renowned (musical) composers and singers of the present
century have come from large towns."[1] Great buildings,
adorned with paintings and sculpture, may indeed be erected
in the country; but it is only in large towns that there is
a sufficiently continuous demand for architecture and the
imitative arts, or sufficient opportunity for studying them. By
an extensive use of all modern inventions which diminish the
inconvenience of distance, future generations may be able to
combine, in a way we can only dream of, the advantages of
both town and country; but those who wish to begin their
social revolution by abolishing everything that did not exist in
the twelfth century, or in ancient Hellas, or in unsophisticated
Japan, or in the Garden of Eden, or wherever and whenever
they place their golden age, are under a strange delusion if
they hope to live in a primeval forest with no governments, no
schools, no institutions of any kind, and yet to hear the music
of Beethoven, or have their walls adorned with frescoes worthy
of the best age of Florence. Rousseau is more consistent than
Mr. William Morris or Mr. Edward Carpenter: art must be
expelled from the ideal state of nature, along with science,
and along with government.

No element of civilisation is possible without the city. But
need the city be for ever what the word is too apt to suggest
to us?—a grimy wilderness of monotonous rows of sombre and
often bad brick, every chimney-pot contributing its pollution
to the atmosphere, the eyes met on all sides by flaring advertisements of soap and pills and mustard, the ears stunned by
ceaseless discordant cries of the latest newspaper with the
latest murder, a pervading odour of horse-dung and of the filth
of ill-cared-for, overcrowded human beings, whilst the more
prosperous are arrayed in coats and hats and trousers that
make sculpture impossible or ludicrous; and beyond all the
dreary noises, beyond everything that offends the senses or
the taste, the ever-present picture of the ceaseless struggle for
existence. May we not rather call up a vision of a city, suggested to us partially even now by some ancient towns, and by

directed to showing how great artists have extended the boundaries of
so-called natural beauty, by their superior insight into the expressive
capabilities of natural scenes and objects." — Bosanquet, *History of
Æsthetic*, p. 4.

[1] *Essays upon Heredity* (Engl. trans.), Vol. II, p. 48.

some parts of some modern towns—a city not too large, but of such size that from the upper windows of the Town-hall the fresh fields can be seen—a city with a smokeless sky and clean streets, no shops, and above all no advertisements, but a large central market for needful exchange, no one interested in making any one buy what he or she does not want, handsome buildings and large leafy spaces, all the inventions of science used to diminish irksome labour, and all the wealth of art lavished not on the gratification of private luxury, but on the adornment of the property of the commonwealth? But it is an odd way of preparing such a commonwealth, to condemn civilisation as a disease, to exalt ignorance above science, and the savage above "the heir of all the ages." Every one of the elements or materials of civilisation may be turned to a bad purpose: is that a reason for wishing them destroyed? On the same principle we might well wish that Prometheus had kept his discovery to himself. There is quite as good reason for blaming him as for blaming James Watt or George Stephenson.

In this revolt against civilisation there are, however, undoubtedly important elements of truth. Civilisation, as it has just been defined and analysed, consists of certain means or instruments (material and intellectual) for human well-being; and these means or instruments are capable of being inherited in the legal or social, not in the biological sense of inheritance. But what is properly an instrument may come to be regarded as if it were an end in itself. Tools and ornaments and institutions were made for man, and not man for tools and ornaments and institutions; and yet the individual may become the slave of the things he has created or, more likely, of the things he has inherited. The miser who accumulates coin is an abnormal product of half-civilisation, and is recognised as such by every one except himself: what is not so generally recognised is the slavery of the ordinary civilised man and woman to clothes, which have to be varied when there is no need, and to customs which change or do not change quite irrespective of use or convenience—all this implying wasteful expenditure and unnecessary fatigue on the part of those who are supposed to enjoy the full benefits of civilisation, and excessive toil on the part of those who do not. Civilisation is not evil in itself, but because its products are so unequally

distributed and so irrationally used. Again, the mere fact of
social inheritance, whilst aiding enormously the advance of
humanity, contains in it the possibility of danger. It implies
to a very great extent a cessation of natural selection. Thus,
what is in many respects a highly civilised race, may become more and more physically enfeebled, till it falls a prey
to internal degeneration, and to the attack of some rudely
equipped, but vigorous barbarian invaders.

This is the too familiar history of the great empires of the
old world. But the success of the barbarian does not prove
the absolute superiority of barbarism over civilisation. The
healthiness and strength of the barbarian, as of the wild
beast, are due simply to the ruthless action of natural selection.
The savage (if the paradox may be excused) is free from
disease, just because he so readily falls a victim to it. Epi-
demics which are comparatively mild among civilised peoples
rage with frightful virulence among people living under
more primitive conditions. Tribes engaged in constant warfare are exposed to a double process of natural selection : the
tribe possessed of the greatest strength, endurance, and
courage succeeds best, and kills off the others ; and within a
warlike tribe the more successful warrior is the more successful man. Peace is generally accounted a blessing, and is
usually lauded by those who preach the return to nature ; but
peace means a cessation of natural selection, and consequent
decay in the average physique. War and hunting are the
only honourable pursuits among the finer savage races, and
both pursuits ensure a high standard of physical excellence ;
but the killing of men, the capture of women, and the chasing
of beasts are not occupations admired by our humanitarian
neo-savages. Infanticide and the habit of killing off the aged
are primitive modes of artificial selection. But these methods
of social salvation also would probably be reprobated by the
higher barbarism of the present day. Even the physical
vigour of savage, compared with civilised, races is frequently
over-estimated, and for the power of triumphing over natural
difficulties more than physical vigour is needed. An authority, quoted by Mr. Edward Carpenter himself, in an appendix
to his indictment of civilisation, admits as much : "In
endurance the African savage beats us hollow (except trained
athletes). . . . But for *sudden* emergencies they are no-

where."[1] And even for those forms of *endurance* which require "pluck" as well as vigour, it may be questioned whether the civilised man is not as a rule superior. To improve the average physical well-being of modern humanity, it is a violent remedy to strip off our clothes, pull down our houses and expose ourselves to the sunshine, which, in this region of the world, "Nature" so often fails to provide. A diet exclusively of fruit and grains, no government, no medical science, are hardly the proper prescriptions for the sufferings of our age.[2] The Greeks, for whose art Mr. Carpenter expresses admiration, were certainly not destitute either of government or of science, and, although living in a milder climate than ours, they did not restrict themselves to fruit and grains. The Athenians of the great artistic age are the very type for all time of a civilised people; and their civilisation assuredly did

[1] Quoted from Mr. H. B. Cotterill in *Civilisation, its Cause and its Cure*, p. 50.

[2] "It may be noted," says Mr. Carpenter (*Civilisation, etc.*, p. 38), "that foods of the seed kind—by which I mean all manner of fruits, nuts, tubers, grains, eggs, etc. (and I may include milk in its various forms of butter, cheese, curds, and so forth), not only contain by their nature the elements of life in their most condensed forms, but have the additional advantage that they can be appropriated without injury to any living creature—for even the cabbage may inaudibly scream when torn up by the roots and boiled, but the strawberry *asks* us to take of its fruit, and paints it red expressly that we may see and devour it! Both of which considerations must convince us that this kind of food is most fitted to develop the kernel of man's life." "Man's life," I suppose, is a nut to crack; but I doubt if Mr. Carpenter has done it successfully. One is glad to see, however, that eggs have a better claim to be eaten than cabbages. This is a mitigated vegetarianism. But are "milk, butter, cheese, curds, etc.," "seeds"? And what if there be mites on the cheese? And if eggs of fowls may be taken without sin against Nature, why not the roe of fishes, when it can be removed without injuring the developed fish (for it is apparently only the fully developed animal that this reformed science holds to be "living")? These are some interesting problems in casuistry for those who would conscientiously apply the Law of Nature. As to strawberries *versus* cabbages, it is not for *us* that the strawberry paints itself red, but for the bird who will help to spread its seeds. And the market gardener who cultivates fruits to such perfection that the seeds are almost absent is surely violating Nature's holy plan.

The late Professor Lorimer, in his interesting development of the idea of *Naturrecht*, speaks of the "rights" of the "last rose of summer" not to be plucked (*Institutes of Law*, p. 325). What becomes of the rights of the *ugly* weeds in a garden? Still, Professor Lorimer's conception of the Law of Nature at least does not dethrone man from his dominion over the creatures.

not lack its dark side any more than ours. He who would really lead us towards the promised land of an ideal democracy, must not merely lead us out from among the flesh-pots of Egyptian bondage, and leave us without a guide and without the tables of the law in the wilderness of savagery—a sure prey to the strongest and least scrupulous amongst ourselves or our neighbours.

The problem is a harder one: can a general equality of social conditions be attained without the loss of any of those instruments of human well-being which we wish to be enjoyed by all, instead of half-enjoyed or abused by the few? In other words, is civilisation possible without a slave class, and without "free" competition? If it is not possible, there are a good many who will think democracy is a barbarian invasion, worse than that of the Goths and Vandals. Some of us, however, do believe and hope that, as in that older invasion the barbarian was gradually conquered by the *civilitas* he at first despised and hated,[1] so in the new society which will grow up, as the barriers of caste are broken through by the peaceful weapons of education and legislation, the new inheritors of an old civilisation will glory in the citizenship to which they are admitted, and in treasures of thought and knowledge and art to which all who choose may have access, along with sufficient leisure in which to use their opportunities; nor will the aristocrat and the *bourgeois* go without their due meed of praise for having attained and kept alive among themselves ideals of culture, and for supplying from among their own

[1] Cf. the passage from Orosius, *Hist.*, VII. 43, quoted by Mr. Hodgkin in his *Theodoric*, p. 1. Orosius tells how Ataulfus, brother-in-law and successor of Alaric, the first capturer of Rome, " was intimate with a certain citizen of Narbonne, a grave, wise, and religious person, who had served with distinction under Theodosius, and often remarked to him that in the first ardour of his youth he had longed to obliterate the Roman name and turn all the Roman lands into an Empire which should be, and should be called, the Empire of the Goths, so that what used to be known as Romania should now be Gothia, and that he, Ataulfus, should be in the world what Cæsar Augustus had been. But now that he had proved by long experience that the Goths, on account of their unbridled barbarism, could not be induced to obey the laws, and yet that, on the other hand, there must be laws, since without them the Commonwealth would cease to be a Commonwealth, he had chosen, for his part at any rate, that he would seek the glory of renewing and increasing the Roman name by the arms of his Gothic followers, and would be remembered by posterity as the restorer of Rome, since he could not be its changer."

members the very leaders and spokesmen of democracy in its
attack on a civilisation which seems evil, not because there is
too much of it, but because it is accessible to too small a portion
of mankind.

As to the burden of civilised life on those who do now share
its advantages, is not that largely due to the barbaric or patriarchal fashion in which we still manage things? We are
only "citizens" in a small fraction of ourselves; for the rest,
we try, if we can, in our separate households to keep up a
museum or an art gallery of an inferior kind. What barbarians we may seem some day—every household doing its
own cookery! Older generations of housewives would have
been as much horrified at sending their clothes to a public
laundry, or at getting their bread from a baker, as their successors are at the idea of public kitchens. Those who boast
themselves most sturdily "individualists" are generally those
whose social ideal is most completely of the patriarchal type.
"The Englishman's house is his castle"—an ideal borrowed
from the barbaric isolation of the household of the robber
baron. The tent of the Arab sheikh, the cave of the Cyclops,
the den of the wild beast with its mate and its cubs—these
are the ideals that are preferred to the life of the Athenian
citizen.[1] If the householder has to be king, high priest,
finance minister, foreign secretary, minister of war, besides
earning his income, i.e. being his own general, waging war
on rival potentates, while his consort is at the same time
queen, minister of the interior, diplomatist, master of the
ceremonies, minister of fine art, minister of education, besides being mother of some of her subjects, nurse of some of
them, and foreman in a domestic factory, no wonder that
little time and energy remain over for them to "possess their
souls before they die." Yet does not such a description answer
fairly well to the model British well-to-do professional or
business man, and the model British matron? To shake off
the burden of things upon us, we may, of course, lower our
standard of living in the intellectual,[2] and not merely in the
economic sense; but a more systematic division of labour and

---

[1] Le Play consciously and deliberately finds his ideal society among
some of the pastoral peoples of Central Asia. (*L'École de la paix Sociale*,
pp. 20 seq.)

[2] We need a word to correspond to the German *geistig*.

a more complete organisation would be a solution that would involve less sacrifice of the higher goods of life.

True, the physical basis is primary. More and more we discover, often too late, how much happiness and usefulness depend on health and vigour. Man must not be content to be a fine animal alone; but of all tools a well-equipped body is the least dispensable. So far, all moralists and social reformers would nowadays agree with the cult of "the friendly and flowing savage" (I do not the least know what that second epithet means: I wonder if Walt Whitman knew). We have shaken off, in words at least, that contempt for the vile body which has been the worst legacy of Oriental and ecclesiastical asceticism. But for that deterioration which is due to the shelter of civilisation and the consequent partial cessation of natural selection, is the only remedy to be found in a return to the savage state. *i.e.* to the unchecked play of the coarse and cruel action of the struggle for existence? Of course, nothing is to be said against, and everything for, an occasional playing at savages by way of a good holiday—weather permitting. The passion for hunting among our well-to-do " barbarians," as Matthew Arnold called them, is a perverted form of a healthy instinct. The serious direct struggle of the savage with nature is imitated in play as the relaxation of civilised life. By all means let us have a crusade against unhealthy, inconvenient, and ugly clothing, let us prohibit starch (physical and social), let us set up a guillotine, not for heads, but for top-hats; but let our revolutionary tribunal be occupied, not by a carelessly modelled figure of Nature, but by those products of civilisation, men of science and artists. Instead of decrying the modern science of medicine, would it not be wiser to turn its practitioners into an "established church" with the primary duty of *preventing* illness, with compulsory sanitary laws to back them up, and with power to prohibit the parentage of the unfit? Either natural or *rational* artificial selection must be at work—at present there is a great deal of irrational artificial selection—or else a race must deteriorate under civilisation. It is well that people should be compelled to face these alternatives; and the assailants of civilisation deserve our gratitude for forcing the problem on reluctant minds. But when these " advanced thinkers " devote so much of their energy to abusing the very sciences to which we must look for aid, when in

the name of Nature they vilify the patient researches of the
bacteriologist, and, as anti-vivisectionists, anti-vaccinationists,
and anti-everything-that-is-scientific, give literary countenance to the suspicion with which the superstitious and the
ignorant have always regarded science, they make one dread
that the remedy is still far off, and that Plato for a long time
to come will be called a foolish dreamer for thinking that the
wise should rule.

Anarchists are of three kinds. First of all, there is the old-
fashioned Radical who repeats the revolutionary creed of 1789
in changed times, to whom an association called a government
is an object of suspicion, whilst an association called a joint-
stock company is an object of admiration. This old-fashioned
Radical does not think himself a survival, but imagines that
he has the verdict of the newest science on his side. He
would abolish legislation, but would leave the judicial functions of government to enforce what he calls natural rights,
but what are really the legal and customary rights resulting
from ancient legislation or want of legislation. He professes
to give every one a fair start, but does not notice that the
runners are unequally weighted. He calls himself an individualist, and is only a half-hearted Anarchist. His anarchy is
anarchy based on the existing economic structure of society.
He believes in Nature, but forgets that it is a Nature that has
been operating for ages among human beings. Nature to him
really means human society under a completely triumphant
" Manchester School." He would contribute to the amelioration of the species by abolishing all sanitary legislation, but
would perhaps lend the tender-hearted private philanthropist
a free hand in encouraging the propagation of beggars in order
to give scope to his altruistic sentiments.

Secondly, there is the thorough-going Anarchist, who does not
consider government a *necessary* evil, but an evil altogether.
He is produced, as might be expected, most easily in Russia.
Outside Russia he is a much more amiable person than those
who belong to the first species; he has an intense belief in the
natural goodness of man, combined with an equally intense
belief in the badness of all the institutions that man has ever
produced. He often calls himself a Socialist. He is a Cynic
without cynicism. While the first type has very little reverence for the past, this milder type has a great love for some

past age, provided it be sufficiently remote; and while in his
own age he can only see darkness, he ignores everything but
the bright side in his chosen period.   He would make us all
healthy, happy. and wise, by reverting to the life of savages,
forgetful that the old cycle would be sure to repeat itself, and
that our own evil "civilisation period" would either be forgotten altogether, or would only be remembered in an idealised
form, just as he thinks of the Iroquois, or the Athenian, or the
mediæval Englishman, without recalling the dark shadows in
the picture.

Lastly, there is a species of criminal, either a reversion to
the savage type, or produced by the cruelty of half-civilisation acting on a sensitive or unbalanced nature.   He borrows
the language of the previous type, with whom he is apt to be
confused by the careless.   To one branch of science only he
is not hostile, and that is the chemistry of explosives.   He
makes war on society by killing and maiming at random.   He
is perhaps able to die like a martyr, or a hero of melodrama,
but is probably half insane.   Such unfortunate and dangerous
beings have existed at all times.   In some communities and in
some periods they would be religious fanatics.   In modern
Europe and North America they call themselves Anarchists,
and sometimes obtain mistaken sympathy from Anarchists
of the harmless sort, and from other sentimental persons.
Assassins who risk their own lives to kill a tyrant, or a
strongly guarded person whom they sincerely believe to be a
tyrant, and therefore a noxious kind of beast, may occasionally
command our respect, and in some extreme cases our admiration; but the dynamiter deserves nothing but a fair trial and
a quick death, or permanent detention in a lunatic asylum.

In all its forms Anarchism is an example of what Hegel calls
"abstract thinking," that is to say, the habit necessary in
ordinary conversation, and encouraged by the unavoidable
limitations of language, of regarding one aspect of a subject to
the exclusion of all the others, the habit of taking up a formula
which may be true enough in its context, isolating it from the
surroundings which made it valuable, and carrying it out re-
gardless of consequences.   In its extremest shape "abstract
thinking" is monomania, which may often take a criminal
form.   In its more familiar aspects, it is that narrow, one-sided
logic which produces religious or social bigotry—a character-

istic which the most wildly heterodox may share with the most rigidly conventional. "Faddists" are abstract thinkers, and so are all those whose acceptance of formulas is not tempered by a genial disposition or by a sense of humour—the only safe substitute for a sound system of metaphysics. Shelley's "Notes" to *Queen Mab* are an exposition, in very temperate language on the whole, of Anarchism of the kind which I placed second. They preach "the return to Nature" precisely in the Anarchist sense. Abstract thinking is apt to extend itself from one matter into another. In a disciple of Shelley's "principles" may be found another very good example of "abstract thinking." Mr. H. S. Salt[1] thinks that to admire Shelley's poetry, while apologising for his "social heresies," is an untenable position. This is a terrible doctrine: may we not eat flesh and yet admire the "Ode to the Skylark," or the "Ode to the West Wind," or "Adonais"? A small portion of "Queen Mab" is perhaps the only part of Shelley's *verse* that for its thorough appreciation needs an acceptance of the "central underlying convictions" of the poet respecting the necessity of abstinence from animal food, etc. Certainly a person who abhors the mere suggestion of any alteration in the structure of society will find a good deal to offend him in Shelley, and may prefer a "safer" poet; but how little of what is best and grandest in literary art depends for our enjoyment of it on the social theories of the writer?[2] Why, even if we turn to works *professedly* controversial (which the best poetry never is), may only Anglicans admire Hooker and Jeremy Taylor, may only Roman Catholics admire Pascal and Bossuet—and not both together, may only Baptists admire Bunyan? Must we accept "the central underlying convictions" of Newman or of Carlyle

---

[1] *Shelley's Principles*, p. 14.

[2] The principle, or "cant," of "art for art's sake" is likewise a result of "abstract thinking": it involves an abstract use of the distinction between style and matter, between treatment and subject. But we must not ignore the unequal development of even the greatest of mortals. An exquisite stylist may be a somewhat superficial thinker—at least on some matters, and a master of psychological analysis, or a teacher of most excellent and necessary doctrine, may fall into terrible dulness, obscurity, or cacophony. It is said that Tennyson once said of Browning: "He is a great poet, but he does not understand the glory of words."—a considerable qualification in speaking of a poet. Shelley did understand "the glory of words"; but that is not in itself a sufficient ground for setting him up as an infallible authority in ethics or politics.

to take delight in them as writers? Thank the Muses, in the Catholic temple of Art the voice of controversy is hushed, and the disputants stand side by side in their niches, as their books may stand side by side on our shelves, and as their dust may rest reconciled in the peace of the grave.

But to return to " nature "—I mean to the uses of the term— —the Rousseanist antithesis between nature and man is a typical example of " abstract thinking." When Cowper says, " God made the country and man made the town "[1] (substituting " God " for Nature, in deference to his own orthodoxy), he utters what quite represents the usual frame of mind of those who preach the " return to nature," but what contains at once very curious theology and very curious history. If man made the town, who then made man? Man, acting under the stimulus of wants and impulses implanted in him by "nature," has manipulated some of the material with which " nature " has supplied him, and a town hideous or beautiful, healthy or unhealthy, is the result. And what of the country? Man, it is true, has written no furrows on the ocean's brow, he has left no footprints on the eternal snows; but what else in "nature" has man not affected, directly or indirectly? What was " the country " of which Cowper thought? English hedgerows, pollard willows, waving corn-fields. Has not man made these in almost the same sense as that in which he makes a great cathedral, when he lifts " out of the populous city, grey cliffs of lonely stone into the midst of sailing birds and silent air "?[2] The difference is one of degree only. These " English elms " own their Italian origin—was it the Romans who brought them first?—by their seeds seldom ripening under our colder skies. Not only the fauna and flora, but the very climate of a country is affected by the action of man; the rainfall is increased or diminished by planting or by cutting down forests. Mr. Carpenter recognises this in order to take a fresh opportunity of blaming man. "Our climate is greatly of our own creation. . . . It is we who have covered the lands with a pall of smoke, and are walking to our own funerals under it ! "[3] Yet the climate of Britain was probably damper even than now, before marshes were drained and forests cut down. Tacitus tells us that " the sky is filthy

[1] *The Task* near the end of " The Sofa."
[2] Ruskin, *Seven Lamps of Architecture* (" The Lamp of Power ").
[3] *Civilisation, its Cause and its Cure*. p. 57.

with frequent showers and fogs." [1] Birmingham and Manchester can hardly be blamed for that. Adapting Cowper's lines, we should have to say, "God made the fog, man diminished it, and then made what was left dirty and deadly." But why, it may be asked, in this apportioning of blame, did not Nature provide us with only smokeless coal? Why should New York be blessed above Liverpool?

When people appeal to "Nature," they appeal arbitrarily to what they happen to like or approve. Shelley, quoted by Mr. Salt, admonishes us to live "like the beasts of the forest, and the birds of the air"; [2] but *which* beasts and birds? We should hardly become mild vegetarians by imitating lions and eagles. As a rule, animal-lovers take their notions of animals largely from dogs; but the dog, as he exists among us now, is almost entirely an *artificial* animal. He has been selected for countless generations for the sake of diverse qualities which happened to be useful or agreeable to man. He is a parasite of human society. The cat is less popular simply because she is still to a great extent in "a state of nature"; she is a truer disciple of Jean Jacques.

How many of the plants on which the advocate of natural diet would have us subsist in this chilly climate are themselves "natural"? Wheat, barley, oats, cabbage, turnips, peas, beans, apples and pears (except the little-eaten wild apple)—I need not prolong the list—are any of these in their "natural" condition? All are due to artificial selection; they have been tampered with by man for his own convenience. If we "return to nature," how can we permit such violations of nature as grafting, as pruning, and the transference of plants out of their "natural" habitat?

When Nature is contrasted with man, it is not fair to single out all that we happen to like on the one side and all that we happen to dislike on the other. Man's action on nature has been twofold. If he has created the horrors of the "black country," he must also get the credit of having turned wildernesses into gardens, and pestilential marshes into fertile fields on other parts of the earth's surface. The remedy for the evils of our civilisation is not a return to nature, but to use all our power over nature and all our power over human nature to

[1] *Agricola*, c. 12 : "Cœlum crebris imbribus et nebulis fœdum."
[2] *Shelley's Principles*, p. 52.

make the world a better place to live in than we have found it. The Republic needs not chemists only, but all the sciences and all the arts and much more of them than have yet existed.

There is no absolute gap between Nature and man. What is dumb and blind in the struggle of plant and animal gains a consciousness of its meaning and a voice to express its needs in human society. And if we look for traces of Divine benevolence in the world, we shall find them less obscurely written in the records of human society than in the ceaseless warfare which has moulded the forms and the habits of organisms lower than man.[1] The outlook would indeed be very hopeless for us, if the history of civilisation were all a movement away from the best life of which we are capable. It is certainly easiest to see the defects in what is nearest us; but it is a very elementary and childish form of criticism which sees only the defects.[2] The good and sound elements are our only starting-point for further progress.

---

[1] To a friend who preferred the beauty of nature to the insides of churches, a pious monitor is said to have remarked: "The fields and the trees may tell you about the power of the Creator; but what can they tell you of redeeming love?" There is an element of philosophical truth in this "evangelical" objection to the worship of mere nature, as if that were the only revelation of Deity.

The philosopher-king, Frederick the Great of Prussia, has expressed this philosophical truth very well. "Man," he says in answer to Holbach's atheism, "is a reasonable being produced by nature. Nature (*including* man, of course), then, must be infinitely more intelligent than he." Similarly his friend Voltaire: "To produce without intelligence entities which possess it! Is that conceivable?" (quoted by Mr. F. Espinasse in his *Life of Voltaire*, London, 1892, p. 172). The argument, however, becomes much stronger if we take account of all man's "spiritual nature," as well as his intelligence. I may refer to what I have said in *Darwin and Hegel*, p. 173.

[2] Cf. Hegel, *Werke*, VIII. p. 323 (*Philosophie des Rechts*, §268). "Fault-finding is easy; what is hard is to recognise the good and the inner necessity in a thing. 'A little learning' always begins with fault-finding: completed culture sees in everything the positive (really valid) element." I have paraphrased, rather than translated literally.

CHAPTER IV

DE DIVISIONE NATURÆ

In this chapter I do not propose to attempt to construct a philosophical system, as the title might suggest, borrowed as it is from the great work of the light of the dark ages, Joannes Scotus or Erigena—John the Irish Scot. M. Littré in his dictionary arranges the meanings of the French word *Nature* under twenty-nine heads.[1] I shall only try to group together for convenience the principal usages of the word which concern us in political science. What is said here will therefore be to some extent recapitulation of some parts of the preceding chapters.

I. First of all, there is that use of the term "Nature" in which it stands for the totality of what exists, for the whole universe. Within this general meaning there are distinctions of fundamental importance for philosophy and theology; but with most of these we are not here directly concerned. Thus we may distinguish between (*a*) Nature as a principle underlying and explaining (if or so far as it is possible for us to know it) all the particular phenomena of space and time, and (*b*) Nature as meaning simply the sum or series of these particular phenomena. This is the distinction which in scholastic phraseology is known as that between (*a*) *Natura naturans* and (*b*) *Natura naturata* We may indeed speak of "Nature doing this or that," personifying and unifying the forces of the universe, without intending to commit ourselves to any definite theory as to the ultimate explanation of things; but whenever we speak of Nature in such a way, we are more or less consciously speaking of *Natura naturans*, of Nature as dynamic, as operating and operating for definite purposes, however much we may qualify our personification by warning others and ourselves that our language is metaphorical. When we speak of Nature as simply

[1] It should be noted, however, that such uses as *Cotelette nature* are counted separately.

a collection of objects, in whose presence we find ourselves and which form the materials for scientific inquiry as to how they stand related to one another, we are speaking of *Natura naturata.*

Natura naturans may be identified, as in Spinoza's philosophy, with God; or God may be conceived of as transcendent, but not immanent, *i.e.* as distinct from *Natura naturans* (the conception of much popular theism), or as both immanent and transcendent, *i.e.* identical with *Natura naturans,* and yet having a kind of existence over and above what can be expressed and understood by such identification (a conception at once more philosophical, and more orthodox); or the term God may be expressly avoided, because of its associations with particular religions and dogmatic theologies, and *Natura naturans* may be called the Unknown, or even (dogmatically) the Unknowable, and otherwise allowed only as a sometimes convenient metaphor.[1]

When we speak of the " laws of nature," we are thinking of *Natura naturata* as produced by *Natura naturans.* However careful a scientific man may be to explain that by "laws of Nature"

---

[1] " Nature is divided by Scotus Erigena into four kinds:—(1) The Nature creating and not created, viz. God as the source of all being; (2) that creating and created, viz. the primordial causes or Platonic Ideas, constituting the intelligible world; (3) that created and not creating, viz. the effects of these causes, constituting the sensible world of becoming, time and space; (4) that neither creating nor created, viz. God considered as the supreme and unchangeable unity into which all things return." I quote this abstract of *De Divisione Naturæ*, i. or ii. 1, from a very lucid and interesting paper on that little-known book by Mr. Clement C. J. Webb, in the *Proceedings of the Aristotelian Society*, Vol. II. No. 1, Pt. ii. p. 125. Obviously (3) in this list is identical with *Natura naturata*, as just explained. (1) and (2) are identical with *Natura naturans*, though they make a distinction, which is very commonly recognised, between God as the ultimate " first cause " and the " laws of nature " (or " thoughts of God," as Kepler called them) by which He works. In (4) the conception is one not so familiar to popular Christian theology; it is the Aristotelian conception of God as the " final cause " of the process of the universe, form apart from all matter, which "moves all things not as an efficient cause, but as the object of desire." Erigena, in Neo-Platonic fashion, represents God in this sense (*i.e.* not as the Creator, but as God the Father, *i.e.* God as He is in His own essence) as " the One " of which we can as truly deny as assert any predicate. Here is a meeting-point, which may to some be unexpected, between mediaeval mysticism and that Kantian criticism from which latter-day " agnosticism " is descended without always being aware of its parentage.

he means only " generalisations as to what does as a matter of
fact happen " (or, more properly, " statements of what, under
certain conditions, would happen " ; for mere generalisations as
to what does happen are " empirical laws " in distinction from
" laws of nature " in which some causation, *i.e.* necessary or invari*able* connection, is asserted)—however careful a scientific
man may be to de-personalise his conception, he is very apt,
and his hearers and echoes are certain, to think of "laws" as if
they were commands issued by a superior to an obedient set of
subjects. Hence people see no inherent absurdity in talking
about " interferences with the laws of nature "—whether they
picture the sovereign of the universe, on grave emergencies,
issuing special " orders," dispensing some portion of his subjects from their habitual obedience, or whether they imagine
human beings acting in such a way as to violate the commands
which Nature has imposed on them.   That is to say, in ordinary metaphorical or picture-thinking, the laws of nature may
be imaged, either as general commands imposed on *natura
naturata*, or as general commands imposed by *natura naturans*.
I need not here enter into the question of the proper definition
of " law " in its political or legal sense.   Admitting that the
primary and historically essential element in " law " is not
command but custom, it still remains true that all human laws
may be regarded as commands of a political superior (in the
fashion which almost all English jurists have adopted from
Bentham and Austin), and that even as generally observed
customs they differ essentially from laws of nature.   A human
law states what is expected to be done, or what is usually
done ; but the expectation may not be realised, the custom may
be broken through.   Laws of nature are, in the strictest sense,
inviolable, *i.e.* there is no meaning in talking of violating them.
When a law of nature appears to be violated, this only shows
that it has not been correctly stated.   If the conditions are
altered, the effect *must* be different.   When people speak of
breaking laws of nature, they mean breaking some maxim of
health, prudence, etc., based upon, or supposed to be based
upon, a knowledge of the way in which nature works.   To the
mischief caused by this confusion between laws of nature and
human laws, I have already referred.   The phrase " economic
laws," when used strictly, implies that economic facts are being
studied by the help of the conceptions applicable to all phe-

nomena in space and time; the phrase "economic laws" implies the assumption, necessary in all the sciences, that, given
the like cause, the like effect *must* follow (does invari*ably*
follow—they come to the same thing; the word "invariable"
is only a device by which the empiricist conceals from himself
the element of necessity involved in causal connection). But
because the subject-matter of economic science is human
society regarded in certain aspects, the confusion is fatally
easy which permits even careful writers to speak of "violating economic laws," "attempting to over-ride laws of
Nature by acts of Parliament," etc.

II. Secondly, within "Nature," in this widest sense, which
includes all human life and conduct, and all the works of man,
we are very commonly accustomed to make the distinction
between (1) what man does and (2) what exists, or is thought
to exist (for here the difference is not always recognised) independently of, and apart from, what man does. We call the
former set of phenomena "human," "social," or "artificial,"
and the latter alone, in antithesis to them, "natural."

III. Thirdly, closely connected with this last use of "Nature"
is a use of it which extends into the human sphere. By the
"natural" may be meant what is "original" as opposed to
what is "acquired" afterwards, as the result *either* of agencies,
conscious or unconscious, external to the organism or thing
affected, *or* of some effort made voluntarily or spontaneously
by the organism itself. Thus we distinguish a man's
"natural" from his "acquired" powers; his "natural" tendencies from the character he has acquired owing to his own
conduct and the environment in which he has been placed.
When, however, we speak of a "natural" manner as opposed to an affected manner, the meaning of natural is a little
different; for human beings can hardly be said to start with or
to inherit manners, though they may inherit tendencies, such
as a self-assertive or a yielding temperament, a capacity or in-
capacity for imitation, etc., which may make certain manners
more easily acquired than others. By natural manners we
mean manners which do not suggest effort or self-conscious-
ness, so that in such a phrase there is more of the contrast
between natural and artificial (the second sense of Nature)
than of the contrast between original and acquired; but the
notions of artificiality and acquisition run into one another,

and so also do the two meanings of "natural." Such a phrase, however, as "natural manners" suggests, further, the idea of rightness or fitness. They are what the person using the phrase considers the proper kind of manners to have; and on the question of what exact degree of artificiality is allowable and right, and what exactly is artificiality, people would differ very much. So here we get an element, at least, of what I should distinguish as a *fourth* sense of the term "Nature"— IV.) the sense in which "Nature" represents our ideal of what ought to be, whether it actually exists as a fact or not. "Natural" is often equivalent to "normal"; and normal contains both the notion of generally happening, though not necessarily happening, and the notion of a standard or rule by which things are judged[1] in respect of quality or merit. In the previous three senses, Nature always means something that *is*; in this sense it means what *ought to be*, but does not necessarily exist anywhere. Now it is in this fourth sense that Nature is properly and intelligibly used when a Law of Nature (*Jus Naturale* or *Lex Naturalis*) and Natural Rights are spoken of. And here, also, in the use of the term "law" we have passed from the scientific sense of generalisation, formula, statement of causal connection, etc., to the legal and ethical sense of the term, as command or expectation of some observance. If the term "natural rights" were always confessedly used in this sense, and in this sense only, no objection could be taken to it, except that it was an ambiguous way of saying what might be less ambiguously expressed by a direct use of the term "ought." But unfortunately the term "natural rights" is constantly used with a mixed connotation, derived partly in varying degrees from some one or more of the other senses of the term "Nature." As we have seen, people are always apt to make a picture of their ideal as some golden age in the past, to think of a reform as renewing some *old* right;[2] and so the meaning of "natural" as ideal is mixed up with its meaning as "original." Two fallacies may thus

---

[1] The English word "judgment" is ambiguous: it may mean ἀπόφανσις, *enunciatio*, or κρίσις, *judicium*. Generally, except in logic, it means the latter (*i.e.* not simply assertion, but estimate of merit or value according to a standard); for this meaning its legal associations fit it.

[2] "Erneut das alte Recht," says Heine, speaking of the Holy Spirit, in the famous poem on the Trinity in his *Harzreise*.

arise. Either our historical notion of some period in the past is vitiated by idealisation of the facts, or the actual facts of the past are taken as of themselves determining what ought to be done now. Further, the notion of "original" overlaps with the notion of the not-human, *i.e.* that which is not, or is not thought of as being, due to human action. Thus we get Ulpian basing the conception of *jus naturale* on the conduct of all animals. In the way of thinking which I have called Rousseanism, we have a combination of the *second* and *third* meanings as determining the *fourth*. Finally, the use of Nature as equivalent to God (I*a*) gives an apparent sanctity to whatever can be described as "according to nature." The "natural" as the ideal may quite reasonably be represented as that which is in accordance with a divine purpose, natural rights described as bestowed on man by the Creator, and the law of nature either identified with the Divine will, or regarded as some more or less complete manifestation of it. But the second and third senses of Nature are apt to gain an association of sanctity to which they have no necessary claim. The original, which may be the imperfect, or the sub-human, which, at the best, is only the incomplete manifestation of the Divine meaning, is apt to be appealed to as determining what ought to be.

The meaning of Nature as the totality of phenomena in the universe, apart from any underlying principle or ultimate purpose, is less apt to cause ambiguity. Yet the mere appeal to fact as of itself settling a question of right may be regarded as a confusion of the meanings which I have marked I*b* and IV respectively. The optimism which asserts the principle that "whatever is, is right" may be described as such a confusion. It assumes that we are able to estimate the worth of isolated phenomena without regard to their relation to the underlying principle or immanent reason of the universe, if we believe that there is such an immanent reason in things, as all except thoroughgoing pessimists or sceptics *practically* do, whatever theories they may profess, whatever speculative doubts and difficulties they may feel. "Whatever is, is right" is the false way of putting the principle that "the real is the rational." The "real" is not any and every particular phenomena; many phenomena turn out not to be realities (*i.e.* not to have worth), but to be "shams."

Perhaps the four (or five) meanings of Nature that I have distinguished may be grouped more logically and symmetrically as follows: Nature may be regarded either (A) "statically," or (B) "dynamically" (I use these terms metaphorically, not, of course, in their strict sense in physics). We may look on it, that is to say, either as existing (without taking time or process into account) or as in process, moving to an end or purpose (assuming that there is a purpose). Under each division we may further mean either (a) the whole of Nature, or (β) a part of it. "Dynamically," the completed purpose will correspond to what statically is the whole (if the whole be looked at not merely as a collection of phenomena, but as the manifestation of one underlying principle). Thus we should distinguish :—

A *a*.   Nature as the whole universe.
A *β*.   The non-human part of it.
B *a*.   The ideal (or completed purpose).
B *β*.   The original (the incomplete).

These divisions will correspond to the previous divisions as follows :—

A *a* = I. *a* and *b*.
A *β* = II.
B *a* = IV.
B *β* = III.

The original division seems to me to be more convenient, and I shall therefore retain it for purposes of reference.

The shortness of this chapter will, I hope, be a compensation for its somewhat scholastic character. It will be obvious that the word "ought," to which I have reduced the fourth sense of "natural," stands very much in need of explanation. To this I must proceed through an analysis of the meaning of the term "a right."

CHAPTER V

In considering the meaning of the term " right," it is best to begin with the definition of right in its *legal* sense. A right generally is defined by Professor Holland as " one man's capacity of influencing the acts of another, by means, not of his own strength, but of the opinion or the force of society." A " legal right," in the strictest sense, is " a capacity residing in one man of controlling with the assent and assistance of the State, the actions of others." [1] More briefly, though with somewhat less precision, we might say that a legal right is the claim of an individual upon others, recognised by the State. A legal right need not necessarily have been created by the State (*e.g.* by statute) ; but it must be such that the law courts will recognise it, and, in all orderly communities, the force of the State is at the back of all legal decisions. It is obvious that there is no meaning in an individual's right unless there are corresponding duties imposed on other individuals. On the other hand, the State itself cannot be said, in the strict sense, to have legal duties, but only to have legal rights : there cannot be a law court before which the State *in its sovereign capacity* (the qualification is essential) can be summoned for redress. A " government" whose proceedings can come before the courts is thereby proved not to be the legal sovereign in that community. By " legal sovereign " I mean the body behind which the lawyer *quâ* lawyer does not go.[2]

On the analogy of the definition of legal right, a moral right might be defined as " a capacity residing in one man of controlling the acts of another with the assent and assistance, or at least without the opposition, of public opinion," or as " the claim of an individual upon others recognised by society,

[1] *Jurisprudence* (Ed. II.), pp. 61, 62.
[2] I may refer to an essay on " Sovereignty," included in the volume called *Darwin and Hegel, with other Philosophical Studies.*

irrespective of its recognition by the State." The only sanction of a moral right as such is the approbation and disapprobation of private persons. In some cases such sanctions may be more binding and more dreaded than many legal penalties. The religious sanction forms, in the great majority of cases, one of the strongest elements in the sanction of a moral right : but it is a sanction which, if not at the same time political or social, must be applied by the individual to himself. The difference between legal and moral rights makes it obvious that moral rights cannot be so precisely determined as legal rights. Different sections of the society to which a person belongs and for whose opinion he cares may hold different views as to various duties, and consequently as to various rights. Conflict is therefore possible about moral as well as about legal rights ; but in the matter of moral rights there is no law court to which appeal can be made to pronounce a binding decision. In homogeneous societies (and that means, as a rule, in comparatively primitive and simple societies) there will generally be very little difference of opinion about moral rights. Such homogeneous societies are the types of all primitive society, in which there is no distinction between custom and law, between moral and legal right. In societies which are held together by a common religious belief, there is generally a court of appeal in matters of disputed moral rights and duties. Roman Catholics, above all, are able to " consult approved theologians," and although " doctors differ," they are able to get more cut-and-dried and legal-looking answers on moral questions than any body of Protestants who profess to submit their authority, the Bible, to private interpretation. Still, any given sect of Protestants will as a rule be found to hold very much the same opinion on most questions of moral obligation. Whenever we have a very mixed and heterogeneous society, consisting of persons of different religious beliefs, of different stages of religious disbelief, and at very different grades of intellectual development, questions of moral obligation become more difficult to decide ; a greater responsibility is thrown on the individuals immediately affected. Is there a moral right to " boycott " non-unionists? Have workmen on strike a moral right to use intimidation towards " black-legs " ? Has a man a moral right to marry a deceased wife's sister, if he be the subject of a country where such a marriage is not yet recog-

nised by the law? In what cases and to what extent has an
individual a moral right, not merely to do what the law of the
land does not recognise, but to do what it positively forbids?
Public opinion may not only consist of varying elements, but
it may undergo change. A change in public opinion is not
something formal and explicit, like a change in the law of the
land, and hence we have a further difficulty in determining
what are moral rights.

To escape such difficulties people have appealed to the Law
of Nature. If we knew clearly the natural rights of the individual, we could deduce from them what are his moral rights,
and what in a well-regulated community should be his legal
rights: we should have a satisfactory system of practical ethics
and a satisfactory theory of legislation. Natural rights are
not identical with moral rights, because in many cases people
have claimed that they had a natural right to do things that
were not recognised either by the law of the land or by the
prevalent public opinion or by the conscience of the *average*
individual.[1] Natural rights, when alleged by the would-be
reformer, mean those rights which in his opinion would be
recognised by the public opinion of such a society as he ad-
mires, and would either be supported or at least would not
be interfered with by its laws, if it had any laws; they are
the rights which he thinks ought to be recognised, *i.e.* they
are the rights sanctioned by his ideal society, whatever that
may be. Not all rights, however, of our ideal society are, in
the strict sense, natural rights. The term " natural rights " is
generally restricted to those of them which are conceived of
as more fundamental than others, from which the others may
be deduced, or to which the others are only auxiliary. Thus,
most of those who have held the theory of natural rights have
not counted among them various political and civil rights, *e.g.*
the right to have a vote for representatives in the Legislature
(though this has frequently been claimed as a natural right), the
right to be elected, the right to sue in the courts, the right to

---

[1] Alleged natural rights may even be guaranteed by the State when
they are refused by the prevalent public opinion of society or of large
sections of it. Thus liberty of opinion in the matter of religion is one of
the most generally recognised " natural rights "; but the history of persecution from the times of Jesus and Paul to the present day shows
how public opinion has often been more intolerant of religious freedom
than the State.

a speedy trial if accused, the right to be tried by a jury of one's peers, etc. All these would generally be regarded as merely means, and not necessarily the sole means, towards the attainment of the fundamental natural rights of liberty and security. It would generally be allowed that some degree of diversity of opinion might quite well exist as to the particular form which these secondary and derivative rights should take. With regard to certain rights, notably the right of property, there is a marked divergency among different believers in natural rights, some giving it a prominent place in their list of natural rights, others denying that it is a natural right at all, or limiting the objects to which such right can apply, or restricting it in various ways, excluding at least some property rights from their law of nature. All such limitations of the meaning of natural rights are clearly connected with that tendency, of which I have already spoken, to regard the law of nature as something that has already prevailed in some primitive state of nature (to identify the natural with the original), and to oppose the "natural" to that which is clearly due to human institution (according to the distinctions laid down in last chapter, meaning IV. of "nature" is confused with meanings III. and II.). A primitive state of nature seems incompatible with an elaborate set of political institutions, and with complicated laws and customs regarding inheritance, freedom of bequest, etc. The law of nature, moreover (as with the Roman jurists), is something behind and independent of the variations of local usage: it is a universal code. Different communities may adopt different kinds of political, legal, and social machinery to give effect to it. Absolute uniformity is not required except in essentials. But what are these essentials? There may be as much difficulty in getting the wished-for agreement among the doctors of the Law of Nature as among the doctors of the Church: and who shall decide as to who are the politically and socially orthodox? What rights *ought* every society at the very least to guarantee to its members? These, if we can agree upon them, will be our "natural rights."

Now what determines this "ought"? To this question three types of answers have been and still are given. They may be denoted by the words *Authority, Nature, Utility*. By "Authority" I mean here authority external to the mind of the individual. Nature, as we have already seen,[1] is thought of as something known by an inner voice, an internal authority. Utility is known by Reason and Experience.

(1) To base natural or fundamental rights on external authority of any kind may seem to involve an obvious contradiction, because these natural rights are supposed to be the very criterion by which the worth of the external authority itself can be judged. If the end of government be the preservation of certain natural rights, we cannot let government itself determine what these rights are. This was clear enough to the reflective framers of the American and French Declarations. But if we go back to the ordinary unreflecting opinion of mankind in comparatively primitive conditions, we shall find that those rights which people think they ought to have are just those rights which they have been accustomed to have, or which they have a tradition (whether true or false) of having once possessed. Rights are claimed because sanctioned in the present or in the past by the authority of social recognition. Custom is primitive law, and custom determines primitive notions of obligation. But even in a reflective age, the thinking of the majority of persons remains of a primitive type; and even people who have become sophisticated enough to distinguish certain things as "natural" from certain others which are merely "conventional," will be found very often to mean by "natural" whatever has the sanction of the longest and the least broken custom, while what is well known to be of quite recent growth or is not very widely adopted can more easily be regarded as "conventional." Thus to the average Greek slavery undoubtedly seemed a "natural" institution; it was familiar to him, and he did not know of any civilised society without it. Similarly the average person in every country at the present day thinks the "natural" position of women to be the position which is assigned to them by the customs of the particular society to which he belongs. A Turk, a German, an American, would give somewhat different accounts of this natural status. The "natural" in each case may perhaps be pitched a little above the average usage of the society in question; it represents the expectations of the society, of which expectations fulfilment may indeed fall short.

Where the customs or laws of a society are ascribed to the

[1] Cf. above, Chap. II. pp. 36, 41, 42.

revealed will of the gods, these rights are expressly based on a
definite authority; and, if the revelation is supposed to be
through oracles, through sacred writings, or through a particular caste or class of society, the authority is an external authority. "Natural law" is, however, generally distinguished from
the revealed will of God;[1] yet the revealed will of God is sometimes used as an argument to prove that something must be in
accordance with or not contrary to natural law, and, on the
other hand, natural law is sometimes appealed to as confirming
the validity of an alleged revelation. According to those theologians and moralists who hold that right and wrong are dependent upon the arbitrary will of the Deity, so that, if he had
so willed it, what is now right might have been wrong, and
vice versâ, there can be no meaning in natural law as distinguished from the revealed will of God. This combination of
" philosophic doubt," with a passive acceptance of Scriptural
or ecclesiastical authority, is a type of thinking very congenial
to a certain order of mind: it gratifies simultaneously the com-
pletest scepticism in the powers of the human reason and the
craving for absolute certainty. To this type of thinking the
theory of Hobbes presents considerable analogy, save that for
the Church he substitutes the *de facto* government. By
"natural rights" Hobbes means simply those powers which
an individual has apart from all human institutions: so that
natural rights are equivalent to natural mights.[2] In the state
of nature, *i.e.* apart from the laws and customs of a definite
political society, every one has a right to everything. The only
sanction of such natural rights is force. Political society has
its justification in the fact that it, and it alone, saves mankind
from the miseries of a condition in which there is no security
or peace: that is the meaning of Hobbes's version of the social
contract theory. With the exception of the natural right of
every individual to preserve his own life, to retain which mankind surrender all their other natural rights, all rights that a
man has in the civil state depend simply on the will of the
sovereign person or persons to whom he has handed over his
natural rights. The exception made by Hobbes in favour of

[1] The *jus divinum voluntarium* of Grotius and others.

[2] "Natural" is thus used for what exists as a matter of fact apart from
the interference of human society. This is the sense of " nature " I have
marked (II.) in Chap. IV.

the right of self-preservation seems inconsistent. "Skin for skin, yea, all that a man hath will he give for his life." True ; but many Englishmen of Hobbes's own time would have argued, and did practically argue : " You take my life when you do take the means whereby I live "; and others thought even life itself not worth having at the cost of depending on the arbitrary will of any human being for the right to worship God according to their consciences. What absolute priority, it might reasonably be asked, has the right of preserving one's life over the right of protecting one's property and the right of following one's conscience in matters of religion ? Hobbes, I fancy, means that the right of preserving one's life is primary, because without life everything else would be of no account. But does it not depend largely on individual temperament whether mere life at any cost is to be preferred to all the things that seem to make life worth living ? If this natural right is to remain intact in the civil state, why not others which are necessarily involved in it? If these others are excluded, why not this also ? It would be a more logical theory to make even the right of preserving one's life dependent on the will of the sovereign. As a matter of fact, it is so dependent, as much as any other right. What difference is there in principle between struggling with the executioner on the scaffold and struggling with the officer who at the first arrests me by order of the king ? And, on the other hand, what right on Hobbes's theory has the government to do anything except such right as depends upon its force to do it, so that if any body of persons can succeed in obtaining the mastery, they have the same right to issue orders and make laws which the dispossessed government had, but no longer has? All rights must depend on the will of the *de facto* government, and natural right means nothing except force. Spinoza eliminates the inconsistency from Hobbes's theory, and preserves natural right " safe and sound " in the civil state.[1] To the question of the relation between might and right I must return later on.

Bentham, Austin, and most English jurists have accepted Hobbes's account of rights in the civil state (" natural " rights being discarded altogether) as perfectly true of *legal* rights. But Hobbes himself (like his precursor, the sophist Thrasyma-

---

[1] *Epistola*, 50 (in the arrangement of Van Vloten and Land, as well as in that of Bruder).

chus[1]) made no distinction between legal and moral rights;
and therefore remains as the most remarkable example of
a philosopher basing obligation simply upon the external
authority of the State. In this "sophistic" theory, custom
or usage becomes explicit as the mere arbitrary will of the
sovereign.

(2) When traditional custom or constituted authority comes
to be unsatisfactory to certain more reflective minds, there
arises a discrepancy between it and what seem to be the
natural instincts or feelings of the individual, a discrepancy
between law and conscience; and so, as we have seen, reformers
try to go back to an authority more venerable than parliaments and kings; more venerable even than immemorial
usage: they "appeal from tyranny to God," from the mere
custom of the multitude to the feelings that Nature has implanted in the breast of each of us. The unfortunate thing is
that these instinctive feelings differ so much in different persons. A little reflection may show a discrepancy between outward law and inward sentiment; but a little more reflection
will show divergence between the sentiments of different persons, or at least between the sentiments of different classes of
persons. The individual's conscience is apt to be the mirror
of the particular environment in which he has grown up; and
even his revolt against existing institutions bears traces of
its unavoidable influence. We may strive to be as individual,
as original, as "singular" in our judgments as possible;
but we cannot escape much more easily from the network of
our social inheritance than we can escape from the inheritance of a particular physical and mental constitution. Plato's
ideal state is the Hellenic state he knew—idealised. Some
of the materials are re-arranged, some latent principles are
clearly seen and carried out to their logical consequences.
"Conscience," says Professor Bain, "is an imitation within us
of the government without us." Hence it is no wonder that
Conscience should be spoken of, as it is by Butler, as if it were
a king, with definite prerogatives secured by the constitution.[2]

---

[1] In Plato's *Republic*, I.

[2] Cf. *Sermon* II. "This *prerogative*, this *natural supremacy* of the
faculty which surveys, approves, or disapproves of the several affections
of our minds, etc." "To preside and govern, from the very economy and
constitution of man, belongs to it." It is the legal theory of the English

Yet there is this all-important difference between the appeal to law and custom and the appeal to conscience or natural feelings, that in the latter case the authority appealed to is an internal, not an external authority. The existing and the customary are being reflected upon and criticised, from the point of view of an ideal which has grown up or been created out of them. And the voice of God and Nature in the heart of every mortal is thought of as a universal revelation: it professes to mean, not what any chance person happens to feel, but what approves itself to calm, reflective reason, and what can be shown to be in accordance with the essential nature of things. The individual conscience, according to the straitest sect of the Intuitionists, should be an infallible Pope in every man's own breast; but this infallible Pope is not in practice treated as infallible, any more than is the other, by those to whom his dogmas or decisions do not approve themselves. Even Catholic theologians are not always agreed, in practice, as to the exact point at which the infallibility comes in; and with "every man his own Pope," the distinctions between certainty and error are even more difficult to draw. Practically we trust, not to every man's conscience, but to the good man's conscience—as Aristotle does,[1] escaping thus the subjectivity of *Homo mensura*. But who is the good man? We have only put the difficulty a stage farther back. What, then, is meant by this further test of conformity to the essential nature of things? Is not this appeal the self-refutation of Intuitionalist theories, and of all individualist or "idio-psychological" (to use Dr. Martineau's phrase) theories of ethics? It is an admission that we must determine right and wrong by reference to experience, and not by the simple irresponsible dicta of an inner light, which every man may claim to possess as well as every other man. Natural rights, then, will not be what any chance person may happen to claim as suiting his private notions of what he ought to have. If the thief justifies himself on the ground that "One must live," it is always possible for any one, who is backed by sufficient physical force, to answer, "I do not see the necessity." Now such a retort is not the appeal from one egotism to another: it is the appeal from individual self-

---

Constitution—rather than the political facts as they were coming to be—to which Butler's theory of Conscience corresponds.

[1] *Eth. Nic.*, III. 4, § 5. Cf. VI. 11, § 6; 13, § 6.

assertion to the self-assertion of a *society* of individuals. And, be it observed, the genuine antique type of brigand or pirate, as distinct from his survivals—his burglars and pick-pockets of a civilised society—has such a social sanction to fall back upon.

In the chaos of conflicting individual impulses, instincts, desires, and interests, we can find no stable criterion. We must go beyond them to the essential nature of things. But what part of the nature of things is here relevant? Is it not simply —human society? If there are certain mutual claims which cannot be ignored without detriment to the well-being and, in the last resort, to the very being of a community, these claims may in an intelligible sense be called fundamental or natural rights. They represent the minimum of security and advantage which a community must guarantee to its members at the risk of going to pieces, if it does not with some degree of efficiency maintain them.

But in this interpretation of Nature we are appealing from mere feelings to reason : conflicting claims can (in theory, at least) come before a court in which their validity can be judicially and impartially examined by the standard of the general welfare. So that the details of a professedly Intuitionalist ethical code are filled up on Utilitarian principles.

The principle of Utility was expressly advocated by Bentham and Mill in opposition both (1) to the mere following of custom or external authority, and (2) to the arbitrary appeal to the voice of nature speaking in the human breast—an appeal which can be made in support of abuses, as well as in support of the revolt against them. In opposition to both Authority and the Law of Nature, Bentham, following Beccaria, sets up "the greatest happiness of the greatest number," as our criterion by which to judge of what ought to be. But the Utilitarian theory is apt to provoke antagonism and revolt almost more than the principle of external authority, for it has not in the same way rooted itself in unreflective sentiment, and feelings will outlive the reasonings that are supposed to have killed them. And thus from Rousseau's time downwards the appeal to Nature is made as much against the Utilitarian Rationalist as it is made against the advocates of authoritative law and dogma.[1] The duel becomes triangular :

[1] A certain person, resisting the pressure of a bibulous friend who was

Dogmatist (or Legalist), Sentimentalist and Rationalist do not belong in life to separate epochs, as they might in the pages of a history of thought ; all three are living and contending among ourselves. Between them who is to decide ?

The Law of Nature, if it really represented " the consent of the human race," would serve to settle controversies ; on the whole it has helped to promote them. An illustration of the difficulty in interpreting the voice of nature, and of the way in which the case comes to be transferred from the court of nature to some other court, may conveniently be taken from the opinions about marriage which have been held by different schools of believers in natural law. The Roman jurist, Ulpian, as we saw, took this very matter of the union of the sexes as one of his illustrations of *jus naturale*, so that we might reasonably expect a fair consensus of opinion on the natural rights involved. If, however, following Ulpian's guidance, we were to refer to the usages of all animals, I fear we should find a very conflicting set of precedents for man to follow. Both monogamy and polygamy are sanctioned by the usages of mammals and birds, though perhaps the *consensus avium* may be allowed to condemn the polyandric practices of the wicked cuckoo. But even when we may use the term " monogamy " of animals, it must be remembered that most unions of animals are temporary, and, as a rule, terminate at the latest when the young are independent of their parents' care.

As representing scholastic theology on the subject, I shall take the opinion of the Jesuit Father Rickaby, an able modern exponent of Thomas Aquinas. In his exposition of Natural Law, he lays down that " by nature " polyandry is excluded altogether, because (1) the absence of definite fatherhood interferes with the good rearing of the offspring, and (2) if the mother has as many " heads " over her as husbands, there will be confusion; if she is head, there is "a perversion of the natural order of predominance between the sexes."   " Against polygamy," he continues, " the case in natural law is not quite so strong as against polyandry. Still, it is a strong case enough in the interest of the wife."   The relation between the

urging another glass upon him, was met by the argument, " You're letting your judgment get the better of you." This is the appeal from Reason to instinct, from Utilitarianism to emotional Intuitionism.

sexes should be a relation of equality, so far as mutual faith is concerned. This limits the natural pre-eminence of the husband.[1] The polygamy of the Old Testament saints is, however, an obvious difficulty to a Catholic moralist. The view "that polygamy is not against the natural law, but only against the positive divine law, which was derogated from in this instance," is rejected by Father Rickaby, as is also a second theory, that God gave the patriarchs a dispensation, strictly so called, from this point of natural law. "A third explanation would be founded on the words of St. Paul to the Athenians (Acts xvii. 30) about 'God overlooking the times of this ignorance.' This would suppose that mankind, beginning in monogamy [Adam had not much opportunity of beginning with anything else], from passion and ignorance, lapsed quickly into polygamy; that the patriarchs in good faith conformed to the practice of their time, and that God, in their case, as with the rest of mankind, awaited His own destined hour for the light of better knowledge to break upon the earth. Whether, meanwhile, by some darkly intelligible stretch of His power He legitimised their unions, who can tell? A fourth explanation suggests a mode by which this legitimisation may have taken place. God, by His supreme dominion, can dissolve any marriage. By the same dominative power He can infringe and partially make void any marriage contract, without entirely undoing it. The marriage contract, existing in its fulness and integrity, is a bar to any second similar contract, as we have proved. But what, in this theory, the Lord God did with the marriages of the patriarchs was this: He partially unravelled and undid the contract, so as to leave room for a second contract and a third [and a seven hundredth, in the case of Solomon?], each having the bare essentials of a marriage, but none of them the full integrity. This explanation, and the one preceding, will stand with our philosophy. As to which of them is to be preferred [I thought the fourth was only supplementary to the third], we answer in the style of the Roman Court, *Consult approved theologians.*"[2]

I have quoted this passage *in extenso* with my own interpolations in square brackets, lest any account of its contents in

[1] *Moral Philosophy, or Ethics and Natural Law.* 2nd Edition, pp. 270, 271.
[2] *Ibid.*, pp. 273, 274.

my own words might be suspected of caricaturing the opinions
of a very able writer. Father Rickaby's problem is indeed a
hard one—to reconcile a due respect for the much-married
heroes of Hebrew history with a belief in the absolute prohibition of polygamy by the law of nature; and he deserves
the credit of having taken his conception of natural law much
more seriously than many modern sentimentalists, who appeal
to nature simply as a means of giving a formal justification of
their private likes or dislikes, and then shirk the trouble of
argument.

Protestantism, in depressing the authority of the Church,
raised in relative importance the authority of the whole Bible;
and the case of the Hebrew patriarchs, combined with a wider
knowledge derived from classical sources of the varying
practices of different peoples, leads Grotius to find no prohibition of polygamy in the law of nature.[1] " Marriage by natural
law we conceive to be such a cohabitation of the male and
female as places the female under the protection and custody
of the male; for such a union we see in some cases in mute
animals. But in man, as being a rational creature, to this is
added a vow of fidelity, by which the woman binds herself to
the man." [2]

Locke, in his *Treatise of Civil Government*, seems to think
that, apart from the positive law of any particular political
society, the mutual obligation of husband and wife depends,
as with the animals, only on the necessity of rearing the
young. Since the young of those viviparous animals that feed
on grass can be nourished by their dams till they are able to
feed themselves, "the male only begets, but concerns not
himself for the female or young to whose sustenance he can
contribute nothing.[3] But in beasts of prey the conjunction
lasts longer. . . . The assistance of the male is necessary
to the maintenance of their common family, which cannot
subsist till they are able to prey for themselves but by the

[1] *De Jure Belli et Pacis*, II. 5, § 9. Luther's sanctioning the bigamy
of the Landgrave Philip of Hesse was probably more due to strong
pressure from a defender of Protestantism, than to an unbiassed conviction following from a study of the Bible.

[2] *Ibid.*, II. 5, § 8 (Whewell's trans.).

[3] This fact might have been appealed to by Shelley and his disciples to
support a connection between vegetarianism and their theories about
marriage.

joint care of male and female. . . . And herein, I think, lies
the chief, if not the only reason why the male and female in
mankind are tied to a longer conjunction than other creatures,
viz. because the female is capable of conceiving, and *de facto*
is commonly with child again, and brings forth, too, a new
birth, long before the former is out of dependency for support
on his parents' help, and able to shift for himself, and has all
the assistance which is due to him from his parents; whereby
the father, who is bound to take care of those he hath begot,
is under an obligation to continue in conjugal society with the
same woman longer than other creatures, whose young, being
able to subsist of themselves before the time of procreation
returns again, the conjugal bond dissolves of itself, and they
are at liberty till Hymen at his usual anniversary season
summons them again to choose new mates.   Wherein one
cannot but admire the wisdom of the great Creator, who,
having given to man foresight and an ability to lay up for the
future, as well as to supply the present necessity, hath made
it necessary that society of man and wife should be more
lasting than of male and female amongst other creatures, that
so their industry might be encouraged, and their interest
better united to make provision and lay up goods for their
common issue, which uncertain mixture or easy and frequent
solutions of conjugal society would mightily disturb." [1]

Locke's object in dealing with the subject of marriage is
simply to show, in opposition to Filmer, that the paternal relation does not determine the nature of political obligation ; but
that, on the contrary, a great deal of what is commonly supposed to be involved in the family depends upon the enactment of the civil magistrate and not upon the law of nature.
Although his opinion is expressed in a somewhat doubtful
way (" the chief, if not the only reason "), it would seem to
follow that, in Locke's view, a childless couple, or a couple whose
children were independent of them, might, according to the
law of nature alone, *i.e.* apart from special positive laws and
apart from any specially revealed divine law, separate from one
another and contract new conjugal ties.[2]   In another place

---

[1] *Treatise of Civil Government*, II. c. vii., §§ 79, 80.

[2] That polygamy is not contrary to the law of nature is also maintained by Locke in his unpublished *Essay concerning Toleration* (1667),
printed in Mr. Fox Bourne's *Life of Locke*, Vol. I.   See esp. pp. 178, 186.
Cf. also a passage in a paper of 1661 (?), *ibid.* p. 163.

(c. vi. § 65), he refers to polyandry without any suggestion that such a form of the family is contrary to the law of nature; he uses the institution of polyandry as an argument against Filmer: "What will become of this paternal power in that part of the world where one woman hath more than one husband at a time?" Locke, of course, must not be understood to imply that all the various systems of relations between the sexes which may not be contrary to the law of nature are therefore equally good: throughout his whole treatise, though the law of nature and the state of nature are frequently appealed to, Locke decides all important points on what we should call "utilitarian considerations." The modern student of sociology may note that, in his reference to the relation between man and the animals, Locke has seen, in one respect at least, the immense significance for social evolution of the prolongation of infancy.[1]

I shall now take the opinion of the late Professor Lorimer, whose *Institutes of Law* bears as its second title the words, *A treatise of the Principles of Jurisprudence as determined by Nature*. This work is probably the best English exposition of the idea of a Law of Nature in the special form which that idea has received at the hands of German jurists and moralists who have adopted the principle of *Naturrecht* as the basis of their systems. Having decided that monogamy is the system approved by the law of nature, because, among other reasons, the sexes are on the whole equal in numbers, Professor Lorimer sees possible difficulties which he discusses by putting a hypothetical case of conscience. Suppose that one man and twenty women find themselves on a desert island without hope of ever being restored to society. There are three courses open to them with respect to the regulation of marriage. *First*, they may adhere to monogamy (and, it is implied, to all the other restrictions on marriage usual among civilised nations) and allow the race to become extinct after the first generation. [We must assume apparently that the women at starting are all

---

[1] Dr. E. Westermarck's formula that "marriage is rooted in family rather than family in marriage" (see his *History of Human Marriage*) might almost serve as a summary of the passage I have quoted from Locke. Dr. Westermarck told me that he was quite unaware of Locke's treatment of the subject, till I pointed out to him the striking anticipation of his own view, contained in the passage I have quoted.

approaching middle life, else the difficulty might be got over by a son of the sole married couple marrying at the earliest possible age any woman still capable of bearing children; but this would spoil the puzzle.] *Secondly*, they may adhere to monogamy and allow brothers and sisters of full blood to marry; or *thirdly*, they may resort to polygamy and avoid any nearer connection than between brothers and sisters of half-blood for one generation: afterwards re-establish monogamy and the ordinary rules as to forbidden degrees. "The first course is that which they probably ought to adopt; but, inasmuch as polygamy is less revolting than incest, the third course would be clearly preferable to the second; and in so far as the teaching of nature goes, a good deal might be said for it even as opposed to the first." [1]

Now it is difficult to see how the final suggestion differs from that which would commend itself to a Utilitarian: and the first course, it might very well be argued, conflicts with the law of nature; for how can nature command the extinction of the species? But the curious thing about the whole statement and solution of the problem is the transference to a chance group of human beings of the ideas and sentiments of particular civilised societies. What human beings so situated *would* actually do, and how far they would consider what they were doing to be right, would depend entirely on who these human beings were, how they had been brought up, and what their feelings towards one another came to be when they were thus thrown together. It is possible the one man might become a Mormon, it is possible he might become a monk—to pick out one wife might be a dangerous experiment. The problem may be commended to the notice of the psychological novelist.

Lastly, by way of change from this casuistical atmosphere, let us consult Shelley, who finds in the law of nature an easy solution of all problems. "Free love" would be his answer to all questions about the natural relations of the sexes; [2] and if by "Nature" be meant what would happen in the absence of all institutions, it is obviously the only true answer (save that "free capture" would probably be the more accurate expression). To Shelley Nature means this; but it also means the ideal. Shelley and his followers are very anxious to make out

[1] *Institutes of Law* (1st edit. 1872), p. 433.
[2] *Queen Mab*, note on Canto V.

that free love and promiscuity are not the same thing. But
" promiscuity " is simply a dyslogistic term for what is eulogisti-
cally called " free love " : a name for the relationships existing
between the sexes where, if anywhere, there are no definite
prohibitions recognised by law or custom. As soon as certain
things come to be approved and other things disapproved, we
have a custom and the elementary stage of a law : therefore, if
in a " natural " society any conduct was liable to be disapproved
of, there could not be absolute freedom. Opinions like those
of J. S. Mill and others, that positive law ought not to interfere with the relations of the sexes, except so far as the
welfare of children is concerned, are entirely and confessedly
of a Utilitarian character—the appeal is to what experience
would show to be best : they admit of argument *pro* and *con.*
A simple appeal to Nature stops the mouth of the person who
wishes to argue from experience.

Now a Roman Catholic moralist, who is able to "consult
approved theologians," would not trouble himself with such
heretical and atheistical vagaries as he would undoubtedly
consider the opinions of Grotius, Locke, and Shelley. (Professor Lorimer might, perhaps, escape condemnation.) But he
only avoids the difficulties of knowing what the law of nature
is because he has an external authority to fall back upon.
The person who discards such authority, and appeals to Nature,
finds that *her* doctors disagree : and between them who shall
decide ? The moment the question comes to be really discussed, considerations of *utility* must come in. Would it not
be better to leave Nature alone and bring in Utilitarian considerations from the outset ?

But it may be, and has been objected, that people are no
more agreed as to what is " useful," than they are as to what
is right or just according to the law of nature. It is true,
the " useful," taken by itself, is quite as ambiguous as the just.
But the useful does not profess to be something incapable of
further analysis. It is confessedly a relative term, useful *for*
something. Useful *for what ?* It is here that the Utilitarian
theory stands most in need of revision and correction. While
rejecting in words the theory of natural rights, Benthamism
retains the abstract individualism which forms an essential
part of that theory. Human beings are treated by the old-
fashioned Utilitarian as moral atoms, all similar in kind, so

that one man's feelings can be quantitatively estimated and
dealt with as if they were identical with another man's feelings.
It is assumed that "lots" of pleasures can be distributed among
these individuals—an idea which justifies, so far, Carlyle's
caricature of the Utilitarian "happiness" as so much attainable
pig's wash to be divided among a given multitude of pigs.[1]
Benthamism is an excellent theory for purposes of attack, since
it demands that institutions and laws shall justify themselves
as being conducive to the general happiness. But it is itself
open to many of the objections that can be made to the theory
of natural rights; and in fact it involves an assumption of the
equality and similarity of all mankind in all times and places,
which is just a part of the theory of natural rights in its crudest
form. We have seen that the appeal to nature combines the
abstract individualism of an appeal to each isolated irresponsible
instinct with an appeal to that abstract universal, the "consent of
all mankind." Similarly, Benthamist Utilitarianism combines
the abstract individualism of treating every human being as
an isolated unit with the view of happiness as an abstract universal which is thought of as if it had a sort of existence apart
from the concrete individuals who alone are capable of feeling
it. That "every one should count for one and nobody for
more than one" can indeed be defended on utilitarian grounds
as the only way, or the easiest way, of escaping the difficulty
of distinguishing exactly between the needs and merits of
individuals, and of avoiding the discontent that arises from a
suspicion of injustice. But old-fashioned Utilitarianism goes
farther, and assumes *practically* that men have, *a priori*, equal
rights.[2] Otherwise, according to Bentham's formula, and assuming Bentham's calculus of pleasures to be possible, *if* in any
case it could be made out that the greater happiness of a few

---

[1] *Latter Day Pamphlets*, "Jesuitism."

[2] Cf. Maine, *Early History of Institutions*, p. 399. "The most conclu-
sive objection to the doctrine would consist in denying this equality; and
I have myself heard an Indian Brahmin dispute it on the ground that,
according to the clear teaching of his religion, a Brahmin was entitled to
twenty times as much happiness as anybody else." The Brahmin has the
advantage of being able to appeal to an authoritative estimate of his
claims to happiness. But without such precise moral arithmetic, might
not a vigorous person of all-round interests, and with a great capacity for
enjoyment, reasonably, on Benthamist principles, demand a fuller share of
happiness than the timid, narrow soul on whom an equal "lot" would
be thrown away?

could be obtained by the less happiness of a majority, and that
the total happiness thus obtained would be greater than if
happiness were distributed equally through the whole multitude, and *if*, further (this qualification is necessarily implied),
the majority being ignorant and apathetic were not discontented or could be easily controlled, I cannot see how, on the
" greatest happiness" principle, we ought not to prefer such an
organisation of society to one based on equality.   We know
that many defenders of aristocratic and caste privileges do
argue more or less explicitly in this way ; and if the end of life
were simply the attainment of the greatest sum of pleasures on
the whole (intensity being reckoned as much as extensiveness),
irrespective of the "rights" of the individuals who enjoy
them, then so long as the merry ruling caste are sufficiently
callous, and the depressed subject caste are sufficiently stupid,
I do not see how this aristocratic argument can be refuted.
But we know that the great Utilitarian reformers to whom
England owes so much had the passion for equality, and John
Stuart Mill, illogically it may be, preferred Socrates dissatisfied
to the pig satisfied : so that, practically, they did not accept
the greatest sum of pleasures as the end of life.

   This objection of inconsistency only applies to Utilitarianism,
if the *feelings of pleasure and pain* be made the starting-point
of our ethical thinking.   It would not apply at all to an ethical theory which starts from a conception of the self as rational
and universal (a theory of which the doctrine of a law of nature,
at least in its Roman and in its scholastic form, seems a rudimentary and unsatisfactory foreshadowing).   If our claims are
based not on our isolated instincts but on the fact, which
seems to be a necessary conclusion from the conditions of
knowledge, that our particular self or *ego* is only the imperfect
realisation of a universal reason, one and indivisible throughout the universe, though manifested in countless forms and
revealed most clearly to us, not in the movements of the stars,
nor in the record of the rocks, nor even in the upward striving
life of plant and animal, but in the work of the human spirit,
that is to say in social institutions, in art, in religion, and
where thought seeks to be at home with itself—in the medita-
tions of the philosopher,[1]—if this be so, every human being may
claim a right to be considered as such, because he *potentially*

[1] See above, p. 70.

shares in this consciousness of the universal reason; he may claim the opportunity of developing this potentiality as far as possible. Each can claim to be an end-in-himself without inconsistency or necessity of conflict, only because none is an end-in-himself, except as partaking of the one " Reason " or " Nature " which is what all the higher religions have meant by God. Such a metaphysical conception of the self will not indeed justify an abstract claim to equality in anything and everything, but only to such equality as is required for, and is compatible with, the highest conceivable form of social existence. And here we come in sight of a means of explaining the nature of rights and a means of reforming Utilitarianism, which can be adopted without the use of what many persons will put aside as unintelligible mysticism. The metaphysics seem to me, indeed, necessary for a *complete* account of the basis of ethics and politics; but having said that, I shall now pass to an easier way of putting the case.

The difficulties which may be raised about the Hedonist basis of Benthamist Utilitarianism do not here directly concern us; the difficulties suggested by the individualism of the theory are sufficient. It is worth particular note that Professor Sidgwick, who in his *Elements of Politics* applies the Utilitarian principle throughout in its individualist form, yet extends his consideration from the happiness of the existing sum of individuals to include that of the future members of the society. We must, he says, " take into account not only the human beings who are actually living, but those who are to live hereafter." [1] " Whatever force there is," he adds, " in the argument urged against the view that the end of government is the happiness of the individuals governed, depends on the conception of these individuals as present, actually existing, members of the particular community in question. I fully concede that there are crises of national life in which it is the duty of the present generation of citizens, the actually living human beings who compose any political community, to make important sacrifices of personal happiness for the 'good or welfare of their country,' and that this good or welfare cannot be completely analysed into private happiness of the individuals who make the sacrifices. I should add that there are cases in which it is the duty of the members of one

[1] P. 31.

political society to make sacrifices for the good or welfare of
other sections of the human race.   But I hold that if this
good is not chimerical and illusory, it must mean the happiness of *some* individual human beings; if not of those living
now, at any rate of those who are to live hereafter.   And I
have tried in vain to obtain from any writer who rejects this
view, any other definite conception of the 'good of the
state.'"[1]

This is a very important passage, because, although Professor Sidgwick still prefers the old-fashioned Utilitarian
phraseology and will not talk about the "social organism," he
practically adopts the important element of truth in that
often misapplied conception, and thinks of society as organic,
i.e. as having a continuous life, within which its individual
members arise and perish, a life which has to be cared for
over and above the sum of individuals at any given time
existing.   Professor Sidgwick complains that writers, such as
Bluntschli, to whom he specially refers, give no definite conception of the "good of the state," beyond what a Utilitarian
can give.   But how if the end of human life, individual and
social, does not admit of a *definite* conception?   It is only with
the progress of time that we discover the natural gifts and
capacities of an individual or of a society; if we say that in
the end of the state should be included the development of a
people's natural gifts, the very word "development" would
suggest growth and progress.   A fundamental defect of the
old Utilitarianism was the assumption of the identity of
human nature in spite of difference of time and place and
stage of growth; it is the characteristic of a crude rationalism
to judge all social stages by similar canons.   The conception
of evolution or, more precisely, the theory of natural selection
has at once corrected the errors and vindicated the truth of
Utilitarian ethics and politics.   That is "good" for any particular society which furthers its success in the struggle for
existence with nature and with other societies; that is "evil"
which hinders such success.   Those societies have succeeded
best which have been most coherent and most vigorous; and
so courage and fidelity to those of the same society have
been "selected" as good qualities; they are the primitive
virtues.   With the growth of reflection and a wider outlook,

[1] *Elements of Politics*, p. 35.

these good qualities and others can be recognised in new and wider spheres: and the society whose welfare determines what is right may come to enlarge its borders and to change its character. The individual naturally and instinctively strives after happiness, i.e. what he takes to be such, not necessarily what a Utilitarian philosopher would advise him to pursue; but the individual's happiness is not what directly determines the difference between right and wrong. "Happiness," as the late Professor Clifford has expressed it, "is not the end of right action. My happiness is of no use to the community, except in so far as it makes me a more efficient citizen: that is to say, it is rightly desired as a *means* and not as an end." This inverts the theory of Hedonist Utilitarianism, while recognising what ascetic theories have neglected, the great value of happiness as a means to social well-being. Happy citizens — and that in the long run means healthy citizens, healthy in mind, body, and estate—will prove the most useful citizens. Clifford's words might indeed seem open to the objection that the good of the community is treated as if it had an existence and a value apart from the good of any of the individuals, without whom the community would have no existence at all: and perhaps the desire to correct the individualism of hedonist utilitarians sometimes leads evolutionist moralists to overstate this aspect of their own theory. The good of a community gives us our only criterion for judging of what is right for individuals to do: but the good of a community is itself identical with the good of its members. A healthy body is a body the parts of which are healthy, but none of which is developed at the expense of others. This metaphor may serve to illustrate the relation between individual and society: though it only brings one in sight of the metaphysical problem of the relation between the particular and the universal self. Rousseau's most sentences The good for man is always a common good; there is no end for the individual apart from a community of some sort — though the community may be thought of as a heavenly city not realised anywhere on earth. What the community is differs from time to time: and it is *in* respect of the nature of the community or society *which* forms the standard of our

Lectures and Essays, Vol. II, p. 178, ed. 1879. Lecture on "Right and Wrong."

moral judgment, that progress takes place. Every extension
of the range of persons who are taken account of, when we
think of the common good, effects changes in our moral judgments. Moral judgments vary because societies vary in
character: conflict of duties and conflict of moral judgments
are possible just because each individual in all highly developed societies belongs to many communities, overlapping
one another. Professor Sidgwick, in the passage I quoted,
recognises that other sections of the human race than our
own section may have to be taken into account; and it is
conceivable that duty towards a higher and better society
might lead people to think it right to destroy a society whose
welfare had previously formed the standard of their moral
judgments. Among conscious and reflective human beings,
natural selection passes into rational selection; and a social
organism may die, while its individual members become absorbed in an organism of a higher type.

" 'Ere's a stranger; let's 'eave 'arf a brick at him."[1] That
is primitive morality—"natural" morality, if natural means
"original." The duty of kindness is only supposed to apply
to members of the same tribe, class, caste, trade-union, or
whatever the group may be. The brotherhood of mankind is
the ideal at the other end of the ethical scale.

There are indeed some sturdy individualists among us
who, whether in the name of "natural rights" or in the
name of "the greatest happiness of the greatest number,"
protest equally against any appreciative reference to the past
and against any consideration of posterity in our ethical and
political judgments. This is a frame of mind against which
argument is difficult, as it implies a non-acceptance of that
continuity of the species which one would have thought was
a patent fact. The human race or, let me say, the inhabitants
of Great Britain do not consist of a certain number of adult
males, or adult males and females, assembled together in a
sort of cross between a debating society and a joint-stock
company, and entitled by the law of nature to divide all the
good things of life among themselves. An assembly or
national convention of all the adults of a community would be
only the trustees inheriting every moment from the old who

_____

[1] Cf. *hostis* = (1) stranger; (2) enemy. "*Hostis* apud majores nostros
is dicebatur quem nunc *peregrinum* dicimus." (Cic.. *De Off.*, 1. 12, 37.)

are dying and obliged to take into account the interests of
those who are being born. Human beings would have to be
artificially cut off from all links of human kinship—to become
like a band of outlaws or pirates—before they could consider
the question of right and wrong without regard to the past
that had produced them and without regard to the future that
was even now amongst them. And with what show of reason
can any one sit in judgment on the past and blame men in old
times for the inheritance of evil their actions or their negli-
gences have left to us, while calmly proposing to decide the
rights of living persons without any " superstition about the
effect on posterity " ? [1]

The transition from Individualist to Evolutionist Utilitarianism—a transition which is being accepted by the great
majority of writers on scientific ethics, from whatever point
of view they set out—makes what one may call a " Copernican "
change in our way of considering the question of rights. The
eighteenth century thinkers looked on society as made by
individuals joining together, in order to secure their pre-
existing natural rights. We, unless we remain uninfluenced
by the more scientific conceptions of human society now
possible to us—we see that " natural rights," those rights
which *ought to be* recognised, must be judged entirely from the
point of view of society. We must return to the method of
Plato : in order to know what is really just, we must call up
a vision of an ideal society. That is the true value of " Uto-
pias " : they are rough attempts to see how our ideas of justice
look when writ large in a picture of a reconstructed society.
Society, as we are always being reminded, has indeed no
existence except as a society of individuals ; but individuals
as human beings with rights and duties, and not as mere
animals, can only be understood in reference to a society.
" Nature," we might say, falling back on the antithesis, made
man an animal ; society has made him a rational animal— a
thinking, intelligent being, capable of moral action. The
person with rights and duties is the product of a society, and
the rights of the individual must therefore be judged from the
point of view of a society as a whole, and not the society from

[1] The phrase is used by Mr. J. M. Robertson in an article in the
National Reformer for Dec. 6, 1891, in which he criticises a lecture of
mine on the subject of " Natural Rights."

the point of view of the individual. As against the Hedonist
Utilitarians, Intuitionalists are quite right in urging that morality is based on personality, and not on a mere summation of
pleasurable feelings, treated as if these feelings had an existence
per se; but the Intuitionalist is apt to treat "personality" as if
that term were the solution, and not the statement of a problem.
Metaphysically, personality can only be explained by a speculative hypothesis about the ultimate nature of the universe—in
more familiar language, about the relations between God, nature,
and man ; but for the purposes of *practical ethics and politics*,
it is sufficient to recognise that personality is a conception
meaningless apart from society.   We have got the word
" person " in its ethical sense from the Roman jurists, and we
should acknowledge our debt by recognising the social—nay,
the civic—character of the conception.   Wherever, as in those
famous theories of " social contract " and " natural rights," a
society seems to be reasonably and legitimately judged from
the point of view of the individual, such theories simply
represent an inaccurate, but possibly convenient way of judging any given society from the point of view of a supposed
wider or higher society.   The rebel against society, whether
he appeals to nature or not, may be of two kinds.   He may be
the precursor of some new and better society, in the name of
which he condemns an existing, but corrupt and decaying, set
of institutions; or he may be the survival of a ruder and lower
stage of existence.   The pirate and the brigand were once
very respectable people, but in a social condition which has
passed the stage to which they belong, they are rightly treated
as dangerous criminals.   Society, indeed, consisting only of
fallible and imperfect beings, is apt to make mistakes, and it
may now and then confuse the two kinds of rebels, and
crucify a true prophet between two ordinary criminals ;
though the ratio of true prophets to ordinary criminals is not
as a rule so high.

Whether we say that rights are in all cases created by the
State or not, is very much a matter of language.   There are
many primitive societies, which have too little definite organisation to be conveniently called States, except proleptically ;
it is usual to reserve the term State for those societies which
have a fairly definite system of government.   Moreover, within
the shelter of the State there may grow up various societies or

associations, of a more or less voluntary character—voluntary in appearance at least—and there may be surviving associations of an older kind, families, clans, village communities, etc., all of which may confer rights on their members, apart from the rights expressly conferred by the State: and some of these associations may be of an international character. The State may recognise some of these rights as legally binding; others it may tolerate, without giving them any legal sanction; others it may expressly forbid, as injurious to the security of the commonwealth, as allowing scope for foreign interference, or as infringing what have come to be regarded as the proper rights of individuals. This last form of State-action forms a principal element in the guaranteeing of "natural rights"; it is interference on the part of an organised State to protect individuals from what has come to be thought undue pressure on the part of other societies. *e.g.* the family, the Church, guilds or corporations of various kinds, old and new.

The appeal to natural rights, which has filled a noble place in history, is only a safe form of appeal if it be interpreted, as just explained, as an appeal to what is socially useful, account being taken not only of immediate convenience to the existing members of a particular society, but of the future welfare of the society in relation, so far as possible, to the whole of humanity. If it is argued that such an appeal is at least as ambiguous as a mere reference to natural rights, I answer, No; for in appealing to social utility, we are appealing to something that can be tested, not merely by the intuitions of an individual mind, but by experience. History is the laboratory of politics. Past experience is indeed a poor substitute for crucial experiments; but we are neglecting our only guide if we do not use it. This means no slavish copying of antique models, but trying to discover, from consequences which followed under past conditions, what consequences are likely to follow under similar or under dissimilar conditions now.

The introduction of the conception of evolution into the study of institutions, if that conception be applied with due care, gives us in one respect a much more hopeful outlook than if we felt bound to apply to every age the same unvarying "natural" code of right and wrong. As an illustration, let me take the institution of slavery. To the scientific student of human history it seems almost certain

that slavery was a necessary step in the progress of humanity.
It mitigated the horrors of primitive warfare,[1] and thus gave
some scope for the growth, however feeble, of kindlier sentiments towards the alien and the weak. It gave to the free
population sufficient leisure for the pursuit of science and art,
and, above all, for the development of political liberty ; and
in this way slavery may be said to have produced the idea
of self-government. By contrast with the slave the freeman
discovered the worth of freedom. Thus slavery made possible
the growth of the very ideas which in course of time came to
make slavery appear wrong. Slavery seems to us horrible :
it is contrary to nature, it violates the feelings that God and
Nature have implanted in our breasts, and so on. It used not
to seem horrible or contrary to nature, even to many people who
talked loudly about the inalienable right of liberty. There
are probably many things existing now, which will seem
" horrible " some day, but which now seem quite "natural "
to most persons. Science must have no prejudices, and therefore we must admit that there was a stage in human development when slavery, being useful to the progress of mankind,
was not contrary to what could then have been considered
" Natural rights," although when slavery is no longer an institution of progressive societies, it becomes contrary to what
people now consider "Natural rights." It is no use to construct hypothetical histories and imagine the civilisation, whose
benefits we reap, and among whose benefits are those ideas
that have abolished slavery, arising among some savage tribe
which had never hit upon this device for securing leisure to
themselves, in which to fight, to govern, to think. But an
historical justification of an institution is no justification for
the continuance or revival of an institution, when it is no
longer socially beneficial, or when the purpose it once served
can be otherwise provided for.

The present competitive industrial system has done marvels
in the way of opening up the material resources of the earth ;
those who have grown up in the shadow of it are apt to

---

[1] That the introduction of the practice of making slaves of captives
diminished the ferocity of war is generally admitted. What is less
generally noted is that, as Sir Henry Maine points out (*International
Law*, p. 131), "One consequence of the decay and abolition of slavery
was an increase of bloodshed."

imagine that it is indispensable. Those who have studied the history of slavery are not bound to any such belief. This very epoch of competitive capitalism has produced ideas which make it possible to believe in a better type of organisation in which the captains of industry shall become essentially, and not merely accidentally, the public servants of the whole community. The growth of joint-stock enterprise, under a system of "free association," suggests the idea of common-ownership on a gigantic scale. The "labour-saving" machinery, which has caused the industrial revolution and brought about an unsettlement of old, comparatively stationary societies, suggests a utilisation of machinery, which shall in very truth be labour-saving and not merely labour-displacing, and which shall provide the leisure that ancient communities could only secure to their citizens by slavery.[1] These visions of a better society are not suggested by vague, irresponsible oracles of Nature; they are inferences from experience, which may be true or false, but which admit of being profitably discussed. And this is the advantage which the appeal to reason and experience has over all appeals to irresponsible instincts, impulses, and claims, whether called natural rights or not. If you appeal to Nature, we may not be able to prove you wrong in your own court of appeal; but neither can you prove yourself right. The oracles of Nature are dumb, save to those who will compel her to speak by torture, *i.e.* by experiment; and, where experiment is inapplicable, by rational interpretation of experience.

Whether we are attacking or defending any institution, it is always well to be very sure that we are doing so on grounds which admit of reasonable discussion. If it could be shown that democratic republics would always fall a prey to military despotism, either from within or from without, then we should have to conclude that democratic republics were incompatible with human well-being, and that monarchical or aristocratical institutions were more in accordance with the "law of nature" than democracy.

If it were certain that the nations of Western Europe or of America, by checking industrial competition and by getting rid of their armies, would fall a prey to a Chinese invasion, just as the peaceful and Christianised Roman Empire succumbed

---

[1] As far as possible we must use machinery as a substitute for "living tools"—the phrase by which Aristotle describes slaves. (*Pol.*, I. 4.)

before the incursion of the northern barbarians, then it would
be right to do all in our power to keep up the military and
industrial pugnacity of the Western peoples, and all socialistic
and peaceful projects would be contrary to the " law of
nature." If it were certain that an equal or nearly equal distribution of the products of industry would lead to the decay
and gradual disappearance of science, of art, and of all intellectual pursuits generally, and a consequent return to savagery,
then any such levelling project would be contrary to the " law
of nature." If it were argued that the " Republic has no need
of chemists," we may be certain that it would be so much
worse for that republic in the long run ; it would go to pieces
before nations that did honour chemists, even if those nations
were ruled by despots. The reformer of society who would
convince those who hesitate to join him, from a fear not of
personal loss but of social retrogression, is bound to prove that
what he advocates is compatible with the welfare of society
and with its progress in the future. The only "law of nature"
to which we can listen must be such as will commend itself to
our reason as a statement of the principles of a coherent and
orderly society which will not throw away the hard-won
achievements of man in his struggle with nature and with
barbarism, and which will at the same time be progressive,
in the sense of being capable of correcting its own faults. Any
" natural rights" which are incompatible with such a society
are only another name for anarchy. " Nonsense upon stilts "
Bentham called them in his *Anarchical Fallacies*. *Fiat
justitia, ruat cælum*, it may be said. But what does that
famous maxim of heroic virtue mean ? " Let justice be done,
though the *heavens* fall "—a maxim admirable as an answer
to those pessimists who would deter mankind from any attempt to better its social organisation on the ground that this
planet cannot for ever support living beings. But whoever
says, " *Fiat justitia, ruat respublica*," whoever appeals to an
abstract justice that is incompatible with the continuance of
orderly social organisation is, wittingly or unwittingly, talking
nonsense—and mischievous nonsense, too. "Justice" may be
incompatible with some particular form or phase of society:
that is likely enough. When people seriously appeal to justice
against society, what they really mean is that a higher form
of society should supersede a lower. But it would be much

better to say so directly, and not to talk about natural rights
or abstract justice at all. A good cause is never benefited by
bad arguments.[1]

If rights are determined solely by reference to human
society, it follows that the lower animals, not being members
of human society, cannot have rights. This conclusion is
resented by many modern humanitarians who, feeling that in
some sense or other we may be said to have duties towards
the lower animals, or at least duties in respect of our conduct
towards them, conclude that the animals in their turn must
have rights against us. If a utilitarian theory be based on a
consideration of the pleasures of all *sentient* existence, then,
whether or not the phraseology of natural rights be used, all
animals must be taken into account in our judgments of
right and wrong. Very difficult questions of casuistry will,
indeed, arise because of the difference in grades of sentience ;
and the undoubted difference in degree of acuteness of feeling
among human beings ought most assuredly to be taken account
of also. If the recognition of Animal Rights is compatible with
the kindly use of a horse as a beast of burden, would not a
kindly negro-slavery be also perfectly compatible with the
recognition of Natural Rights generally ? And if we discriminate between what may be rightly done to the mollusc
from what may be rightly done to the mammal, on grounds of
different grades of sentience, should we not also—if sentience
be our sole guiding principle—discriminate between what may
be rightly done to lower and higher races among mankind—
the lower and less civilised being undoubtedly less capable of

---

[1] In his excellent little book, *First Steps in Philosophy*, with the
" physical " part of which I entirely agree, Mr. W. M. Salter says: " It
might be better that there should be no animal or human life than that
it should maintain itself by violating ethical requirements " (p. 107).
Unless for those who believe ethical requirements to be determined by
arbitrary and irrational volitions of Deity, I can see no meaning in Mr.
Salter's proposition. Morality *may* include more than can properly be
expressed as "social duty," *e.g.* the " intellectual virtues " and the duties
of cultivating science and art and learning *may* not be capable of
analysis into social virtues and duties (I cannot discuss that question
here); but morality that would lead to the destruction of all human life
seems to me a very immoral kind of morality, though a kind of morality
of which we have had a good deal too much in the past. As to the
animals—I discuss that question. Is it the tiger's ethical standard or
ours, which is to decide ?

acute feeling? An ethical theory which is based on the social
nature of man is not directly troubled by these difficulties,
though in the details of practical conduct these grades of
sentience do enter in as one of the factors determining our
moral judgments.

The most recent English book of which I know on the subject of *Animals' Rights* is that of Mr. H. S. Salt. "Have the
lower animals 'rights'?" he asks, and answers his question,
"Undoubtedly—if men have." But the question whether and
in what sense men have rights, Mr. Salt refuses to discuss.
He takes for granted that in some sense they have rights,
and treats the controversy about rights as "little else than an
academic battle over words, which leads to no practical conclusion." The term "academic" is apparently used as a term
of dispraise. For this, unfortunately, the past traditions of
learned societies may be to blame; or is a disparagement of
logic and of all careful use of language merely one of the notes
of the higher barbarism of the new school of Rousseanists? I
have tried to show that there is a sense in which the term
"natural rights" may be harmlessly used, but it is a sense
which needs caution; and therefore, if the term be used at
all, it should not be used except in "academic" discussions.
Otherwise its use can only be regarded as a rhetorical device
for gaining a point without the trouble of proving it—a device
which may be left to the stump-orator or party-journalist, but
which should be discredited in all serious writing. Mr. Salt's
justification for his assertion, that animals have rights if men
have, must be discovered incidentally. First of all, I note that
he appeals to the actual state of the law in England. "It is
scarcely possible, in the face of this legislation [for the prevention of cruelty to animals], to maintain that 'rights' are a
privilege with which none but human beings can be invested;
for if *some* animals are already included within the pale of
protection, why should not more and more be so included
in the future?"[1] Because a work of art or some ancient
monument is protected by law from injury, do we speak
of the "rights" of pictures or stones? Further, are animals
capable of being parties to a lawsuit? It might be answered,
they are on the same footing permanently on which human
"infants" are temporarily (*i.e.* until they attain full age). But

[1] *Animals' Rights*, p. 8.

if there are rights, there are correlative duties. And whereas
infants may be tried on a criminal charge, I do not know,
apart from a *cause célèbre* in Aristophanes, of any such trial
of animals in any advanced legal system. Thus it will hardly
do to appeal to existing law in proof that animals have rights
in any *legal* sense. Again, I note that Mr. Salt quotes with
approbation the maxim of the "Buddhist and Pythagorean
canons"[1]—"Not to kill or injure any innocent animal," and
the words of Bentham: "We have begun by attending to the
condition of slaves; we shall finish by softening that of all the
animals which assist our labours or supply our wants."[2] Why
these limitations of the *jus animalium*? If the animal as such
has rights, who are we to pronounce judgment, according to our
own human convenience, on his "innocence"? What is the
"guilt" from the tiger's point of view of her raid on a human
village? Why do we commend a cat that kills mice and punish
her if she attacks a tame bird? If the animals were consulted,
they would choose to be tried by a jury of their peers, before
the question of guilt or innocence were decided. The most
despotic kings have always been quite willing to leave in
peace those of their subjects who contributed to their convenience, or whom they regarded as harmless. The Czar of Russia
does not oppress any one whom he regards as "innocent."
The claim of natural rights among men has meant something
very much more than a claim that the innocent should be
kindly treated, the arbitrary government against which they
protested being free to decide the question of innocence.

It may be admitted, however, that towards the lower animals
we must always stand in the relation of despots; but it may be
urged that our despotism ought to be guided by a recognition
of their rights. Well, then, in our exercise of our power and
in our guardianship of the rights of animals, must we not protect the weak among them against the strong? Must we not
put to death blackbirds and thrushes because they feed on
worms, or (if capital punishment offends our humanitarianism)
starve them slowly by permanent captivity and vegetarian diet?
What becomes of the "return to nature" if we must prevent
the cat's nocturnal wanderings, lest she should wickedly slay a
mouse? Are we not to vindicate the rights of the persecuted
prey of the stronger? or is our declaration of the rights of

[1] *Animals' Rights*, p. 3.   [2] *Ibid.*, p. 6.

every creeping thing to remain a mere hypocritical formula to
gratify pug-loving sentimentalists, who prate about a nature
they will not take the trouble to understand—a nature whose
genuine students they are ready to persecute? Mr. Salt
injures a needed protest against certain barbarities of "sport,"
and against the habitual callousness of the ignorant in their
treatment of animals, by his attacks on men of science and his
opposition to the use of animal food. If all the world were
Jews, it has been well said, there would be no pigs in existence;
and if all the world were vegetarians, would there be any sheep
or cattle, well cared for and guarded against starvation? Perhaps a stray specimen in a zoological garden: turnips being
all needed for human food. Cruelty to animals is rightly supposed to be an offence against *humanitarian* feeling. Our duty
to the animals is a duty to human society. It is an offence
against civilised life to cause any unnecessary suffering, or to
do any unnecessary damage—" unnecessary " meaning, as it
means even in Mr. Salt's theory, unnecessary for *human* well-
being. This consideration will explain also why we regard
cruelty to domestic animals, especially to pets, with more
horror than cruelty to wild animals—especially to dangerous
or injurious wild animals. We have admitted certain animals
to a sort of honorary membership of our society; and we come
to think of them as standing in a quasi-human relation to ourselves, especially when we give them names of their own, as if
they were persons. Of Schopenhauer, that poodle-loving hater
of man, it might almost be said that he and his dog (the reign-
ing sovereign for the time) formed a society by themselves. In
a metaphorical sense we may be said to have duties towards
these honorary human beings.[1]

Pain is in itself an evil, not in the special moral sense of the
term "evil," but in the sense that it is an impediment to the
maintenance and development of life: it is an impediment
which every normal sentient being "naturally," *i.e.* by mere
instinct, strives to escape, and this instinct is kept alert by
natural selection. The growth of sympathy and of imagination makes it possible for human beings to feel mental pain at
the sufferings of other human beings, even of those not specially connected with them, and of other animals, in a manner

[1] Comte holds that the animals that help mankind form a part of
humanity. *Positive Polity* (Eng. trans.), IV. pp. 33, 312.

and to an extent impossible in a more primitive stage of existence. (The real savage and our sentimental neo-savage are
very different persons in this respect.) And thus the avoidance of pain for other beings capable of feeling it, as well as
for oneself, comes to be thought of as a duty, except when the
infliction of such pain is necessary and unavoidable in the
interests of human society and human progress. Thus we
may be said to have duties of *kindness towards* the animals :
but it is incorrect to represent these as strictly *duties towards*
the animals themselves, as if they had rights against us. If
the animals had in any proper sense rights, we should no more
be entitled to put them to death without a fair trial, unless in
strict self-defence, than to torture them for our amusement.
It is our duty to put animals to death as painlessly as possible,
when we wish their death for any human end; and similarly,
in experiments on living animals for scientific purposes, it is
right to prefer the less highly organised animal to the more
highly organised, wherever the lower type is clearly sufficient
for the purposes of the experiment. It is a duty also not to
cause any suffering which is unnecessary for the properly
scientific purpose of the experiment. The evil of pain is the
element of permanent truth in the Hedonist protest against
Asceticism; but to make the mere fact of sentience the determining principle of right and wrong in ethics is the abstraction that renders Hedonism, even in its universalistic form, an
inadequate ethical theory. I have already suggested the difficulties which would be involved in any consistent attempt to
recognise in animals equal rights with human beings: on the
other hand, to fix a scale of unequal rights solely from the
point of view of human convenience is practically to give up
basing ethics on the mere fact of sentience, and implicitly to
recognise the interests of human society as our ultimate
criterion of right and wrong.

In the foregoing discussion of the ethical end I have included
the notion of the progress, as well as that of the maintenance,
of human society. And on this difficult conception of " progress" I must therefore say a few words. In the first place,
it must be pointed out that progress is not identical with
evolution, as that term is used by biologists.[1] Natural selec-

---

[1] A confusion on this subject runs through the whole of Mr. Benjamin
Kidd's book on *Social Evolution*.

tion produces degeneration of organisms as well as advance.
In the struggle for existence, success may be obtained by
assimilation to a simpler type. Success does not necessarily
imply increasing complexity and differentiation of structure.
And so it is with human beings regarded from a purely biological point of view. The highly cultured European, who
would adapt himself to the environment of the Esquimaux,
must discard those habits of life which raise him above the
Esquimaux from the point of view of sociology. A man may
succeed in the competition of the commercial world by greater
skill and efficiency in the management of his business, by
stricter honesty, by turning out better goods, by employing
more highly paid and capable workmen than his rivals. He
may succeed by these means, under sufficiently favourable
conditions, in the long run—if he gets a sufficiently long run.
But under other conditions he may succeed, and may more
easily obtain a rapid success, by skilful unscrupulousness, by
extensive advertising, by judicious underselling and driving
his rivals out of the field, etc. An old business man is said to
have enforced the maxim, "Honesty is the best policy," by
adding, "I've tried both"; but there is a good deal of evidence
to support the inference that "to get honest" is only the best
policy for those who have already managed "to get on." The
big, successful business can be conducted on better principles
than the struggling one.

When by reflection we have once reached an ethical standard, when we judge human conduct from the point of view
of an ideal society, we become very fully conscious of the
discrepancy between "adaptation to environment," which
means pleasure and the absence of pain, and advance towards
ideal excellence; and the pessimist is at hand to declare that
all intellectual and æsthetic and ethical advance means only
an increase of sorrow. Increasing complexity of structure
makes adaptation to environment more difficult, *except in so
far as the environment can itself be controlled and altered.* But
this control and alteration of the environment is just what the
intellectual conquests of mankind make possible. As we
understand nature better, and as we understand human nature
better, we can secure adaptation and adjustment by bending
nature in many ways to ourselves instead of bending ourselves
in every respect to nature. The torrent that sweeps away

the rude hut of the savage, if confined within barriers and regulated by sluices, will grind corn and supply electricity for the service of civilised man. The energy and desire to excel which makes the Indian scalp his enemies is identical with that "last infirmity of noble mind" which may stimulate the researches of the savant, lighten the labours of the legislator, and even add inspiration to the imaginative work of the creative artist, as it undoubtedly does to the performance of the actor or of the musician. We change the channels in which competition runs, and it becomes beneficial instead of hurtful.

May we then attempt a definition of Progress, in the only sense in which Progress can be an end of action, as such increasing complexity of structure as is compatible not only with increasing "integration" but with increasing, or at least undiminished adaptation to environment? This definition, it may be objected, is only the old commonplace about "Order and Progress" disguised in a new form of Spencerian phraseology. Well, in a sense it is, but it is the old commonplace divested of the fallacy which, by separating progress from order, identifies progress with mere change—with mere instability. The old practical difficulties still remain, of course. Change, variation, increasing complexity necessarily unsettle the existing adjustments, which, however, are apt to seem more settled and stable than they really are. But the merit of the suggested definition of progress is this: that, while the preference is given to the more highly developed structure, the need of adaptation to environment is not ignored, and the practical importance is indicated of adapting the environment, so far as possible, to the higher structure. The mere fact of adaptation to environment, *i.e.* the mere fact of contentment, pleasure, absence of pain, absence of effort, is of itself no proof of excellence. The more complex structure, it must be noted, is not *per se* the higher, unless there is greater "integration," as well as greater differentiation.[1] If the complexity be such

[1] Complexity in any case is not the same thing as mere complication. When "simplification" is accepted as an ideal, it must be clearly understood that simplification does not mean loss of organs. "Simplification" is really an ambiguous way of expressing "greater integration" as an ideal, because it may also mean degeneration. A concrete illustration may help us to see more clearly the true relation of complexity to progress. A man who can talk several languages with ease, who is well acquainted with history and literature, who has some knowledge of

that in no conceivable conditions could the organism work
well, the more complex is not higher than the simpler. But
the more complex structure which is capable of working better
in suitable surroundings than the less complex may work
worse in inferior surroundings; and yet we should not be justified in calling it ethically inferior, simply because of that
want of adaptation. This is one way in which the defect of
the strict Hedonist ethics becomes apparent. To the Hedonist
the mere fact of contentment should be enough. Socrates dissatisfied, however, is better, as J. S. Mill says, than the pig
satisfied; but Socrates dissatisfied is not the ideal. The want
of adaptation and the consequent pain is a proof of imperfection. The higher natures have always to suffer just because
they are in advance of their surroundings.[1] But for the future
well-being and better-being of society, even this suffering is to
be preferred to an adaptation attained by the sacrifice of any
form of realisation of human faculty which is not incompatible
with the general well-being of an improved society. Even a
sufficient dole of bread all round would be dearly purchased at
the cost of stopping the work of the savant and the artist.
Those who try to live by bread alone will soon have to live on
an inferior kind of bread. As I have tried to show in a previous chapter, the only consistent assailants of civilisation are
those who, like the Cynics, are deliberately prepared to go back
to savagery: and if they try to put their precepts into practice, whether by using dynamite, or by refusing to submit to
sanitary laws, civilised society must take the necessary measures against them.

several natural sciences, who can climb mountains, and ride, and row,
who can keep his health and vigour either in town or country—"an all-
round man," in fact—is a more efficient person in every way than one
who can only get on in a particular groove. But he who *can* get on in a
particular groove, though only in one, is more efficient than the person
who knows several languages, but cannot express himself intelligibly or
easily in any one of them, who can do many things, but does them all
badly, etc. Dr. Johnson's warning is always useful: "A man may be so
much of everything, that he is nothing of anything." (Hence the sound-
ness of the precept in learning—to aim at knowing everything about
something, and something about everything.) When we ask, not which
individual stands "higher," but which society, the problem is necessarily
much more complicated.

[1] Of course, the lower natures in a superior environment suffer also.
Punishment is one form of that suffering.

In conclusion, there are two questions about "natural rights" which might claim to be noticed. The first concerns a matter of scientific or theoretical convenience; the second concerns a matter of practical or political convenience. (1) Ought a treatise on politics to begin with a statement of individual rights? (2) Ought the constitution of a country to guarantee certain rights to its citizens, and to protect them from legislative interference?

With regard to the first of these questions, I should only say that such a treatment presents some apparent logical advantages, but has the drawback of being chiefly associated with theories of Natural Law, which assume that we can formulate natural rights irrespective of, and prior to, any consideration of society.

The second question is practically the question whether a rigid constitution, like the American, or a fluid constitution like our own, is preferable. Now that is a question which hardly admits of a general or abstract answer. In some cases a written constitution is an inevitable necessity. The stability of the *Federal* constitution of the United States has been of an undoubted advantage to that country; in the reverence for its written constitution its citizens have found a safeguard against the instability that might have been expected to arise among a people whose independent history began in the violence of a revolutionary war and in a professed breach with the traditions of the past, and whose numbers are constantly being recruited by the fragments and separated atoms of alien societies. On the other hand, the rigidity of the constitution made a war necessary in order to get rid of the institution of slavery, and of the idea that there was a "right" of secession. And it is possible that other questions may arise in which a conflict between modern needs and the theories of the eighteenth century about individual rights may prove harsher and more terrible because of the barriers placed in the way of change. With regard to the *State* constitutions in America, the jealousy of legislatures leads to the citizens every now and then making the attempt to legislate for themselves on minute points, the result being called a "constitution." This can only be regarded as a very clumsy method of legislation. A far better and safer way of guarding against the recklessness or corruption of legislators is the Swiss device of the *Referendum*

—to let the legislators do their work, and then subject it as a whole to the approval of the electorate.[1]

In regard to some particular rights, as we shall see in the following chapters, something may be said for permanent and express guarantees such as we have not yet been accustomed to feel the need of in this country.

[1] The case for written constitutions and for the *referendum* is very lucidly and ably argued in Dr. Charles Borgeaud's work, *Établissement et Revisions des Constitutions en Amérique et en Europe* (Paris, 1893). Many of those, who in this country are most willing to adopt political innovations, feel that the time has hardly yet come when it would be safe to crystallise our fluid constitution; and even the *referendum* might, if prematurely introduced, impede some salutary changes. The arguments for and against the *referendum* do not, however, belong to my present subject.

PART II

PARTICULAR NATURAL RIGHTS

I PROPOSE, in this and the following chapters, applying the results now reached, to examine in detail the most prominent of those "natural rights" which have been claimed in the American and French declarations. In several of the American State-constitutions are specially enumerated those "of enjoying and defending life and liberty, acquiring, possessing, and protecting property, and pursuing and obtaining safety and happiness."

The right of *life* or the right to *life* may reasonably be considered first. Now, what does this mean? (*a*) There is the animal instinct of self-preservation, which undoubtedly is "natural." It represents a tendency which we may trace farther back even than the animal world, and may identify with the *vis inertiæ* of the physicist, with what Thomas Aquinas calls the tendency of every substance to seek the preservation of its own being,[1] with what Spinoza calls the *conatus sese conservandi*.[2] But what sense is there in calling this natural instinct a "right"? If by natural rights be meant those rights which a well-constituted society ought to guarantee to its members, then whether preservation of life is to be guaranteed or not must surely depend on whether the life is valuable to the society or injurious to it, or on whether, though not valuable, or even to some extent injurious, other considerations of general security, etc., make it expedient to give the preservation of such life the support of the organised force of the community. The natural instinct to preserve life is an instinct which may be furthered by reflection, and it may come to be thought a *duty* to preserve one's life. But, on the other hand, the natural instinct may be overcome by reflection, and it may come to be thought a duty not to preserve life, or only a secondary duty, subordinate to others.

---

[1] *Summa*, 1a 2ae, qu. 91, art. 2.　　　[2] *Ethica*, III., Prop. 7.

Even apart from reflection the instinct to preserve life often
gives way before other instincts, *e.g.* the desire to preserve offspring, or even the desire to gratify passion.

The principle that there is an inalienable and imprescriptible
right in all men to preserve their lives, however much social
utility may demand the sacrifice of some lives—still more the
principle that all sentient beings (for where among them are
we to draw the line, if we once pass beyond the circle of
human society?) possess such a right—would bring all regulated action to a standstill, and would lead to a rapid disappearance of the civilised men who adopted such a principle
before barbarians who did not, or, if all mankind adopted it, to
a disappearance of human beings before wild beasts. Restricted to human beings, the idea of such an inalienable
natural right undoubtedly lies at the back of the objection to
capital punishment, although the plea for its abolition is usually
supported by utilitarian arguments, such as, that a convicted
person may afterwards be discovered to be innocent and that
therefore no penalty should be incapable of being reversed, etc.
Now, if the right to preserve life has any meaning, it must
include the right to defend life, and that may involve as a
matter of necessity the right to take the life of others (men or
beasts). It is easy for the theoretical moralist to say that
self-defence is justifiable, but that under no circumstances is
aggression justifiable ; as a matter of fact, those who justify
aggression among civilised communities justify it, as a rule,
on the ground that what appears aggression is really, directly
or indirectly, self-defence. All preventive measures may be
classed, by an unsympathetic onlooker, under the term
" aggression." To be able to call a measure "a measure of
self-defence " does not of itself prove that measure to be justifiable, nor does calling it "a measure of aggression " of itself
prove it unjustifiable. We must know *what* is being defended,
and on *what* aggression is being made, before we can know
whether the defence or the aggression is justifiable in the
interests of some particular society, or of humanity as a whole,
or of some important part of it.

Now on the same general principle on which the man who
is attacked may, with the conscience of the world approving
him, kill his assailant, if he has reasonable grounds for believing that so strong a measure is necessary for preserving

his own life—on the same principle an organised society
may use the necessary force (which may include destruction of
life) in order to secure its members against loss of their
various guaranteed rights of life, liberty, security, etc. This
will justify at least some wars, and the use of such penalties
for the punishment of offenders as will save the community
from danger. If possible, punishment should aim at the
restoration of the offender to the character of a good citizen;
but whether in any case that is possible or not, punishment
must *at least* serve as a deterrent to other possible offenders,
and it must keep the more dangerous criminal from doing
further injury. Whether the punishment of death is necessary
or not, and to what offences it should be limited, is thus a
question of social expediency; and among the elements that
must be taken account of in determining this social expediency, the prevalent opinion on the subject is an important
factor which it is always unsafe to neglect. If there is a
widespread horror of the infliction of the punishment of death
for some offences or for all, the legal enactment of the
punishment may do more harm than good. When juries are
induced to bring in a verdict of "not guilty" because, contrary to their sentiment, death is the penalty for the offence
of which they really believe the accused to be guilty, society
suffers by having a criminal let loose upon it, and by a
weakening of the sense of responsibility on the part of those
called to discharge a public duty. On the other hand, whereas
to many sensitive and cultured natures a long term of imprisonment may seem a much more terrible penalty than a
quick and probably almost painless death, the popular sentiment about death may make it expedient to retain the penalty
for the gravest crimes, experience seeming to show that, if
really enforced, it serves the purpose of a deterrent better than
any other penalty. The growing attention paid to the element
of heredity in the production of crime leads many persons to
recognise that hereditary criminals should, if possible, be kept
from propagating their undesirable qualities. This in some
cases may reinforce the argument for the death-penalty, especially as life-long imprisonment is not only very cruel to
the individual, but very costly to the community, it being
impossible to make the labour of convicts profitable without
competing in the labour market to the disadvantage of the

non-criminal population. On the other hand the sense of the value of all life is on the whole a useful moral factor in society, and, wherever it seems safe to do so, the penalty of death may with some advantage be abolished. To put a human being to death means to give up the problem of making anything of him. Some criminals who have not committed murder may be more dangerous than some who have, but the popular feeling about a fitness between penalty and offence may render it desirable to restrict the death-penalty to such cases, unless and until the popular sentiment can be altered. The murderer, provided that he be not an insane person afflicted with homicidal mania, is indeed less likely, if let loose on society, to repeat his offence than the thief, the forger, the person guilty of cruelty to children or of assaults on women; and if the protection of society from those who have already committed crimes against it were the only matter to be considered, the penalty of death might seem quite unreasonable as applied to the murderer alone. But the effect of the penalty as a deterrent to others is the more important matter, and the average sentiment on the subject is therefore of essential moment. As has frequently been pointed out, the chief or sole reason for visiting murder with a severer penalty than any other crime, is to remove the inducement which the person committing any other offence (such as robbery or rape) might otherwise have to add murder to the crime already committed. If you hang for everything that moves your indignation strongly, the criminal is tempted to get full value for the price he may have to pay, especially as murdered persons cannot appear as witnesses in court. The growth of a sentiment against any use of the punishment of death was chiefly due to the reckless use of the penalty for offences of very different kinds.

The individual has no inalienable right of preserving his life against the society which secures him from aggression. This is admitted, I believe, by all the theorists of natural right except anarchists. Continued obedience, including the acceptance of laws which in certain cases impose the penalty of death, is indeed made conditional on the general security and protection afforded by these laws. But what rights of self-preservation has the society itself? The necessity of a society's preserving itself is, on the principles of evolutionist utilitarianism, made the basis for those rights which the society as a whole has against its members—rights which might be called "natural" in the sense of being necessary to the existence of the society, but which are not usually called "natural," because the theory of natural rights belongs to an individualistic type of thinking. On the other hand the right of the society as a whole to maintain its existence against rebels within it, or against the hostility of other societies, may be called "natural," in the sense of not depending upon any human institution. Such "natural right," however, as we have seen, is identical with might or force. Even civilised nations are still to one another in Hobbes's "state of nature"—a state of war mitigated only by the growth of a certain international moral sentiment and the consequent observance of a certain code of honour, as it might be called, which, having a quasi-legal character, is termed International Law. The idea, however vague and ill-defined, of a community of civilised nations, and the still vaguer and less-defined idea of a possible community of all mankind, do give a certain rudimentary social meaning to the "rights" of political societies; and it is a convention of International Law to treat each society which can manage to assert and maintain its independence as a unit which has a certain right of self-preservation. The point at which a group of rebels becomes a separate and independent State, or the point at which a revolutionary party becomes the *de facto* government, are matters on which other nations may decide differently without necessarily contravening any principle of international law or morality. The existence of any *particular* social organism (either a political society or any other), not being of an absolute value, but simply a means towards the well-being of individuals,[1] there can be no absolute moral right of self-preservation in a society against some higher or better type of society in which these individuals may be absorbed, or against the formation of more closely coherent and better societies out of an ill-compacted unity. Thus we do not consider that humanity lost, but the reverse, by the absorption of Tuscany in Italy, or by the separation of Belgium from Holland. The right of self-preservation in a society is only valid against individuals who would break it up into mere chaos, not against

[1] I emphasise the word "particular," because the existence of a social organism of some kind is essential to the well-being of individuals.

any better form of society (whether previously existing, or in process of formation) which may take its place. Where societies are in a process of transition, it may indeed be very difficult for individuals to decide where their strongest duty of allegiance lies; and in our historical judgments we are frequently compelled to give our warmest praise to some of those who from unselfish motives have been loyal to lost causes or to causes successful at the time, which we have come to consider mistaken. In judging about the value for mankind of revolutions, of secessions, of unifications, of annexations, we gain nothing in clearness of thinking, but the very reverse, by talking about all nations or tribes as if their unity was of an absolute character, and as if the rights of such units as against one another had any existence except in the opinions of human beings, which opinions may change, although in regard to such matters historical prescription is one of the most important factors in keeping opinions uniform. Past history, or past tradition belief is more important than fact in influencing popular sentiment), determines to a great extent what societies seem " natural " units with rights worth struggling for, and what societies do not.[1]

(b) Does the right to preserve one's life imply the right to put an end to it? If the right possessed by an individual over his own life is analogous to the right possessed by him over property, it might be argued that the right to retain implied the corresponding right to destroy. On the other side it might be urged that the destruction of life, by putting an end to all rights, contradicted the very idea of individual rights (which are all based on the primary right to preserve life), and therefore could not be one of them. Between these two abstract arguments I shall not attempt to decide. If, on the other

[1] In dealing with the question of the right of self-preservation, I have unavoidably been led to refer also to the right of liberty or independence. It is one of the proofs of the abstractness of the theory of natural rights, that it obliges us to separate elements that are inseparable in fact. This is an objection which applies, indeed, to every attempt to arrange human relationships under distinctive categories, though it applies much less to the grouping of them according to institutions. e.g. the family (or if that seems to assume a definite type of organisation, say the relations of the sexes and the relation of parent and child), industrial relations, etc., than to the grouping of them according to the recognised or alleged rights of individuals.

hand, self-preservation be regarded as a social *duty*, the question will still arise whether a life that is no longer of any utility to the community may not rightly be taken; and if so, whether we may not say that the individual in question has a right to take it. It is clear, however, that, when we look at the matter from the social point of view, it must be the society and not the individual that ought to judge. Individuals who may feel their life a burden to themselves may still be capable of some social service; and, if they were occupied in doing such service, would most probably feel their life less of a burden: while those who are of no social utility, and are, in fact, a burden to others, may not be inclined to remove themselves. Very different views have been held respecting suicide at different times; and the tendency to seek refuge in death varies greatly among different races. The Christian Churches have universally condemned it in all circumstances: but popular sentiment among Christian nations has been ready to find excuses for it in certain cases. The conflict between law and sentiment in our own country leads to the customary verdict of "temporary insanity" wherever a plausible pretext can be found, and sometimes where it cannot. At the most, however, suicide is excused, but not approved. When a detected scoundrel takes his life in order to escape his trial or his punishment, people may agree with Aristotle [1] in calling the act the act of a coward, rather than of a brave man: and yet there is often a feeling of relief at his disappearance, and sometimes even a qualified admiration for the relative courage of the act. The unsuccessful patriot, who kills himself to avoid dragging out a dishonoured existence, or in despair at the failure of the cause to which he had devoted his life, is looked on with admiration, in spite of the effect of Christian teaching. Philip Strozzi, who killed himself through fear that torture might extract from him revelations injurious to his friends, is said to have prayed that, if he must be damned, he might occupy the same part of hell with Cato.[2] In the case of some suicides, we blame social conditions rather than the individual; a poem like Hood's *Bridge of Sighs* represents a very widely diffused sentiment.

Thomas Aquinas (*Summa*, 2a, 2æ, qu. 64, art. 5) lays down

---

[1] *Eth. Nic.*, III. 7, § 13.

[2] Lecky, *European Morals* (ed. 3.), II. p. 56.

unequivocally that "to kill oneself is altogether unlawful, for three reasons. First, because naturally everything loves itself, and consequently everything naturally preserves itself in being, and resists destroying agencies as much as it can. And therefore for any one to kill himself is against a natural inclination, and against the charity wherewith he ought to love himself. And, therefore, the killing of oneself is always a mortal sin, as being against natural law and against charity. Secondly, because all that any part is, is of the whole. But every man is of the community; and so what he is, is of the community; hence, in killing himself he does an injury to the community. Thirdly, because life is a gift divinely bestowed on man, and subject to His power 'who killeth and maketh alive.' And therefore he who takes his own life sins against God."

The last of these arguments is identical with that used by Socrates in Plato's *Phædo* (62). The second is that of Aristotle in the fifth book of the *Ethics*.[1] The first, which Father Rickaby (from whose translation I have quoted) considers "perhaps the best of the three," is the only one that turns on the idea of a Law of Nature. If there is any force in the argument, it seems equally applicable to all actions contrary to natural inclination, and certainly to many ascetic practices and abstinences, which may be regarded as slow suicide, and which, so far from being condemned by Catholic theologians, may even constitute a claim to saintship.

Sir Thomas More, who died for his constancy to the Roman Catholic faith, suggests in his *Utopia* the expediency, not merely of permitting, but of recommending suicide to those suffering from incurable diseases: no suicides, however, are to receive honourable burial who have not received public authority for the act. Something like this suggestion of the *Utopia* was actually the custom in the Greek colony of Massilia (Marseilles). If a man wished to die, he must apply to the Six Hundred; and if he made out a good case, he was allowed a dose of poison.[2] Not a few physicians have felt the terrible cruelty of a moral code which makes it a positive duty on their part to prolong hopeless suffering. Yet it is clearly a matter that cannot be left to individual responsibility. Would a license to die necessarily be a more injurious institution than "that

[1] *Eth. Nic.*, V. 11, § 3.   [2] Valerius Maximus, II. 6.

charitable perjury of juries " as Mr. Lecky calls it) to which we are accustomed ?

(c) The subject last discussed may suggest the question whether the right to life does not mean something more than the mere right to maintain life under certain conditions—a right which is fully secured to all inhabitants of the United Kingdom by our Poor Laws. The American declarations speak of *enjoying* life ; and this implies an assertion of a natural right to a life worth living. But this includes all the other natural rights, and cannot, therefore, be discussed as a right by itself apart from them. As a matter of history, the demand to enjoy and defend life is simply part of the protest against arbitrary government; it is the demand to belong to a community with responsible government.

(d) A very important, but often neglected question remains. Does the right to life include the right to be well-born ?—that is to say, the right to start with a hereditary equipment which at the least shall not foredoom its possessor to hopeless misery ? If *this* right is to be recognised, there must be a good deal of interference with some other alleged natural rights.

When Robespierre put forward his " Declaration of the Rights of Man " in the Jacobin club, it was opposed by one member only, Boissel, who proposed in place of it another, which began : *Les droits naturels des sansculottes consistent dans la faculté de se reproduire, de s'habiller, et de se nourrir.* " The natural rights of the unbreeched are to breed, to dress, and to feed." This Declaration, we are told, was received with general laughter, and no one supported it.[1] The order in which these " natural rights " are stated corresponds on the whole to the order in which the " proletariat," true to the etymology of the word, exercise these " natural rights." The precept " to be fruitful and multiply " is observed with very little regard to the possibilities of food and clothing. The instinct of reproduction and the instinct to obtain food are the primary " natural" instincts of all animals ; the desire for clothing among human animals, insufficiently covered by Nature, may be regarded as having developed out of the natural impulse to seek shelter, except where, as in warm climates, it exists under " natural " conditions simply as the desire for ornament or

---

[1] Duvergier de Hauranne, *Histoire du gouvernement parlementaire*, I. p. 277.

from ideas about decency. In such a statement of natural
rights there is certainly no "sacrifice of the natural rights of
living people to a superstition about the effect on posterity."[1]
Posterity is provided with life; but there is no regard paid to
the quality of the life bestowed on those who have never been
consulted. Might it not be argued that, as children have no
voice in choosing their parents, those who are called into
existence without their own consent should have such a life
secured to them that they would have consented to accept it
had it been possible to consult them? Such an argument
however strange it may seem, is of the very same kind with
the argument that a government, if it is to be obeyed, must
either have been consented to by the subjects, or be such as
they would have consented to. Both arguments, it may well
be said, refute themselves by being unworkable. Obedience
cannot depend merely on consent; else every government, and
the coherence of every political society, would be perpetually
at the mercy of every discontented or disorderly individual.
A *liberum veto* in the hands of every citizen would produce
anarchy more surely even than did the *liberum veto* of the
Polish aristocracy. Similarly, no ameliorations of the evils of
human life, that we can conceive of in this world, will ever
prevent some of the children of men from uttering, in the
bitterness of their soul, the wish that they had never been born.
A society of sincere and consistent pessimists, if such persons
exist, and if a society of them could exist, might decide that
the gift of life was not worth handing on; but such a society
would thereby rapidly become extinct. The inevitable working of natural selection determines that those who, blindly or
knowingly, believe in the worth of life must always supplant
those who, wisely or foolishly, disbelieve in it. The creed of

---

[1] In his exposition of Natural Law, Prof. Lorimer lays down that
"the right to be involves the right to reproduce and multiply our being";
but at the end of the paragraph which expounds this natural right, we
are told that "A man who cannot bestow a human education on his
children has no more natural right to marry than a man who cannot
beget them" (*Institutes of Law*, pp. 176, 177.) What is the good of
declaring rights one moment and revoking them the next? But this is
what has to be constantly done by the theorists of natural rights, when
they are not anarchists. And when they are anarchists, the ungratified
natural rights of every one land us very soon in the *bellum omnium
contra omnes*.

pessimism by its very nature cannot prevail; it can never be
anything but a " bye-product" of growing reflectiveness. But
the growth of reflectiveness, and of imaginative sympathy,
must make one generation take thought for those who are
to come after. Yet those who denounce the wickedness of the
rulers of mankind in the past, and those who treat the question
of political obedience in the anarchical fashion to which I
have just referred, are often very ready in their turn to disregard the interests of posterity, and even to proclaim such
disregard as a part of the natural rights of those now
living.

It may be objected that any attempt to establish the right
of the unborn is hopeless, because the very last thing to which
human beings will submit is interference in such a matter as
sexual relations. The objection is false as to fact. At the
present time the vast majority of people in every orderly
society do submit to a great number of "interferences" of
custom and of law. Even amongst savage tribes there are
some set prohibitions as to marriage, rigidly observed. Among
ourselves, and in kindred societies, over and above the legal
preference given to monogamy, the exclusion of marriages
within certain prohibited degrees, the penalties attached to
certain sexual acts, and, in addition to legal enactments, the
sentiments which are connected with what the law allows
and forbids, we have, especially among the upper and middle
classes, a whole series of interferences on the part of "society"
with the freedom of individuals—interferences expressly intended to check the "natural" consequences of "natural"
instincts. The social prohibition of what are considered "unsuitable" marriages is a very strong one, and interferes greatly
with the operation of natural and sexual selection. A great
deal of what is often blamed as the selfishness and worldly
ambition and money-grubbing of the middle class is the outcome, not of direct individual selfishness at all, but of a
highly-developed feeling of responsibility towards offspring.
The pity of it is that so much of the suffering and sacrifice
of individual happiness, caused by the social or parental prohibition of an imprudent or an unsuitable marriage, does
nothing to improve the character of the race, and is often
directly injurious. But the moral pressure exerted in behalf
of an imperfect or false idea is a sufficient proof of what a

more enlightened public sentiment could do in the way of
direct or indirect control of parentage. Wherever the standard of living rises, and a greater security of economic
condition is attained, the " virtues " of the middle class are
assimilated ; the most improvident, as might be expected, are
those whose economic condition is the most uncertain. The
children of the slums marry, or at least produce offspring, too
early ; among the dwellers in villas marriage is frequently
postponed too long for the physical and moral well-being, both
of the persons directly concerned and of their offspring. In
this bourgeois prudence, considerations of health occupy a
very minor place. The practice of life-insurance serves, among
the men at least, to introduce a certain minimum standard of
fitness ; and business success is, of course, some test of a certain
degree of vigour—a test that again applies to the men only.
But natural selection in this matter operates under great
limitations : the value of " ability to marry " as a test of fitness for parentage is vitiated by the inheritance of property,
and sexual selection, so far as it operates freely within the limits
of persons considered "eligible," only excludes some of the
extremer cases of physical unfitness. Now, is it quite vision-
ary to suppose that, at least among those persons who exercise
this aristocratic and bourgeois virtue of prudential forethought,
the meaning of *mésalliance* and of unsuitability might come to
be altered, and that cancer, insanity, consumption might be
substituted as impediments to marriage for a deficiency of
quarterings, a grandfather in retail trade, or (most usually
now) a grandfather who did not leave behind him a sufficient
sum of money, however acquired ?

But no alteration in the implications of parental prudence
will affect those whose economic condition is the worst. A
general improvement in economic conditions would, of course,
mean a higher standard of living. But until that is brought
about, the deterioration of the race goes on unchecked. The
famines and pestilences of ruder stages of society exercised a
severe natural selection by killing off those least fit for the
struggle. But sanitation and philanthropy have checked the
ravages of the most deadly of these pestilences, and, although
there may be great want and suffering, deaths from starvation
are rare. It is true that natural selection still works with
cruel license among the children of the poor : so that in the

lowest economic stratum there is more selection of children
than among the middle class, while there is less check on the
instinct of propagation. If the children of the proletariat
were better cared for by the community, the check of natural
selection would cease; and it has been very seriously argued
that free education, if supplemented by free food and free
medical attendance, would simply tend to increase the physical
deterioration of the race by removing natural selection, and
at the same time to increase population by removing such
prudential checks as may now operate to some extent among
those who are not in the very lowest depths of hopelessness.
This argument contains a certain element of fallacy: for anything that helped to give the new generation a lift up in
respect of proper nourishment, intelligence, and standard of
comfort, might do more than counterbalance any weakening
of the almost non-existent sense of parental responsibility,
which, when it is roused, works so often at present in wrong
directions. But the argument contains this important truth,
which those who use it and those against whom it is used are
alike slow to recognise—that the assumption of responsibility
on the part of the community towards the children of the
community points logically to the assumption by the community of some control over the existence of these children.
Those who may become parents cannot be indefinitely relieved
of responsibility; if they are relieved of it in one direction,
they must be made to feel it in another. If the State i.e. the
community) should ever come to guarantee to every citizen,
not a bare minimum of subsistence, but a fairly comfortable
subsistence, requiring the necessary amount of work from
every one capable of it, the State must take precautions to
ensure that the number of incapables shall be as small as
possible; in other words, if the State becomes a general
employment agency and insurance company, it must exercise
the same kind of prudence which such societies have to
exercise at present. If it does not, the quality of its citizens
must deteriorate, and the conditions of work for those who can
work will become more unpleasant, or else there must be a
continual degeneration towards a lower and lower scale of
existence, till the society sinks into barbarism, or falls a prey
to some stronger community, which, either through remaining
more under the sway of natural selection, or through having

adopted some system of rational selection, has not entered on the campaign with an army of hereditary wastrels.

Many persons are ready to accept the idea of responsibility towards the unborn, but not to accept the idea of State-interference in the matter. Such things, they say, must be left to the conscience of the individual; the family is a sphere too sacred for legal interference. Unfortunately for this argument, the State has already interfered with a great many of the institutions of the patriarchal family. The *paterfamilias* can no longer chastise his wife or even his children according to his own irresponsible judicial decisions; he can no longer decide whether they shall have any education or none; he can no longer hold his house as a castle against the sanitary inspector. The law, as I have already pointed out, decides that certain marriages are unlawful, and consequently that certain children are illegitimate. How if the meaning of illegitimacy were to be changed? or, if that suggestion sounds too startling, how if it were to be enlarged? The fatal defect of trusting to private prudence and conscientiousness is that it operates least just where it is most wanted; the prudent and conscientious therefore increase in a smaller ratio than the imprudent and careless. In a democratic community, or, indeed, in any community, a large amount of public sentiment on the subject would be necessary to carry a law enforcing a health-certificate as a requisite for lawful parentage, or to make the law effective if it were carried; but that does not prove that the reform could operate without the law. A law is the judgment of the people when sober, and it serves as a check on what they might do when drunk with passion. A law against bigamy does not absolutely prevent bigamy, but it diminishes the number of bigamists.

The view of criminality as to a great extent of the nature of disease is a strong argument for certain punishments which at first sight it might seem to condemn. The criminal who is put to death, or who receives a very long sentence of imprisonment, is, at least, prevented from propagating his species.[1]

---

[1] The ferocious penalties enforced till lately under the criminal law produced a reaction against all corporal punishment, a reaction which some legal reformers feel has now gone too far. The making of eunuchs for reasons of luxury, or jealousy, has caused the idea of sterilisation to seem repulsive, so that a defender of *Animals' Rights*, like Mr. Salt (p. 41),

There is another aspect of this question of the right of the unborn. As I have said, we cannot separate the discussion of each "natural" right from the others. The question of the equality of the sexes is very constantly treated as if it stood by itself, and could be settled on its own merits. Supposing all occupations opened to women, and women put on a footing of equality with men so far as legal and political rights (and so far as legal and political responsibilities—for that also would follow) are concerned, a little thinking will show that the *average* woman would always be at an economic disadvantage in competition with the *average* man (I am not dealing with cases of exceptional ability), because of the interruption caused to her work by the bearing and rearing of children. And in the interests of the children to be born, that interruption ought to be much greater than it is at present in the lives of women who are wage-earners. The average man at present works for such wages as will support himself, a wife and children; the average woman, for what will support herself alone, and generally on a lower scale of expenditure than the man. The man "without encumbrances" gets the economic advantage of the standard set by the average man. The woman with encumbrances gets the economic disadvantage of the standard set by her unencumbered sisters, who are often moreover partially supported by relatives or in other ways. In addition to this we must add the fact, that in many pursuits the woman worker is apt to be less valuable than the man, because marriage takes her away from her work just when she has learnt it thoroughly, while marriage gives the man a stronger inducement to continue and improve. Seeing this, some women are far-sighted enough to urge that their services as mothers should be taken into account by the community, which could not continue to exist without such services. If, however, maternity is to be regarded as a public service, and rewarded as such, the community must, in its own interests, take care that it receives a due equivalent for its

suggests that even the mutilation of domestic animals "could scarcely survive the critical ordeal of thought." But when we consider the numerous cases of semi-imbeciles who are found guilty of certain crimes, is not the question worth asking whether (at least, for any repetition of the offence) a surgical operation would not be a more beneficent and more socially useful penalty than a very long sentence of imprisonment?

expenditure. When the compulsory military service, which is normal in many countries, and may be required in all, is urged as an argument for the political privileges of men in distinction from women, the advocates of "women's rights" ask, with considerable relevancy, "Where would your soldiers be without mothers?" The defect in this retort is that it overlooks the fact that the State does not support any and every male as a soldier; a certain minimum of fitness is required. The State must similarly reject those would-be mothers who are physically or morally unfit. To burden the State with paupers and imbeciles is the reverse of a public service, and should certainly not be rewarded as such.

NEXT to the right of life is generally named the right of
"liberty," and to many persons this seems the primary and
most essential right of all.[1] As many crimes have been done
in the name of Liberty (and a still greater amount of nonsense
talked in the name of Liberty), there are some who think they
gain a point or two by substituting the Saxon term "Freedom." Liberty, it is admitted, is something French, foolish
and frivolous. Freedom is English, solid and sensible, if just
a trifle dull. Any such distinction is mere playing with
words; it matters not whether we choose to take the Romance
or the Teutonic term between which our conveniently compo-
site language offers us the alternative. John Locke writes
indifferently of "natural liberty" and of "freedom." I have
shown sufficiently in Chapter I. that we cannot shuffle off
upon French fanatics the sole responsibility of having proclaimed, even in the most extreme forms, the natural rights
of liberty, etc. The same ambiguities lurk in the one term
and in the other. Whether any one demands the liberty to
do something, or asks to be left free to do something, he is
making the same sort of claim; and if he supposes that for
liberty *as such*, or for freedom *as such*, there is any *a priori*

---

[1] In a work entitled *The Natural Right to Freedom*, by Mr. M. D. O'Brien
(recently published; no date), I had hoped to find a reasoned statement
of the Individualist theory. But, save for some fragments of Stoic
moralising, I have found nothing except vituperation, misprints, and
bad grammar. Of the vituperation I am one of the objects; but in the
distinguished, if somewhat oddly assorted, company of Professor Flint,
Sir J. F. Stephen, M. Zola, and Walt Whitman. To Mr. O'Brien's
vituperation of myself and my arguments I do not in the least object,
but I do object to having put in my mouth, and in that of Tacitus, such an
atrocious piece of individualist Latin as " *Principis mortalis, republica
æterna*" (p. 81). Mr. O'Brien would seem to claim a natural right to
freedom from the rules of grammar, as well as from the authority of
civilised society.

justification as against the claims of "restraint" *as such*, or
" interference" *as such*, he has become a prey to the old
fallacy which consists in taking relative terms as absolute.
The modern reader of Plato's *Euthydemus* is apt to dismiss the
captious puzzles of the old Sophists with a superior smile,
saying, "Such things belong to a very childish stage in
human thought." When Euthydemus argues that my father,
because he is a father, is also the father of all other men, and
also of all gudgeons and puppies and pigs; and when Diony-
sodorus reverses the position, and argues that Ctesippus's dog,
because a father, is the father of Ctesippus himself,[1] the
reasoning is so ridiculous, if one may say so, that it hardly
raises a laugh. But a great many arguments based upon the
appeal to " freedom " are arguments of the same kind, though
the fallacy is more deeply hid, since "freedom" is not on the
face of it a relative term in the same way that "father" is.
If I call a person "more learned," the question at once
suggests itself: "More learned than whom?" But when a
person is called "learned," or "prudent," or "sane," or
" honest," the question is not always asked: "By what
standard?" Yet that is a very important question to ask.
A tall Esquimau would be a short Englishman; and a learned
pig would be ignorant for a Justice of the Peace. The
relativity of the term "drunk" has frequently come before
the notice of the law courts. The definition of drunk as " not
capable of lying on the ground without holding on" would not
satisfy a "total abstainer." Now the term "free" is more
obviously relative than some of these terms. Not only, like
all adjectives of quality, does " free " imply some standard by
which it can be measured—a free man, under the despotism
of Nero or Domitian, would hardly be accounted free by those
who looked back on the Republic—but the very word ought
to suggest the incompleteness of the description, till we know
from what a person is free, or what he possesses the liberty
to do.

The editor of Sir George Cornewall Lewis's excellent little
book on the *Use and Abuse of Political Terms*—Sir R. K. Wilson[2]—quotes from a speech, so far as he can remember, of Mr.

---

[1] *Euthyd.*, 298.
[2] P. 151, *note.* I have not followed Sir R. K. Wilson's commentary on
the phrases in every respect, though I am greatly indebted to it.

Joseph Chamberlain, in which an "advanced" political programme was put forward under the phrases "free land, free labour, free religion, and free schools." If this combination of words was not actually used by the orator to whom it is ascribed, it is likely enough to have been used by somebody else in the days when the creed of "Advanced Liberals" was manufactured at Birmingham. The adjective "free" in each of these cases is meant to commend the policy advocated to the minds of the party of "freedom." But what confusion of thought that little word conceals! By "free land" is meant apparently any measures which would facilitate the legal transfer of land; and among such measures one of the most effectual would be an interference with the "freedom" of bequest, and with the "liberty" of landowners to tie up real property. "Free labour"—well, what does that mean? In more recent years it would probably mean the putting of restraint upon trade-unions in their interference with the employment of non-union men.[1] In earlier times, in many lands, it would have meant the abolition of slavery, or the removal of restrictions which hindered the migration of workmen from one district to another. Sir R. K. Wilson suggests that it may mean "the repeal of all laws for punishing manual labourers as criminals for mere breaches of contract," or "a shortening of the hours of labour by means of legal restrictions on the freedom of contract." I give up the problem of what it meant as originally used. "Free religion" might mean freedom from legal and political disabilities on the ground of religious opinion, and the legal right of every citizen to worship God in his own fashion: in the mouth of some ecclesiastics it would mean the liberty of one Church to restrain all other forms of religion, and its exemption from any responsibility to the civil courts, in all those matters in which it did not choose to be responsible. As used at Birmingham, however, the words would only mean the disestablishment and disendowment of State Churches, *i.e.* an extensive interference on the part of the State with the property of various corporations (sole and aggregate), and the abolition of all legal provision of free, *i.e.* gratuitous, religious teaching and worship. "Free schools" means the institution of gratuitous teaching at the cost of the nation; so that the

---

[1] Cf. the phrase about every man's right to do what he likes with his labour, quoted p. 15 above.

word "free" in these two last formulæ has exactly opposite meanings.

It would be easy to multiply examples of the ambiguities of the words "liberty" and "freedom." "A free monarchy" to Bacon and to King James meant an absolute monarchy, so that "a free monarchy" is incompatible with what we call "free government." The "liberties" of corporations, classes, or individuals, mean their special privileges, and thus involve considerable interference with the "liberty" of the non-privileged. "Freedom of contract" may result in a practical bondage of one of the parties to the other. A "Free Church" may allow less "liberty of thought" than Churches which are not "liberated" from the State.[1] Where Bishop Burnet wrote, "The Earl of Argyle was free of all scandalous vices," Dean Swift, in correction or malignity, wrote on the margin, "As a man is free of a corporation, he means." The last example suggests forcibly what is perhaps the most important of all the differences in the signification of the term "liberty"—the difference, namely, between *negative* and *positive* liberty. Negative liberty means simply "being let alone." Whether that is a good or a bad thing in itself is a perfectly useless question to discuss. It is (to adapt an illustration of Sir James Stephen's) just like asking whether a hole is a good thing in itself.[2] All depends on what the hole is made *in*, and on what you want to put into the hole. A hole in my coat is useful, if it is a button-hole or the place my arm has to go through; but a hole in the wrong place is not desirable. And so it is with liberty in the merely negative sense of non-interference. We must know who or what is being left alone, on what occasions, in what places, and who it is that is leaving any one alone, before we can profitably discuss the good or evil of freedom. To give a baby its freedom on the verge of a precipice and to attempt to supervise every act of grown men are both foolish and culpable proceedings. When people praise liberty, it may simply be a way of expressing their strong detestation of some particular form of restraint; but more often, there is implied also in the praise the ideal of some *positive* powers of doing something which they consider worth doing.[3] Positive or real liberty, as

[1] Cf. below, p. 220.
[2] Cf. *Liberty, Equality, Fraternity* (Ed. 2), p. 197.
[3] Cf. T. H. Green, *Works*, III. p. 371.

we might call it, to distinguish it from the negative or merely
formal liberty of being let alone, means the opportunity or
capacity of doing something.   Such liberty is, in its turn,
good or bad according as the things which can be done are
good or bad.   That there is a natural right to liberty might be
understood to mean (in accordance with the sense of "natural"
explained above, p. 75) that every well-regulated society ought
to secure to all its members, so far as possible, the opportunity
of developing their various natural (*i.e.* inherited) gifts and
powers so far as they can without detriment to one another
or to the well-being of the society as a whole.

But this positive and qualified meaning of liberty has not
always been recognised as clearly distinguished from the mere
negative sense of being let alone ; nor is it always realised how
very much any real positive liberty depends upon the existence
of elaborate social arrangements, and on a strong and stable
government.   In this country no one is hindered by law from
reading all the works of Mr. Herbert Spencer.   That is negative
liberty.   But if a man cannot read at all, or if he can read but
has not any money to spare for the purpose of buying so many
volumes, or if he has no access to any public library, or if the
managers of any library to which he has access refuse to permit
such works on their shelves, or if, having access to them, he has
no leisure in which to read them, or if he has not had such an
education as enables him to understand what he reads, he cannot
be said to get much good out of the fact that the law of the land
does not prohibit him from reading Mr. Spencer's works.   Thus,
in order that the great mass of the inhabitants of this country
should really enjoy the privilege of appreciating the philosophical basis on which Mr. Spencer founds his objections to State
education, State libraries, and all such forms of interference
with individual liberty, it is necessary that such forms of
State interference with individual liberty—and a good many
others—should be in active operation ; at least experience has
not yet shown us any instance in which opportunities of
culture have been accessible to all, or nearly all, the inhabitants of densely populated countries without some such interference with the liberty of being ignorant, the liberty of
keeping children ignorant, the liberty of working for excessive
hours, and other individual liberties of that kind.

Thus, liberty in the sense of positive opportunity for self-

development, is the creation of law, and not something that
could exist apart from the action of the State. It is, indeed,
conceivable that at least in small communities the pressure of
public opinion alone might suffice to keep up a strong sense of
parental responsibility in the matter of education, and a standard of living which would ensure among other things a fair
amount of leisure. But, where any approximation to such conditions has existed, it will be found that a Church not tolerating
nonconformity has practically exercised effective compulsory
powers, backed by sanctions such as excommunication, for
which an equivalent can only be found in State-enforced penalties when the Church ceases to be identical with the civil community, and when citizens may belong to other religious bodies,
or to none at all. Even in such cases of ecclesiastical, or, one
might say, theocratic compulsion, the sword of the civil magistrate has generally been at the service of the Church. Scotland and the New England colonies in the seventeenth and
early part of the eighteenth centuries might be cited as examples of countries where illiteracy was exceptional before
Compulsory Education Acts—in the modern sense—had been
passed; but a powerful Puritan clergy enforced reading-lessons
on their flocks with the same stringency they would have used
to prohibit the teaching of such doctrines as those of Mr.
Spencer. The only alternative to the penalties enforced by the
law courts are the often more terrible penalties of religious
excommunication enforced by an exclusive and necessarily intolerant Church, or of a " boycott " enforced by some irresponsible association, too much believed in or too much feared to
be lightly disobeyed. Most persons who care for liberty—in
the sense in which alone it is worth caring for, *i.e.* opportunities
of self-development—will prefer the compulsion enforced by a
State in which the whole community is in some way represented, and which is strong enough to secure toleration for
those who dissent from the prevailing religion or who dread
the arbitrary edicts of private associations or secret societies.

The American Declarations of Rights have contented themselves with claiming the natural right to liberty, but with more
prudence than respect for logic have abstained from giving
any definition of the term:[1] the attempt might possibly

[1] Here is a charming specimen of the casuistry to which the doctrine
of a natural right of liberty may lead. In a case arising out of the South

have led to some awkward and premature differences between
the northern and the southern States. The French Declaration
of 1789 (prefixed to the Constitution of 1791) seriously grapples
with the difficulty. "Liberty," according to its fourth article,
"consists in the power to do everything that does not injure
another; thus the exercise of the natural rights of every man
has no limits except those which assure to the other members
of the society the enjoyment of these same rights." The corresponding article in the Declaration of 1793 has its first clause
almost identical with the words used in the Declaration of
1789: "Liberty is the power which belongs to man of doing
everything that does not injure the rights of another." What
follows is a somewhat rhetorical flourish: "Nature is its principle, justice its rule, the law its safeguard: its moral limit is
to be found in the maxim, *Do not do to another what thou
wouldest not have done to thyself*"—the negative side of an
ancient and venerable moral precept. Mr. Herbert Spencer
enunciates the "formula of justice" in very similar terms:
"Every man is free to do that which he wills, provided he
infringes not the equal freedom of any other man" (*Justice*, p.
46). Mr. Spencer tells us that "for more than thirty years"
he supposed that he was "the first to recognise the law of
equal freedom as being that in which justice, as variously ex-
emplified in the concrete, is summed up in the abstract." At
length he has learned that Kant had said something similar.
In a translation of Kant's *Philosophy of Law*, he finds these

---

Carolina liquor law, which prohibits the sale of alcoholic drinks except
in State dispensaries, Judge J. H. Hudson, "the ablest of South Carolina's
eight judges" (I quote from the *Boston Transcript* of July 11, 1893, laid
down that the law was unconstitutional, because it deprived the people
of the right to pursue a lucrative branch of trade, and gave the State a
monopoly therein; but that it would be lawful to prohibit the sale of in-
toxicating liquors altogether. Thus, apparently, the individual has a
natural right to sell drink, but no natural right to get it! It is only in
a very commercial community that the right of selling could seem more
primary and fundamental than the right of using the article sold; but to
regard it as more "natural" is stranger still. As the South Carolina
liquor law has been enforced, *i.e.* has caused riots quite recently, I fancy
that Judge J. H. Hudson's decision must have been overruled, on equally
plausible grounds doubtless.

Since writing the foregoing note I see that the Supreme Court of South
Carolina has decided that the liquor law is unconstitutional, whether on
Judge Hudson's grounds or not I do not know.

words : " The universal Law of Right may be expressed thus :
' Act externally in such a manner that the free exercise of thy
will may be able to co-exist with the freedom of all others,
according to a universal Law.' " [1]   (See Mr. Spencer's *Justice*,
pp. 263, 264.)   Kant's *Rechtslehre*, it may be observed, was first
published in 1797 (or, rather, in the latter part of 1796).   Mr.
Spencer apparently has not yet heard of the still earlier anticipation of his own formula in the French Declarations, nor of
the deduction from a more ancient maxim introduced in one of
them.   " The Golden Rule," of course, in its *positive* form is a
maxim of Benevolence rather than a maxim of Justice, and it
is only the negative side of it which has any proper place in a
formula of Justice to be used as a principle of legislation.

All these formulae of Justice or definitions of liberty, it
should be noted, bring in the conception of *equality* as well as
that of liberty.   As I have already pointed out, we cannot
keep the several alleged natural rights apart from one another.   At first sight, Mr. Spencer's phraseology may seem
the simplest and the most distinct.   Liberty is taken to mean
"doing what one wills"; but the right of doing what one
wills is limited by the equal freedom of everybody else.   The
formula obviously implies a manner of thinking about human
action analogous to that which underlies a very common version of the Social Contract theory.   Every individual human
being (I assume that Mr. Spencer means "man" to be con-
strued as of common gender) is thought of as having in himself
a right to do anything he likes ; but as every one has the same
right, the various absolute rights conflict and make a war of
all against all, except for the Social Contract which sets limits
to the rights of each.   The Social Contract theory may however be used, as it is by Hobbes, to solve the difficulty about
rights, by denying what are commonly called natural rights
(though not what Hobbes himself would call rights according
to the law of nature) altogether ; it may be used, as it is used
by Locke, to modify somewhat seriously some of the alleged
natural rights.   According to Mr. Spencer's view of Justice,
this principle of equal liberty is an absolute principle which no
convention or law can rightly abolish or destroy, and which
can always be appealed to for the criticism of positive institu-

[1] Hastie's Kant's *Philosophy of Law*, p. 46; Kant, *Werke* (ed. Rosenkranz), IX. p. 55.

tions. We must think of the formula as a principle underlying any possible social contract, and not as resulting from it. Now let us see what it means, and what help we can get from it, in settling practical difficulties. People will generally admit that they wish to do what is just; but *what* is just in any particular case is often the very thing in dispute. And it would indeed be a great help if we had a formula applicable to all cases.

At the first glance this formula of justice seems to offer me a most charming license. I may do anything whatever that I like—except— "Ay, there's the rub." I must leave "equal freedom" to everybody else. Now, what is *equal* freedom? Have I no right to stand up and speak at a meeting unless everybody else may also stand up and speak at the same time? If others are prevented, they are certainly deprived of their equal freedom; if they are not, it would be rather awkward to be the chairman of that meeting—if, indeed, the formula of justice allows any one to be chairman without everybody being chairman. This last illustration will suggest the obvious and reasonable solution. Why is any one allowed to stand up and speak at a meeting at all? Why is any one allowed to sit in the chair and regulate the proceedings? Is it in virtue of any *a priori* principle of natural justice or equal freedom, and not simply and solely because the persons attending the meeting find it convenient to make or to follow certain conventions as to the conduct of business? Anybody's "right" to do or say anything is derived entirely from the consent of the society of persons forming the meeting; there is no such right in any one prior to, and independent of, the society in question. A public meeting is indeed a very temporary type of society; and if it were not for the traditions and conventions inherited by one meeting from others, or from the procedure of assemblies of a more permanent kind, public meetings would always be more chaotic than they sometimes are.

It may be objected that I am quibbling with Mr. Spencer's formula; and that by equal freedom is meant, not necessarily the right to do exactly the same thing at the same moment in the same place, but only the right to do similar things at the same moment in the same place, or to do the same thing at different times and in different places. My right to stand up and speak at a meeting depends on the right of other people to stand up and speak after me, and on other people's rights to hold other meetings at different places, and so on. But suppose I am speaking at the most advantageous time and in the most convenient place, the other people who only get the right of speaking at the inferior times and places are deprived of their *equal* freedom. And, even among the persons present at one meeting, can it be said that no one has a right to speak at all, unless every one has a right to speak afterwards? Meetings would be more terrible ordeals even than they are now, if there was a natural and indefeasible right in everybody to bore everybody else. Whether anybody is allowed to speak at all, how long he may speak, and how many people may speak—all depend ultimately on the willingness of the audience to hear them. But, it will be said, can you not appeal to the sense of *justice* in a meeting in order to get a hearing? Undoubtedly. But why? It is because the persons are accustomed to certain modes of conducting meetings which have gradually grown up under the shelter of firm government and stable social order. These modes may vary, and one or another be adopted according to the particular purpose for which the meeting is held. People may have come together simply to listen to a lecture: nobody but the chairman introducing the lecturer, the lecturer himself, and perhaps some persons moving and seconding votes of thanks, may claim the right to be heard at all. Or, again, questions may be invited by the chairman, but any person taking advantage of the right thus bestowed upon him may be strictly limited to the asking of questions, and checked if he begins to wander off into a little oration of his own. Or, again, the meeting may be one in which " free discussion " is invited, but all persons except the speaker or speakers who have opened the debate may be restricted to ten or to five minutes. In none of these cases—all familiar enough—is there any absolute principle of " *equal* freedom." There are, however, meetings—most notably, the usual type of legislative assembly—in which every one of a certain determinate number of persons constituting the assembly is presumed by the constitution of the assembly to have an equal right to speak, just as he may have an equal right to vote. But I do not think there exists any assembly of this kind anywhere, or that any such assembly

would be likely to exist long, in which an absolute and indefeasible right is conceded to every member, however fatuous
and however dull, to speak as frequently and as long as the
most eloquent, the most trusted, and the wisest statesman
present.   Some venerable legislative bodies do occasionally
seem to be approximating to such a condition; but it is
generally regarded as a bad sign when an assembly, professedly met together for the transaction of business, comes
to waste its time in a weak concession to the natural rights of
bores and buffoons. As a rule, the right of speech is dependent
on the goodwill of the audience ; and, though there may be a
general willingness to give every one a hearing, that willingness is usually and wisely limited by the conviction that,
unless a person has something to say that is worth listening
to, the less he is heard the better.   Any assertion of an
absolute claim to equal freedom of speech would probably be
met by disapprobation and clamour; and a continued assertion of it would certainly lead to a general chaos and confusion—the claim of "equality" destroying the "freedom" of
all by destroying the order that alone makes freedom possible.

To the connection between the idea of justice and the idea
of equality I shall have to return. Meanwhile, I think this
discussion of what is practically meant by the right of free
speech in meetings for special purposes illustrates sufficiently
well the source of such rights generally.   The right of making
a speech is the creation of a society, and is limited by the
goodwill of the society as a whole, and, as a rule, is both protected and restricted by the authoritative decisions of some one
presiding person, to whom the society hands over its powers
in this matter for the time being, and who is aided and
supported by the accumulated traditions of the past.   The
principle of justice should be a principle that holds a society
together; but any absolute claim of equal freedom on the part
of every individual could only mean the break up of the
society, and cannot therefore be the principle of justice.

The French Declarations, however, do not leave the definition of liberty open to any such anarchical interpretation.
The Declaration of 1789 makes the limit of individual liberty
depend upon the question whether any *injury* is done to other
persons or not; the Declaration of 1793 approaches more nearly
in appearance to the anarchical principle of Mr. Spencer's

formula, since it substitutes for "injury to others," "injury
to the *rights* of others." But injury to the rights of others is
in any case something very different from interference with
the equal freedom of others; for among these rights are included in the Declaration of 1793 the right of security and the
right of property. Without referring now to the difficult questions which are raised by an assertion of a natural right of property, it is enough to point out that the recognition of a right
of security alone is incompatible with any absolute assertion of
a right to equal freedom under all circumstances. It implies,
however vaguely, the right to have order maintained by a
government of some sort. And the article on liberty in the
Declaration of 1793 goes on to say that "the law is the safeguard of liberty"—an expression much more ambiguous,
indeed, than the clear language of the Declaration of 1789,
which expressly lays down that the limits of liberty "can
only be determined by the law." Now, if this is once recognised, it follows that the right of equal freedom, or the right
of any freedom, whether equal or not, is not prior to positive
law but dependent upon it. The French Declaration is a
protest against arbitrary government; but it is a protest in
favour of the determination of rights by fixed and known laws.
It is conceived quite in the spirit of John Locke, who, in
spite of all his phrases about natural rights, says that "Where
there is no law there is no freedom." [1]

It might be shown in other ways that the right of any
individual to do what he wills must be limited by other considerations than the right of other individuals to do the same
or similar acts. Most people now-a-days in this country
would, I fancy, agree that a person has not a right to spread
the infection, say, of scarlet fever or small-pox, provided only
that he concedes to all others a similar right. The others
might not consent to his liberty in return for his concession
of equal liberty to them. We have come to consider certain
things expedient in the interests of the general well-being, and
certain things injurious. And we have come to consider it
expedient to prohibit certain things simply because they are
injurious, quite apart from considerations of equal freedom.
We have indeed come to consider that restraints are inexpedient, unless they are imposed upon all persons similarly

---

[1] *Treatise of Civil Government*, II. § 57.

situated, so that in a certain sense we recognise a principle of
equal restraint ; *i.e.* we hold that the law should be impartial.
The reasons for this principle of equality I shall have to discuss later. Meanwhile, let me point out one obvious reason
for it. A law is more likely to be accepted under a democratic
constitution, and is more likely to be obeyed and to be enforced
if it seems to apply to all equally. But to recognise the need
of satisfying the demand for equality to some extent is a
very different thing from making equal freedom our guiding
principle. A few strong, well-armed men might be quite
willing that every one should have an equal right to kill and
plunder; but this willingness of the brigand to adopt the
formula of Mr. Herbert Spencer would not (in the judgment
of most persons) justify a settled modern society in going back
to

> " the good old rule . . . the simple plan.
>   That they should take who have the power,
>   And they should keep who can." [1]

The principle of equal freedom, if taken as the ultimate basis
on which the fabric of law and government is to be built up,
would either compel a complete abstinence from all action on
the part of every individual—that would be one way of every
one having an equal right to do everything,—or it would mean
the equal right of every one to do everything in the sense of
Hobbes, *i.e.* the war of all against all. The intermediate meanings, which *seem* to make the principle of equal freedom a
plausible account of what justice is, all presuppose an orderly
fabric of society in which the rights of individuals are settled
for them by a fixed system of law. In the blank spaces left
unfilled by definite law or established custom, people do act
on a rough general principle of give and take.

Liberty in general is too ambiguous a term to permit us to
decide how far the right to liberty is a right which ought to
be recognised by a well-regulated society. The principle that
the liberty of every one should be limited only by the equal
liberty of every one else has been shown to be incapable of
any literal application as a fundamental principle of society :
on the contrary, it is a principle which is either absurd or

[1] Wordsworth, *Rob Roy's Grave.* According to the poet, "in the
principles of things, *He* sought his moral creed."

anarchical, or both. I proceed now to examine some particular
kinds of liberty which have been claimed as natural rights.
In the life of man we very commonly distinguish three main
forms in which his natural powers can be exercised—thought,
speech, action. Action is a very wide term, and clearly requires subdivision; but we may take these three main forms
as distinguishing three spheres in which freedom may be
claimed. Freedom of thought in one sense, which may fairly
be regarded as the strictest sense of the words, every one has,
and nobody can restrict. The Holy Office may forbid a man
to utter any doctrine of which it does not approve, but no
power that priest or tyrant has ever wielded can limit the
freedom of a man's inmost soul. And, under oppression and
amid bigotry, the closed lips of the intellectual rebel have
often smiled bitterly but proudly, conscious of a freedom
which even stone walls and iron bars cannot limit or confine.
But to think what may not be uttered becomes a torture which
eats away the soul. And the intellect which is shut up in its
own dark chamber tends to pine away and perish, missing
alike the fresh air of controversy and the sunshine of human
sympathy. Indirectly, if not directly, even this sad privilege
of freedom of thought is destroyed by systematic repression of
freedom of utterance. And in any sense of the words which
goes beyond the merely negative one—that what goes on in
one's mind cannot be directly [1] controlled by others—freedom
of thought cannot exist except in a stimulating intellectual
atmosphere. For freedom of thought, in the positive sense
of the development of intellectual capacity and the earnest
pursuit of truth, implies the existence of a good system of
education, of a high average of intellectual culture in at least
some class of the community, and of the possibility of a satisfactory career for those who devote themselves specially to
intellectual pursuits.

The mere absence of laws interfering with intellectual
liberty will not of itself lead to the growth of a genuinely
scientific spirit in regard to matters of belief. The public

---

[1] A person hypnotised may be said to have his thoughts controlled by
another; but the control is not exercised directly by mind over mind,
but through the medium of suggestion. Further, a hypnotised person
is not a specimen of a person "thinking," in the only sense of that term
we are here concerned with.

opinion of a society of uneducated or slightly educated persons, who are more or less under the sway of the same beliefs in religious, political, or social matters, may be far more adverse to the growth of any true positive intellectual liberty than even the existence of considerable legal restrictions on the free expression of opinion in popular discourses, provided that a certain degree of license is permitted. or winked at, in the case of those who address a limited audience of the learned. In a democratically governed society there may, owing to the strong pressure of popular prejudice, be less intellectual liberty, negative or positive, than under certain kinds of aristocratic and even of despotic governments. In the latter cases freedom of thought may be the privilege only of the few, and it may be a privilege dependent on the somewhat uncertain caprice of those in power; but in the former case it may be practically non-existent. A strong government, even of a despotic or arbitrary kind, is often necessary in order to secure the person who holds some unpopular opinion against the hatred of the bigoted multitude. Under the early Roman Empire, Greek sceptics and Christian believers enjoyed an amount of security and liberty which no champions of new and unpopular opinions could possibly have enjoyed in a small Swiss democracy or in Puritan Massachusetts, so long as such communities remained homogeneous in their religious belief.

Freedom of thought is thus not necessarily connected with the existence of what is called "free government." In spite of what is sometimes alleged, religious and political liberty do not always go together. The struggle for civil liberty, *i.e.* for self-government, for institutions that are to some extent at least democratic, still more the struggle for national liberty, *i.e.* independence of alien rule, may even be directly hostile to religious liberty—as we understand it. The necessity of homogeneity, as we shall see, may compel or seem to compel a degree of intolerance which is not necessary under a strong despotism. In the long run, however, religious liberty is placed on surer foundations if it is based upon a principle deliberately adopted by a free people than if it rests solely on the caprice, or carelessness, or individual tolerance of a despot. On the other hand, if liberty of thought is once granted, it is not likely to be limited to religious questions: freedom of opinion respecting the other world will lead to freedom of opinion respecting this.

And on this account the liberty of thought and speech is, as Milton saw, the very foundation of all other liberties. A democracy of uniform religious belief may stagnate through centuries; an absolute monarchy which tolerates independence of thought will prepare the way for something else than absolute monarchy, though the transition may be violent.

When people speak of freedom of thought, they generally mean, not the mere freedom of thinking for yourself, but the "right to the free expression of opinion,"[1] the freedom of speech and the freedom of writing and circulating opinions. The French Declaration of 1789 asserts that "the free communication of thoughts and opinions is one of the most precious rights of man. Every citizen therefore may speak, write, and print freely, save that he must answer for the abuse of this liberty in the cases determined by the law." In the first section of the Constitution of 1791 (to which, as already said, the Declaration of 1789 is prefixed) it is written: "The Constitution guarantees as natural and civil rights . . . liberty to every man to speak, write, print, and publish his thoughts, without his writings being submitted to any censorship or inspection before publication." The Declaration of 1793 asserts the right to free expression of opinion in less guarded terms: "The right of manifesting one's thought and one's opinions, whether by means of the press or in any other manner . . . cannot be interdicted." This ambiguous "cannot be," which provoked the wrath of Bentham,[2] is clearly meant to mean "ought not to be." Thought cannot, as a matter of strict fact, be subjected to legal penalties: the manifestation of thought may be so subjected. The Constitution of 1793 "guarantees to all Frenchmen equality, liberty, security, property, the national debt,[3] the free exercise of religious worship, a system of public education, State relief (*des secours publics*), the unlimited freedom of the press (*la liberté indéfinie de la presse*), the right of petition, the right of meeting in popular societies [we might interpret this—the

---

[1] Cf. Dicey, *Law of the Constitution*, Ed. 3, p. 224.

[2] See his *Anarchical Fallacies*, in *Works*, Vol. II. pp. 499, etc.

[3] Art. 122. "La dette publique." This means, I suppose, that the State will not repudiate its debts. It sounds a little odd to name the national debt among the privileges of citizenship; though it does not need much reflection to see, that the financial honesty of a State is a thing in which its citizens are most deeply interested.

right of association and of public meeting], the enjoyment of all the rights of man." The last clause makes a double guarantee of all the preceding rights; but (alas for promises!) the events which followed the promulgation of this Girondist Constitution are an unfortunate commentary on its unrestricted liberality. In the Declaration of Rights and Duties prefixed to the Constitution of 1795, the right of free expression of opinion is conspicuous by its absence. But it may be presumed that the authors of that Declaration thought the right sufficiently secured, though with the necessary restrictions, by the definition of liberty which is adapted from the original Declaration of 1789: "Liberty consists in doing what does not injure the rights of another." To the body of the Constitution (*Titre* xiv. § 353) is transferred the provision that "No one can[1] be hindered from saying, writing, printing and publishing his thought. Writings cannot [*i.e.* must not] be submitted to any censorship before their publication. No one can be made responsible for that which he has written or published, except in the cases contemplated by the law." The Constitution of 1795 thus returns, so far as intention goes, to the position taken up in the Constitution of 1791. Only the short-lived Constitution of 1793 ventures to proclaim an absolute and unqualified liberty of the press. The important feature of both the other Constitutions is their acceptance of the principle, which had been laid down in England by Lord Mansfield in these words: "The liberty of the press consists in printing without any previous license, subject to the consequences of law,"[2]—that is to say, I am free to publish what I choose, but if I libel any one, or if I infringe a copyright, I may have an action raised against me; and if there are on the statute-book laws against treason, or against blasphemy, or against indecency, I may be made responsible before the courts for any offence against such laws.

In calling attention to this resemblance between these two

---

[1] The "can" must be understood as meaning "shall by any law or executive order," since there is apparently no intention of coercing publishers and editors, who know various ways of hindering people from manifesting their thought—not always entirely to the public detriment. Even the compositor *can* hinder a person from publishing his thought, by misreading the author's "copy."

[2] Quoted by Dicey, *Law of the Constitution*, Ed. 3, p. 222, from *Rex v. Dean of St. Asaph*, 3 T. R. 431 (note).

revolutionary Constitutions and the principle of the English
law on the subject, I am not forgetting the difference, which
Professor Dicey points out so lucidly,[1] between the usual Continental practice of dealing with press offences before special
tribunals and the English tradition of recognising no special
class of press offences. This difference is of great importance
to any one who is tracing the history of the liberty of the press
in different countries. But I am here only concerned with the
general principle, that the liberty of free expression of opinion,
even when explicitly proclaimed in a Declaration of Rights,
must, if we are to avoid anarchy, be subject to *some* restrictions. What these limits should be, and by what procedure
they should be enforced, are very important questions of
practical legislation. But in the solution of them, is any help
to be got from the principle of natural rights? It would be a
mere quibble to say that a preliminary censorship interferes
with a natural right, while a subsequent prosecution does not.
If there is a natural and indefeasible right inherent in every
individual to express his opinions freely, it is equally wrong to
punish him for having exercised that right, and to prevent
him exercising it. If the right to express opinions freely
is from the first regarded as necessarily checked and limited
by the need of avoiding "injury to others," such checks, so
far as the principle of natural rights goes, may seem to be
better applied before any injury is done than after the mischief
has actually taken place. Prevention is better than cure: and
that is exactly the principle on which such institutions as a
literary censorship have been defended.[2] It might even be
argued that the individual has a natural right to be protected
by government against the insults, indecencies, and profani-
ties of reckless scribblers, just as he expects to be protected

[1] *Law of the Constitution*, ch. vi.
[2] Cf. the argument of Dr. Johnson in his *Life of Milton*: "It seems not
more reasonable to leave the right of printing unrestrained, because
writers may be afterwards censured, than it would be to sleep with doors
unbolted, because by our laws we can hang a thief." Our laws do not,
however, oblige the policeman to find out where every man is going
to, lest one or two should be thieves. Dr. Johnson was not likely to
sympathise with Milton's *Areopagitica*; but he seldom goes as strongly
against the current of his century, as when he says, "If every murmurer
at government may diffuse discontent, there can be no peace; and if every
sceptic in theology may teach his follies, there can be no religion." For
peace and piety now-a-days we should have to go to Russia.

against assaults upon his person. Both claims might be classed under the general claim of a natural right of security.

If a distinction be drawn between injuries to the body and injuries to the mind or character, it is drawn on grounds of expediency and convenience. Injuries to the mind and character may be worse than injuries to the body, but they are injuries respecting which the ordinary person has more difficulty in deciding. No government—except under revolutionary or exceptional conditions—undertakes to arrest intending criminals: the habitual arrest of persons on suspicion becomes itself an evil as great as the occasional commission of crimes. An author's manuscript is more easily inspected than the intentions of a person of whom the police are suspicious; so that a censorship cannot be put aside simply on the grounds of impossibility. On the other hand, a censor presumes to judge for a great mass of human beings and for the future. It is a great and difficult responsibility. "Who kills a man," says Milton, "kills a reasonable creature, God's image; but he who destroys a good book kills reason itself, kills the image of God, as it were in the eye." "It cannot be denied," he says farther on in his immortal *Areopagitica*, "but that he who is made judge to sit upon the birth or death of books, whether they may be wafted into this world or not, had need to be a man above the common measure, both studious, learned, and judicious." If the censor, he argues, is such a person, how irksome a drudgery are we imposing on him; if he is not, how badly will the work be done. The stupidity of censors, their venality, the wretched subterfuges to which they drive authors—such subterfuges as those practised by Voltaire,[1] and which help to make him so strange a mixture of the knight-errant and the monkey—such things are the best practical proof of the mischief of a censorship. And it is well worth noting that it was the practical inconveniences of the licensing system which led to the abolition of a censorship of the press in England. The House of Commons discontinued (in 1695) the temporary Act which placed the press under the control of licensers, and induced the Lords to give way on the subject, not on any general grounds of a

---

[1] "A Genevese worshipper would sometimes take up in church a book lettered as, and looking like, the Psalms, only to find that it was a copy of the one-volume edition of the *Dictionnaire Philosophique*."—Espinasse, *Life of Voltaire* ["Great Writers" Series]. p. 151.

natural right to free expression of opinion, nor even on the grounds urged by Milton of the injury done to truth by impediments put in the way of its pursuit, but "on account of the petty grievances, the exactions, the jobs, the commercial restrictions, the domiciliary visits which were incidental to"[1] the enforcement of the Licensing Act. "Such were the arguments," says Macaulay, "which did what Milton's *Areopagitica* had failed to do." The reasons given by the Commons for dissenting with the Lords, when the latter proposed to continue the Licensing Act, were supplied, it seems, by John Locke.[2] And it is specially to be noted that here Locke makes no use of the doctrine of natural rights. Locke proposes exactly the system now always accepted in this country. "I know not," he says, "why a man should not have liberty to print whatever he would speak; and to be answerable for the one, just as he is for the other, if he transgresses the law in either. But gagging a man, for fear he should talk heresy or sedition, has no other ground than such as will make gyves necessary, for fear a man should use violence if his hands were free, and must at last end in the imprisonment of all who, you will suspect, may be guilty of treason or misdemeanour. To prevent men being undiscovered for what they print, you may prohibit any book to be printed, published, or sold without the printer's or bookseller's name, under great penalties, whatever be in it. And then let the printer or bookseller whose name is to it be answerable for whatever is against law in it, as if he were the author, unless he can produce the person he had it from, which is all the restraint ought to be upon printing."[3]

Under this system, what we call the liberty of the press and the freedom of thought have gradually, though not in an untroubled course, progressed in this country. No such right as the liberty of the press has ever been recognised by the law. The "practical right" has come solely from the fact of responsibility to the ordinary law only. The laws about sedition and about blasphemy might seem to make liberty of the press, as we understand it, impossible, even after the censorship was abolished. The uncertain security of the writer in the free expression of his thought has lain only in the institution of

---

[1] Macaulay, *History of England*, ch. xxi.
[2] See Fox Bourne, *Life of Locke*, II. pp. 311–316.
[3] Lord King's *Life of Locke* (Bohn's edition), pp. 202–208.

trial by jury. We have had no special tribunals for the trial of press offences. " Freedom of discussion," as Professor Dicey puts it, " is in England little else than the right to write or say anything which a jury, consisting of twelve shopkeepers, think it expedient should be said or written. Such 'liberty' may vary at different times and seasons from unrestricted license to very severe restraint, and the experience of English history during the last two centuries shows that under the law of libel the amount of latitude conceded to the expression of opinion has, in fact, differed greatly according to the condition of popular sentiment." [1] The question is well worth raising : whether a security, which has proved effectual when the majority of the class from which jurymen are drawn had a general tendency to give a verdict against the government, is likely, when political and social conditions have changed, to prove a sufficient security for what many would consider legitimate freedom of thought. An extended franchise and the removal of the disabilities of Dissenters have made the sentiment of the average juryman less sympathetic with some types of intellectual rebellion than he was in the days of Pitt. Suppose a still more extended suffrage and the Church disestablished, the average juryman would be relatively still more "conservative," and it is just conceivable that the free expression even of political opinion might not be so well safeguarded as we think, if an anti-revolutionary panic should overtake the country. Suppose, further, that the qualification of jurymen were lowered or abolished, it might still happen that in any community of very homogeneous belief in religious matters and of very settled social conditions, the author, whom we may regard as exercising only a reasonable liberty of expressing his opinions (whether we agree with his opinions or not), might find himself punished for offending against the religious or political belief of the majority. Suppose Shelley to be tried before a jury of Welsh Calvinistic Methodists, or Mr. Herbert Spencer before a jury in a Collectivist community ; would either of them be sure of getting a fair trial ? The absence of homogeneity in religious beliefs, and the fact that so great a mass of the population wish the liberty of airing *different* grievances and of advocating *different* reforms, is a great security for the liberty even of the more daring intellectual rebel.

[1] *Law of the Constitution*, Ed. 3, p. 231.

A consideration of the degree of liberty or license allowed under our system of dealing with the press calls attention forcibly to the dependence of such liberty on the prevailing mood of public sentiment. No formal declaration of the liberty of the press or of the freedom of opinion will of itself secure the habitual exercise of such " rights," unless public opinion continues to support the idea. But it may very well be argued that the existence of such a formal declaration, even if it cannot, without risk of anarchy, be made constitutionally or legally binding, has a very important moral effect in restraining the prejudices or the passions of the multitude. And that is really the chief use which such Declarations serve.

I HAVE been assuming that a very wide, though undefined, degree of toleration for diversity of opinion is a good thing. It may reasonably be urged that, if the theory of natural rights is rejected, such an assumption needs proof. In saying a little about "toleration," it will be most convenient to go beyond mere freedom of expressing opinion in speech and writing, and to take account also of that form of freedom of action which consists in the free exercise of religious worship and the carrying out of religious principles into outward conduct. I have used the word "toleration" because it is the name under which the struggle for liberty in matters of belief has been generally fought out. In itself the word, on the whole, has the advantage, rare in terms of controversy, of being neutral. It does not ostentatiously claim to be a good thing; there was, at least, no absurdity of language in the denunciations of the wickedness of toleration, so common in the seventeenth century. It is still intelligible, and not uncommon, to speak of the toleration of vice or of political corruption as being a bad thing. It is true that in its original use the word implied a certain set of opinions and beliefs and practices approved of by the Church or by the State, while certain other opinions or beliefs and practices, though not accepted nor indeed approved of by the powers that be, might yet be "tolerated." In any case the word implies that the right is granted by the community to individuals. It is this suggestion in the term of a special favour or gracious condescension which provoked the indignation of Paine. "Toleration," he says, "is not the opposite of intolerance, but is the counterfeit of it. Both are despotisms. The one assumes to itself the right of withholding liberty of conscience, and the other of granting it. The one is the pope armed with fire and faggot, the other is the pope selling or granting indulgences."[1] Paine urges it as a special

---

[1] *Rights of Man.* p. 31 (Ed. 1883).

merit of the French Constitution that it "hath abolished or renounced Toleration and Intolerance also, and hath established Universal Right of Conscience." The Constitution to which Paine is here referring is the Constitution of 1791, not that of 1793, in the framing of the original form of which he had himself some part. In the Declaration of Rights of 1789 (Constitution of 1791), as we have already seen, the limits of liberty are expressly said to be determinable only by the law, and not therefore by the conscience of any one and every one. The tenth article of the Declaration asserts that "No one ought to be molested on account of his opinions, even on matters of religion (*pour ses opinions, même religieuses*), provided that his 'manifestation'[1] of them does not disturb the public order established by the law." In both articles the "law" is made the arbiter of liberty, so that the very idea which Paine objects to in the word "toleration" is introduced. The Declaration of 1793 omits these qualifications, and may therefore be taken as representing better Paine's own ideal. "The right of expressing one's thought and one's opinions . . . and the free exercise of religious worship (*des cultes*) cannot be prohibited." If such "rights" are supposed to be incapable of limitation, they will certainly come into conflict with the principle of not injuring the rights of others, especially as "security" and "property" are included among these rights. Suppose an individual were to declare that his conscience or an express revelation from God commanded him to offer up his son in sacrifice as a part of his religious duty (the son consenting), Paine would have been more ready to denounce the detestable superstition than to guarantee the free exercise of this piece of religious worship, and he would not have shown much respect to any kind of government that did not endeavour strictly to prohibit any such "free exercise." The assertion of a "Universal Right of Conscience" in any absolute and indefeasible sense would oblige a government to take the word of every individual for his own sincerity in saying what his conscience ordained. If we refuse to allow the individual to judge in his own case (as every well-regulated society must in a great many instances refuse to do), we give up any absolute

---

[1] The word is *manifestation*. Paine's translation "avowal" is not quite enough. We might paraphrase "way of expressing them." The word "even" (historically interesting) must have jarred on Paine.

right of the individual conscience and fall back upon the
authority of the legislature and the law-courts, which decide
to "tolerate" certain kinds of acts and utterances within
limits determined by the law, and not to tolerate other kinds
of acts and utterances, *i.e.* to punish those who are convicted
of them. We may very well rest content with the word
"toleration," which correctly expresses the nature of the liberty
allowed, and suggests the source of that liberty, and has, moreover, received a sufficiently honourable consecration from the
use of it in the long struggle against ecclesiastical intolerance.

This matter of toleration is very apt to be thought much
simpler than it really is. We flatter ourselves that we no
longer persecute people for their religious or other opinions,
and we condemn the persecutions inflicted in past time by
Church and State. We seem to have a difficulty in understanding how Christian people came to persecute ; for persecution is
supposed to be inconsistent with the religion they professed, and
inconsistent also with the true purposes of government, which
seem to us necessarily to include the safeguarding of liberty of
conscience. Now, in the first place, it must be pointed out that
"persecution" is a question-begging term. It means "repression," or "compulsion," of which the person using the term "persecution" disapproves. Public opinion has undergone great
changes as to the kind of actions which ought to be legally
repressed, or may be legally repressed without attendant evils,
that are too great to be risked. At all times people have been
ready to tolerate certain kinds of acts and utterances, but have
regarded it as a duty to suppress other kinds, if possible. The
line between what might be tolerated and what might not
has, however, been very differently drawn at different times,
and the methods of repression adopted have also differed very
greatly. Nowadays we blackball *our* heretics at a club, or
we try to subject them to what is called (in journalistic ignorance of a Greek institution) "social ostracism," where our
ancestors would have used for *their* heretics the coarser methods
of the pillory and the stake. The "heresies" differ ; the
methods of punishment differ. The spirit which leads to
persecution remains, and it is a spirit which, in some form,
is necessary to the cohesion and existence of any society. A
universal and absolute toleration of everything and everybody
would lead to a general chaos as certainly as a universal and

absolute intolerance. We are all "dogmatists" on some questions, while prepared to treat others as relatively matters of
indifference on which we can tolerate diversity of opinion.
We are all ready to "persecute," *i.e.* to use the force of government and the pressure of popular sentiment, in support of our
dogmas where it is otherwise expedient and safe to do so, sometimes even where it is not. We persecute "conscientious"
persons in support of the "dogma" of vaccination; we "persecute" the Peculiar People who quote Scripture to sanction
their neglect of getting medical attendance for their dying
children; some people would like to "persecute" scientific
men, who have by their experiments defied the "dogma" of
anti-vivisection and violated the natural rights of frogs and—
microbes. Those who hold the "dogma" of monogamy, still
more those who hold the "dogma" of the equality of the sexes,
persecute the polygamist, who is, at a humble distance, following the example of those saints of the Old Testament, whose
lives have edified many generations of Christian people. The
"persecution" of Mormonism in a land of professed "religious
liberty" like the United States is an instructive comment on
the notion that Declarations of natural rights will protect individuals who do what is unpopular. To the onlooker it is
even a little grotesque that in a society which permits such
varied "experiments in living" as the easy-going divorce laws
of some States allow, there should be so little toleration for an
experiment in restoring a primitive and venerable type of the
family[1]—the only form of it which, in old countries with an
excessive female population, could give a fair chance of becoming "a wife and mother" to every woman; and, according to the
view many persons profess to hold about the "natural sphere"
of woman, such a fair chance might be reasonably considered
every woman's "natural right."

Of course the objection is ready to hand, that I am here confusing the repression of acts which are obviously injurious to
society with persecution because of belief in theological doctrines, that I am confusing martyrs for religious faith with
criminal and vicious persons. "Criminals," it may be as well

[1] Cf. J. G. Schurman, *The Ethical Import of Darwinism*, p. 263. "Blind
to the havoc which divorce is making in the old family system, we atone
for our manners by embodying the principles of our fathers in denunciation of the Mormons." See note B at end of this chapter.

to point out, means simply—those who have done actions which the law of the land classes as "crimes." If the law of the land makes heresy of any particular form a "crime," the heretic is a criminal. Put yourself for a moment in the place of the persecutor of old days, and you will see that he looked at religious persecution (as *we* call it) exactly in the same manner in which you look upon the repression of polygamy, or of vivisection, or of indecent literature, or of the liquor traffic, or whatever may happen to be your special aversion among what you regard as the evils of the time. Opinion has changed as to the things which ought to be forcibly repressed, as to the things which can safely be repressed, and as to the methods of repression which it is right or expedient to use. We are all (except Count Tolstoi and a few benevolent anarchists) agreed that *some* kinds of conduct ought to be repressed by force, if it is possible and safe to do so; we differ as to what kinds of conduct these are. It cannot even be said that we have limited ourselves to the repression of *acts* of which we disapprove, and that we leave people to express their opinions quite freely in speech or writing, however much we disapprove of these opinions and however mischievous we think them: a speech which contains incitement to murder or violence is punishable by law, and certain kinds of literature are liable to suppression on the grounds of indecency, even where the conduct to which they may be supposed to incite is not made "criminal" by the law of the land, though condemned as "vicious" by prevalent popular opinion. That is to say, limits are in all civilised countries, however "tolerant," imposed on the liberty of speech and writing as well as on the liberty of action.

We consider that to circulate false coins is rightly made a crime and punished very severely by the law of the land. St. Thomas Aquinas considers that heretics are much more mischievous persons than the utterers of false coins. "For it is a much heavier offence to corrupt the faith, whereby the life of the soul is sustained, than to tamper with the coinage, which is an aid to temporal life. Hence if coiners or other malefactors are at once handed over by secular princes to a just death, much more may heretics, immediately they are convicted of heresy, be not only excommunicated, but also justly done to die." But although such immediate capital punishment of heretics is just, the Church is merciful. "On the part of the

Church is mercy in view of the conversion of them that err;
and therefore she does not condemn at once, but 'after the
first and second admonition,' as the Apostle teaches (*Titus* iii.
10): After that, however, if the man is still found pertinacious,
the Church, having no hope of his conversion, provides for the
safety of others, cutting him off from the Church by the sentence of excommunication; and further, she leaves him to the
secular tribunal to be exterminated from the world by death." [1]
It is worth observing that St. Thomas Aquinas here assigns
as the reason for the punishment of the heretic, not simply a
desire to vindicate the honour of God, a desire which we might
say modern legislation had found it right or expedient to leave
unsatisfied, but "the safety of others."

There should really be nothing startling in this passage
of Aquinas: it is difficult to see how a theologian, sincerely
believing that the Church is in possession of absolutely certain knowledge (so far as God has been pleased to reveal it)
respecting the destiny of the human soul and the principles
of right and wrong, can hold any different view about the
treatment of heretics, where the Church has sufficient power
to keep itself free from the taint of corruption. He may, indeed, hold that burning was too cruel a punishment, though
the blame for that rests with the temporal powers, the Church
handing over heretics with the merciful request that they
were to be put to death "without the shedding of blood"!
he may hold that imprisonment or even exclusion from the
privileges of citizenship would be a sufficient penalty and
bring less discredit on the Church from its unsympathetic
enemies. But he cannot consistently admit the claims of the
Roman Catholic Church to universal dominion over the souls
of men and to the possession of absolute truth, and yet hold
that the heretic ought to be left quite free, and should even
be defended by the arm of the law, in propagating his soul-
destroying opinions. The modern Roman Catholic theologian
may admit that manners have become milder, even among

[1] 2a 2æ, qu. 11, art. 3. I quote from Father Rickaby's translation,
which puts quotation marks before the words "After that, etc.," but has
no indication of where the quotation ends. They ought to come *at latest* at
the word "excommunication." The passage in *Titus* cannot possibly be
stretched to mean more than that. As I understand St. Thomas, the
words "ut Apostolus docet" are meant to apply directly to the immediately preceding phrase alone.

theologians, and that the Church's claws are cut and her jaws muzzled: he cannot admit that she ought never under favourable conditions to use her teeth or to get the civil power to scratch and bite for her. Let me quote Father Rickaby's commentary on the passage just cited from the Angelic Doctor:—

"*Are heretics to be tolerated?* A question to ask in the nineteenth century! The changes of the last six hundred years may be reduced to three heads.

1. The formation of heretical bodies of long standing, the individual members of which, never having professed the Catholic faith, and being ignorant of it, and from infancy prejudiced against it, cannot without distinction be called heretics.[1]

2. The fallen estate of the Church as a political power.[2]

---

[1] This is a point very often ignored by, or unknown to, the Protestant controversialist who is stirring up intolerance against Roman Catholics.

[2] I assume that Father Rickaby in these words is referring generally to the diminished influence of the Church in political affairs: but his words would include a reference to the loss of the temporal power in a portion of Italy. On this matter of the temporal power I think it worth while to quote a passage from the *Catholic Dictionary* of Addis and Arnold. (I purposely take my quotations from representatives of a very tolerant and very enlightened Catholicism. Mr. Addis is no longer a Catholic.) The passage may serve as a further illustration of the way in which earnest modern Catholics feel obliged to look at the subject of toleration. In the article on the "States of the Church" we are told that "Protestants themselves, or the more reasonable and enlightened among them, view with grief and scorn the process by which Rome is being reduced to the level of an English or American town. They would prefer that at least one place should be left on earth where Catholic principles of government and maxims of life might be applied without disturbance. They would wish to see the Sacred Congregations again discharging their critical and judicial functions. It might be said that the discipline so set up must be ineffectual; a Roman could obtain the works of Renan or Paul de Kock at Florence, if the sale were forbidden at Rome; he could turn Methodist and rant in public at Naples, if this luxury were denied to him at home. But what then? Is it nothing that an *example* of right practice should be given, towards which European society, dislocated as it now is, might gradually tend?" The tourist in search of the picturesque, who complains that Rome (which never was a typical mediæval city) is losing some of its mediæval quaintness, is dragged in as a witness on behalf of the claim of the Pope to "mismanage the drains of a third-rate European city." He, or she, would like to have a good specimen of a kind of spectacle that has become obsolete. It would be *so* interesting to see the Sacred Congregations at work: to see a Giordano Bruno, for instance, being roasted. But perhaps another class of tourist might think it equally interesting to see the spectacle of an older Rome, to witness a gladiatorial contest in the

3. The irritation set up in modern minds at the sight of men punished for opinions, whether political or religious: a fact that the Church would have to reckon with, even if she had might on her side, and consider whether it would be prudent in her nowadays to visit heresy with all the ancient penalties. For the Church's punishments are medicinal;[1] and the same medicine does not suit every age and constitution of society. The Church, however, still insists on her right to punish by corporal inflictions. Pius IX. condemned this proposition (Syllabus, 24): 'The Church has no authority to use force.'"

In his manual of *Moral Philosophy* Father Rickaby discusses the right of the *State* to control the expression of opinion. At the end of his section on "Liberty of Opinion," he says: "Penalties for the expression of opinion are available only so far as they tally with the common feeling of the country. When public opinion ceases to bear them out, it is better not to enforce them: for that were but to provoke resentment and make martyrs"—a most valuable lesson from the experience of history. No regulation can be maintained except in a congenial atmosphere. "Allowance, too, must be made for the danger of driving the evil to burrow underground" (p. 370)—a most important matter to be considered in all schemes for enforcing a uniform type of opinion or conduct. As to the duty of the State to prevent the spread of what he considers pernicious opinions, Father Rickaby has not the least doubt "where the atmosphere is congenial," *i.e.* where the State can carry on an effective persecution of heresy. "Silencing discussion," he says, "is an assumption, not of infallibility, but of certainty" (p. 366); so that, even on matters where infallibility is not claimed, the State may silence discussion. A great and, on the whole, reasonable distinction is drawn between "free discussion among competent persons" and "free discussion among the incompetent and incapable."[2]

Coliseum, or to see the Christians as living torches lighting up Nero's gardens. The tourist in search of strange and vivid sensations, who looks on the whole of Italy as if it were a spectacular exhibition in an American circus got up for his amusement, might even find the more ancient spectacle the more attractive and exciting performance of the two. As to "reasonable and enlightened" persons, Protestant or not, a little knowledge of how the Popes used to govern, and a little imagination as to how "the example of right practice" would work out if gradually followed by all European countries, would probably be sufficient to deter them from doing anything to revive the experiment of putting the sword of the civil magistrate into the hands of the priest.

[1] Very nasty physic sometimes.

[2] This distinction was made by Laud in England. He was tolerant

In answer to the objection "that it is immoral to interfere with conscience and to attempt to stifle sincere convictions," Father Rickaby writes: "The State has nothing to do with convictions as such, nor with the inward convictions of any man. But if the State is sincerely convinced that the convictions openly professed and propagated by some of its subjects are subversive of social order and public morality, whose sincere conviction is it that must carry the day in practice? It is of the essence of government that the convictions, sincere or otherwise, of the governed shall on certain practical issues be waived in the external observance in favour of the convictions of the ruling power. After all, this talk of conscience and sincere convictions is but the canting phrase of the day, according to which conscience means mere wild humour and headstrong self-will.[1] Such teachings as those which we would have the State to suppress, *e.g. An oath is a folly;*[2] *There is no law of purity; There is no harm in doing anything that does not annoy your neighbour*: are not the teachings of men sincerely convinced: they deserve no respect, consideration or tenderness on that score. . . . When a man proclaims some blatant and atrocious error in a matter bearing directly upon public morals—and it is for the restraint of these errors alone that we are arguing[3]—there is a decided *præsumptio juris*, that the error in him, however doggedly he maintains it, is not a sincere, candid, and innocently formed conviction." "Sincere conviction" is to be respected; but *we* are the judges of who is sincere, and we decide that every one who maintains any opinion about public morals which is contrary to what we believe (since it has been revealed to us by the Law of God or the Law of Nature) is insincere, and therefore is not to be respected! I think it a pity that Father Rickaby did not

of learned discussion in big folios, but not of theological arguments and political conclusions in sermons before the ordinary laity. Cf. Gardiner, *History of England*, 1603–1642, Vol. VII. p. 121. Pitt is said to have given as his reason for not prosecuting Godwin for his *Political Justice* that "a three-guinea book could never do much harm among those who had not three shillings to spare"—toleration for high-priced heresy only.

[1] How precisely all this expresses what the average Roman magistrate must have felt in dealing with obstinate Christians, who refused to offer incense to the Emperor's statue.

[2] What about the teaching that an oath is a *sin*, because forbidden by Jesus Christ?

[3] "In this particular book or place," I assume, he means.

avoid suggesting this time-honoured way of dealing with dissenters, religious or social—to deny the sincerity and to assail
the character of those who differ from you even on questions
of morality.[1] He is on safer and surer ground when he says
that "the convictions, sincere or otherwise," of some persons
may have to be overridden in the interests, or what are supposed to be the interests, of the well-being of the community
as a whole. So far as this general statement goes, we all—
except a few amiable anarchists—agree with Father Rickaby.
We may not like to admit the principle in words ; we adopt it
in practice, and it is well that we should realise clearly that
we do so, because we shall then be more fully alive to the responsibility we undertake in all legislation which is intended
to protect individuals, especially the young, against what we
consider indecent literature, pictures, etc. If a person accused
of disseminating indecent literature pleads that he sincerely
believes the incriminated works to be of real artistic value, or
to contain sound doctrine wholesome and necessary for these
times, the plea is not likely to weigh with a jury who sincerely
believe the works in question to be detestable and pernicious
rubbish. Wiser persons and a later generation may differ
from the jury in their estimate : the typical juryman is not
exactly the person whom the lovers of art and literature would
like to entrust with the power of drawing up an *Index Ex-
purgatorius*. Still, if the law prohibits indecency, as most
persons probably think it should, it seems safest to leave the
interpretation of "indecency" to fair representatives of the
community as a whole. Otherwise, who is to judge? We
have given up the plan of a censorship, except in the case of
stage plays : and the licensing functions of the Lord Chamberlain are often severely criticised.

---

[1] In his attitude to those whom he regards as in error as to matters of
morals, Father Rickaby seems to me to come short of the principle of St.
Thomas Aquinas, who holds (1a 2æ, qu. 19, art. 5) that "when an erroneous reason proposes something as the precept of God, then it is the same
thing to despise the dictate of reason as to despise the precept of God,"
which seems to imply that a person may sincerely have opinions about
matters of morals and doctrine which St. Thomas Aquinas regards as very
grave errors, *e.g.* that to abstain from fornication is evil, or that to believe
in Christ is evil. These are Aquinas's own illustrations, and they are
evidently chosen by him as opinions the most hateful to a mediæval
theologian.

But while Father Rickaby's statement in its general form expresses the principle which is accepted with the consent of the majority in our legislation and in the administration of the law, there would be great difference of opinion as to the particular "teachings" which we would have the State suppress. And I doubt if any British legislature, or any British jury, would be likely to regard as an incitement to immorality the doctrine *that there is no harm in doing anything that does not annoy your neighbour*, which is just the definition that the French Declarations give of "liberty." I do not think the officials of the Post Office would consider a copy of *The Rights of Man* to be an obscene publication, or that any one is likely to be successfully prosecuted by a Vigilance Committee for selling a copy of Mill's *Liberty*; and yet both of these works preach this "blatant and atrocious error" which Father Rickaby thinks that no one can sincerely maintain. The doctrine seems to me, indeed, so extremely vague and ambiguous that it is useless as a general principle or law of nature from which to deduce safe maxims of morals or legislation. It is a formula which implies the fallacious theory, as it seems to me, that there exist purely self-referrent actions, and that these can always be easily distinguished from those that affect others. The word "annoy" and the word "neighbour" stand also in need of definition. On the other hand, the formula does express in a very crude and rough way the great ethical principle which is coming more and more to supplant both the old theory of the Law of Nature and the appeal to external authority—the principle, namely, that right and wrong are to be judged by the standard of social well-being. The principle is expressed in a way open to misinterpretation, because it implies the conception of society as consisting merely of mutually exclusive and repellent atoms. It is the Utilitarian principle, still hampered by the individualistic basis which belongs to the theory of natural rights. It is by this very principle of social well-being that we must judge what limits are to be assigned to free speech and free action. And it is because the conception of the ethical end has itself undergone such great changes, and because the structure and environment of different societies have varied so much, that we can explain the extraordinary differences between different ages and countries in the matter of toleration.

Sir Frederick Pollock, in an essay on "The Theory of Persecution,"[1] has distinguished the grounds of persecution as
(1) tribal, (2) political, (3) theological, and (4) social.

(1) The Jewish persecution of Jews who became Christians
will serve as an illustration of the first kind. In all societies
of the more primitive type—I mean societies held together by
the bond of real or fictitious kinship—the god or gods worshipped are the gods of the tribe, and to desert the worship of
these gods, or worship them in a way not approved by tradition, is to be disloyal to one's own family, one's own kith
and kin. Persecution of this kind, though we should certainly
call it "religious persecution," is best understood by us, if we
think of the feelings of parents towards undutiful and rebellious children, who have been led away by evil example.
Persecution of this kind is not exercised towards aliens, so long
as they do not interfere with the religion of the tribe; but any
wrong done or insult offered to the tribal god will readily provoke persecution. The *popular* hatred of the Christians which
was apt to break out in various places throughout the Roman
Empire is to be explained in this way. The Ephesians would
not have molested the Apostle Paul if they had not thought
their special goddess was being injured,—commercial interests,
as often happens, supporting the prevalent religion.

(2) The *political* reasons for persecution are closely connected
with the preceding, and grow out of them. A sharp line cannot, I think, be drawn between these two divisions. When
the Athenians put Socrates to death for impiety, it was not, as
has been well said, because he introduced *false* gods, but because he introduced *new* gods. The religion of a Greek city-
state was an inseparable part of its political and social life.
The Sophists and Philosophers were exposed to attack on the
grounds of introducing dangerous innovations into the State.
With the establishment of the Roman Empire we see clearly
the predominance of political over tribal grounds of persecution. Under the Roman rule, local cults were not interfered
with. The Romans tolerated every kind of religion, except
(*a*) those whose rites seemed to conflict with public morals
and public order—like the orgiastic worship of Bacchus—and
(*b*) those which seemed to threaten the stability of the Empire.

---

[1] *Essays in Jurisprudence and Ethics*, pp. 144 *seq.* I have followed
out in my own way some of the ideas suggested in this admirable essay.

Druidism and Judaism both suffered at the hands of the Romans, because and in so far as they stirred up political rebellion; but the Jewish *religion* was treated with great toleration on the whole. So far as the Christians suffered molestation or punishment from Roman magistrates, it was because their missionary spirit disturbed the peace of families and of towns. their secret meetings roused suspicion of social danger, their attitude to existing institutions seemed to be anarchical, and their refusal to offer incense to the Emperor's statue appeared a clear proof of disloyalty. They were punished, not on the ground of their beliefs, unless we except their belief in the speedy destruction of the world—not, however, on the ground of any of those beliefs which have remained a permanent part of Christian *theology*, but on the same sort of grounds as those on which Social Democrats have been punished in Germany, and Nihilists in Russia. So far as religion goes, the Roman Empire was perhaps the least persecuting government that ever existed on a great scale before the present century, and under no condition of affairs that had previously been known in the world had a missionary religion greater opportunities for spreading itself. The general attitude of the Roman official to the Christian apostle was to protect him from the fanatical vengeance of the offended "tribal" religion of the Jews. His enemies accused Jesus of blasphemy before the Jewish high priest, but before Pilate they accused him of treason against Cæsar. Pagan Rome tolerated all religious doctrines, and tried to keep the peace between rival religions in the same way that the British magistrate does in India.[1] We have prohibited widows from burning themselves, and we endeavour to prevent disorder. But the model civil servant is as "indifferent" to a theological quarrel between two sects of Mohammedans as was Gallio to what seemed to him a mere squabble between two sects of Jews.

(3) Persecution, in the sense of repression for the purpose of maintaining true doctrine, is the outcome of Christianity.

[1] In what I have said about the treatment of the Christians under the Roman Empire, I do not think I have said anything inconsistent with the views either of Prof. W. M. Ramsay in his book on *The Church in the Roman Empire*, or of Mr. E. G. Hardy in his *Christianity and the Roman Government*. My statement is a rough, general one, taking no special account of variations of time and place; but I think it is true on the whole, and certainly true of the *earlier* history of the Church.

Such an assertion may seem a malignant slander, inexcusable
in any one who remembers the words ascribed to Jesus in the
Gospels " Forbid him not," spoken of one who followed not
with the disciples, and yet used the name of their Master to
cast out devils;[1] or the rebuke addressed to James and John,
when they wished to call down fire from heaven on the
Samaritans who would not receive their Master;[2] or the
lesson taught, but so often overlooked, in the parable of the
Good Samaritan,[3] where the alien and heretic is held up as a
model to be imitated, because of a kind action, rather than the
priest and Levite of orthodox Judaism; or the passages in
which, in the spirit of the greatest of the old prophets, deeds of
justice and mercy done in the service of humanity are made
the passport to the kingdom of God, and not the profession of
sound belief;[4] or the parable of the tares and the wheat,
where the lesson of tolerance seems very explicitly taught.[5]
Still more strongly might persecution seem to be excluded by
the precepts of non-resistance[6] (which most Christians have,
however, decided to be impracticable in their literal form), and
by the prayer of divine pity on the cross: "Father, forgive
them, for they know not what they do."[7]   The words "Compel them to come in"[8] have, we know, been used to sanction
the attempt to save souls from everlasting fire by penalties of
terrestrial burning; but such a use of the words is just one of
the many mischievous absurdities which result when any book
whatever is taken as a series of " texts " to be quoted, without
reference to time and occasion, as absolute and final authorities

---

[1] *Mark* ix. 39 ; *Luke* ix. 50.   [2] *Luke* ix. 54, 55.
[3] *Luke* x. 25-37.   [4] *Matt.* vii. 21-23 ; xxv. 31-46.
[5] *Matt.* xiii. 24-30.   This parable is referred to by St. Thomas
Aquinas, 2a 2ae, qu. 11, art. 3, as an argument that might be used for the
toleration of heretics. On the same side he mentions also (1) 2 *Timothy*
ii. (24-26) : "The Lord's servant must not strive, but be gentle towards
all, apt to teach, forbearing, in meekness correcting them that oppose
themselves, if peradventure God may give them repentance unto the
knowledge of the truth," etc. ; for, as Aquinas says, if heretics are not
tolerated, but put to death, the power of repentance is taken away from
them. And (2) 1 *Cor.* xi. (19), "There must also be (*oportet esse*) heresies
among you, that they which are approved may be made manifest among
you." Against toleration he quotes only the passage from the *Epistle to
Titus*, iii. 10, 11. Yet he sums up, as we have seen, against toleration.
The "Conclusio" only is given in Father Rickaby's translation.
[6] *Matt.* v. 38-42.   [7] *Luke* xxiii. 34.   [8] *Luke* xiv. 23.

on matters of belief or practice. "I come not to send peace, but a sword," [1] is a prophecy, a warning of sufferings to come, and most certainly not a precept of persecution. We have already seen how the words of the *Epistle to Titus*, which imply a much more definite religious organisation than any of these sayings of the *Gospels*, are used by St. Thomas Aquinas to justify persecution. But in the *Epistle to Titus* not one word is said of anything beyond spiritual excommunication: "A man that is heretical (or factious) after a first and second admonition refuse (or avoid), knowing that such a one is perverted, and sinneth, being self-condemned." [2] It is very easy, however, to see how, when Christianity had become the prevailing religion in any district or community, the avoidance of intercourse with a heretic might come to be as effectual a measure for repressing the utterance of opinions disapproved of by the majority, or by those who controlled their conduct, as the "boycott" has proved to be in more recent times. The maintenance of uniformity of belief and practice and the exercise of a strict censorship over doctrine and morals within any Christian community thus prepared the way for the use of the secular arm in the repression of heresy, when the Roman world became converted to Christianity.

When we speak of "Christianity" in any comparison between it and other religions, we mean, of course, the Christianity which has actually manifested itself in history, and not what any one may conceive to be the ideal of the religion as originally taught. It is manifestly unfair to compare an ideal of one religion with the actually prevalent precepts and practices of another. Now, in the sense in which we say that Christianity became the religion of the Roman world, in the sense in which we say that Christianity is now the religion of the most progressive and civilised part of the world, in the sense in which we compare the numbers of Christians with the numbers of Buddhists and Mohammedans, in that sense Christianity has been a persecuting religion, and persecution has been of the essence of it in a sense in which that could not be said of any of the older tribal or political religions which it supplanted. This is the historical sense of Christianity—the only sense which the term can bear in any scientific discussion; in any other sense its meaning will vary

[1] *Matt.* x. 34.   [2] *Epistle to Titus* iii. 10, 11. Cf. above p. 162.

according to those passages of the *Gospels*, or of the *Pauline Epistles*, or of the whole of the *New Testament*, or those interpretations of them which approve themselves to this or that person.[1]   Christianity in this historical sense is a religion which to elements derived from Jewish prophets has added elements derived from Greek metaphysics, and elements derived from Roman political administration : it is a religion with definite theological doctrines and a definite system of government and discipline ; and it was only as such that Christianity could possibly have been the vehicle through which the northern barbarians, who destroyed the old civilisation, could have received, as they did, an inheritance—maimed, indeed, and mutilated—of Greek intellectual culture, and of Roman legal and political institutions.

The importance assigned to the possession of truth—of *the* truth—is one of the most fruitful ideas which Christianity has diffused in the modern world. From it has grown up that scientific spirit which is proving fatal to some traditional beliefs—a devotion to truth as such, which in the ancient world

---

[1] Thus, if some one quotes the dicta of St. Paul as expressing the Christian theory of the status of women, it is replied that the true Christian theory is not to be found in the Pauline Epistles, but in the teaching and life of Jesus (who, however, though he had women among his followers, is not recorded to have chosen a single woman among his Apostles). The relation of Christianity to the status of women is a subject capable of, and deserving, historical study ; but we must take the whole range of Christian thought and practice on the subject, and not a few arbitrarily selected "texts" interpreted for the occasion. There is an interesting article on the subject of "The Position of Women among the Early Christians" in the *Contemporary Review* for September, 1889 (vol. 56, p. 433 *seq.*), by Principal Donaldson; and this is what so scholarly and impartial a writer feels obliged to say : "It is a prevalent opinion that woman owes her present high position to Christianity and the influences of the Teutonic mind. I used to believe this opinion, but in the first three centuries I have not been able to see that Christianity had any favourable effect on the position of women, but, on the contrary, that it tended to lower their character and contract the range of their activity." Like other writers (*e.g.* Mr. Galton), Dr. Donaldson calls attention to the mischief done to the race by the exaltation of virginity above marriage, and the consequent survival of the morally and intellectually unfittest. Yet, even on this, one must not exaggerate. How much more have the celibate Latin clergy done for civilisation than the married Greek clergy ! Even if all the celibate Christians of the first three centuries had married and left offspring, this, so far as one can see, would not have hindered the barbarian invasions.

was known only to a few philosophers.[1] But this very exaltation of the importance of knowing the truth was the source of
"the persecuting spirit" when the truth was preached and
thought of, not as something to be sought for by patient
inquiry, as something towards which the "Spirit of truth"[2]
would gradually guide mankind, but as a precious treasure, or
"deposit of doctrine," already possessed and enjoyed by the duly
accredited teachers of the Church. Such a treasure might
well seem fit to be defended and protected from everything
that would diminish its size or impair its beauty. Among
the rude barbarians out of whom the Church has moulded the
nations of modern Europe, this was the only way in which
"the truth" was likely to be thought of. Add to this manner
of conceiving truth the necessity of enforcing a rigid discipline,
especially whilst the State was in so many ways a weaker
power than the Church, and the claim of the Church to be the
one universal religion of the whole world, and it is difficult to
see how an orthodox theologian of the thirteenth century, or
any of those who derive their ideas from him, can escape from
believing in the duty of repressing false doctrine where it is
possible to do so, and by such means as experience has shown
to be best for the purpose. The growth of large and powerful
communities of "heretics" has obviously made it inexpedient
or difficult to use the secular arm in direct defence of orthodoxy; and certain forms of punishment have gone out of
fashion.

A large part of the arguments used by Locke in his *Letters
on Toleration* are arguments which involve a complete *ignoratio
elenchi*; they are completely irrelevant, if supposed to be addressed to a Roman Catholic or to any one who holds, as the
early Puritans mostly did, that his religious body is in sole
possession of the one truth about the highest and most important of all subjects. Thus Locke assumes that ordinary
morality is more important than the unity of the Church in
faith and doctrine, an assumption which would not have been
admitted by a great many Protestants of his own time. He
assumes that he can lay down precisely the functions of Church
and State respectively, and that "the care of souls cannot

[1] This affiliation was suggested to me, I think, by a remark of M.
Tarde's in one of his works, but I cannot at present find the passage.
[2] Cf. the words in *John* xvi. 13.

belong to the civil magistrate," which he interprets to mean
" that the magistrate's power extends not to the establishing
of any articles of faith or forms of worship, by the force of his
laws "—a principle which Anglican High Churchmen *of the
seventeenth century type*[1] would not have accepted, and which
Roman Catholics could hardly accept in its generality, because
the magistrate might be using his power under the guidance
of the Church. Locke defines the Church as " a voluntary
society of men, joining themselves together of their own accord
in order to the public worshipping of God in such manner as
they judge acceptable to Him and effectual to the salvation
of their souls "—a definition of the Church which Roman
Catholics, Anglicans, and Presbyterians (as they were in the
seventeenth century) would all have considered unsatisfactory.
He condemns persecution solely because he cannot find it in
the New Testament—an appeal to the sole authority of Scripture interpreted by mere private judgment, which a Catholic
theologian could not allow.[2] And we have already seen how
St. Thomas Aquinas deals with the argument from the New
Testament. When Locke says that " every Church is orthodox
to itself; to others, erroneous or heretical," he makes what
many people would consider a very sensible remark, even if it
be somewhat of a truism ; but to an ardent theologian the
remark may seem " a blatant and atrocious error," or to savour
too much of flippancy to allow a belief in the writer's sincerity.
Locke draws the line between essentials and matters indifferent
in religion at a different point from that where Roman Catholic
or strict Anglican or Presbyterian would draw it. He lays
down that " there is absolutely no such thing under the gospel
as a Christian commonwealth," a proposition which very few
Protestants even would have accepted in the earlier part of the

[1] Cf. Gardiner, *Hist. of England*, 1603–1642. VII. p. 127.

[2] In *Religion's Peace: or, A Plea for Liberty of Conscience* (1614), by
Leonard Busher—a work which is claimed by the Baptists as one of " the
first articulations of infant liberty "—the plan of toleration proposed includes this provision : " that it be lawful for every person or persons, yea,
Jews and Papists, to write, dispute, confer and reason, print and publish
any matter touching religion, either for or against whomsoever, *always
provided they allege no Fathers for proof of any point of religion, but
only the Holy Scriptures*" (*Tracts on Liberty of Conscience*, 1614–1661,
published by the Hanserd Knollys Society, 1846, p. 51). Such limited
" liberty of conscience " would certainly have told hardly against many
of the more learned controversialists of the seventeenth century.

seventeenth century, and which many even of those opposed
to State churches would hesitate to accept now. He holds that
"the care of each man's salvation belongs only to himself"—a
doctrine of extreme individualism in religion which would be
rejected by the great majority even of Protestants. Locke,
that is to say, argues throughout from the point of view of a
"Liberal Christian" of very rationalistic tendencies, and his
arguments could only appeal to those who had gone a very
long way in his direction, and could not be accepted even by
the most liberal of Catholics without very important qualifications.

A change in the notion of what constitutes a Church, and
a change in opinion as to what is essential in religious belief and what is not, and furthermore, a diminished sense of
the importance of correct intellectual conceptions about the
nature of God and the Divine plan of the universe, with, perhaps, some scepticism as to the possibility of attaining complete certainty in such deep matters—these are the necessary
preliminaries to an acceptance of Locke's views on toleration.
Contrast Locke's position with that of St. Thomas Aquinas or
Father Rickaby, and we have a very excellent measure of the
gap between the premises from which persecution (where
convenient) is a necessary deduction, and the premises which
exclude persecution, with some exceptions. For Locke's
limitations are worth taking note of. Milton, in his *Areopagitica*, excludes from the toleration he advocates "Popery and
open superstition." Locke has no objection to tolerate what
he would consider "superstition." "It may be said, what if a
Church be idolatrous"—what most Protestants said of Roman
Catholicism, what most Puritans said of the Church of England—"is that also to be tolerated by the magistrate? I
answer, what power can be given to the magistrate for the
suppression of an idolatrous Church which may not in time
and place be made use of to the ruin of an orthodox one?"
a good diplomatic argument. But Locke holds (1) that those
ought not to be tolerated "who will not own and teach the
duty of tolerating all men in matters of mere religion," and
(2) that "that Church can have no right to be tolerated by
the magistrate which is constituted upon such a bottom that
all those who enter into it do thereby *ipso facto* deliver themselves up to the protection and service of another prince."

Under either of these heads it would be easy to refuse toleration to Roman Catholics. The important thing to note is, that
in both cases Locke's reasons for excluding these two classes
from toleration are not theological or religious, but purely
political, and the same remark applies to his reasons for excluding Atheists. "Promises, covenants, and oaths, which are the
bond of human society, can have no hold upon an Atheist." A
Roman magistrate in the same way might have argued that a
person who would not burn incense to the emperor's statue
could not possibly be a safe subject.

Locke's minimum of belief requisite in those who are to
be tolerated comes to very much the same as Rousseau's
"dogmas of the religion of the citizen as such" (if so we
may paraphrase "*la religion civile*"), which are as follows: "the
existence of a God whose attributes are power, intelligence,
beneficence, foreknowledge, and providential care; a future life
with rewards and punishments, the sanctity of the social contract and the laws—these are positive dogmas. As to negative
dogmas, I limit them to one only—intolerance. . . . One
should tolerate all those who tolerate others, so far as their
dogmas contain nothing contrary to the duties of the citizen.
But whosoever dares to say, *Out of the Church no salvation*,
should be driven from the State." "It is impossible," Rousseau says, "to live in peace with those whom one believes
damned," so that theological intolerance by itself excludes
from citizenship on political grounds.[1] Rousseau's dogmas
seem, indeed, rather more numerous than those of Locke; and
the citizen of Calvin's Geneva anathematises in a sterner tone
than the countryman and admirer of the mild and judicious
Hooker. But Locke and Rousseau alike base the "persecution" they justify on purely political grounds.

Very many persecutions, which have been regarded by those
who suffered from them, and even by critical historians, as
"religious persecutions," *i.e.* forcible interferences on the part
of the State with liberty of expressing opinion on theological
matters and with liberty of worship, are much more properly
classed as "persecutions" in the interests of political security
and social peace and order. The persecutions of the Christians
under the Roman Empire, certainly those under the early
Empire, were acts of repression in the interests of political

[1] *Contrat Social*, IV. ch. viii., "De la religion civile."

stability. The Roman magistrate, as I have already pointed
out, did not punish the Christians for preaching the theological
doctrines distinctive of their faith, as magistrates in Catholic
countries afterwards punished Protestants, or as magistrates in
Catholic and Protestant countries have often punished Socin-
ians and Atheists; to the Roman magistrate it was a matter
of comparative indifference whether the Christians worshipped
as a God one whom the Jews declared to be a man guilty
of blasphemy, and whom a Roman magistrate had, foolishly
perhaps, put to death as a rebel against Cæsar; but to the
Roman magistrate and to the Roman Emperor it did seem
important to discourage secret assemblies and movements
likely to cause a breach of the peace, and to ensure the political loyalty of the subjects and citizens of Rome. Now the
persecution of Roman Catholics, and specially of the Jesuits in
England in the days of Queen Elizabeth, was a persecution,
in the main, for political reasons,—certainly *after* the Pope,
Pius V., had issued a bull of excommunication against the
queen. After that, how could any one believe that a conscientious Roman Catholic could be a loyal subject?[1] The writings of some Jesuits—whether disapproved or not at Rome
—had, moreover, undoubtedly justified the assassination of
heretical princes who persecuted the true religion; and every
Jesuit was therefore—presumptively—an instigator of treason.
The methods of enforcing uniformity of religious worship
adopted in Elizabeth's reign are, indeed, uncongenial to the
modern mind; and it may very well be argued that the persecution of the Puritans was the beginning of a fatal policy which
led to the civil dissensions of the following century, and was
thus a most mistaken piece of statecraft. But with regard to
the repression of Roman Catholicism, the case is somewhat
different; and it is quite possible for the historian, who regrets

[1] The Earl of Southampton asked Mary's (the Queen of Scots) ambassa-
dor, Bishop Lesley, whether, after the Bull, he could in conscience obey
Elizabeth. Lesley answered that, as long as she was the stronger, he
ought to obey her. (The story is referred to by Hallam, *Const. Hist.*, ch.
iii. [" World Library " edit., p. 115 *note*].) If that was a widespread sentiment, Elizabeth's supporters had strong motives for keeping her the
stronger; the rest was a question of means. And it may be very well
argued that a toleration such as commends itself to us might have been
fatal to the maintenance of Protestantism in England in the time of
Elizabeth.

that Catholic emancipation was so long delayed in this century,
to recognise that to statesmen of Elizabeth's day stringent
measures may have seemed necessary purely on political
grounds. Was her government sufficiently stable to afford to
tolerate those whose interest it undoubtedly was to upset her
government if possible? The rigid uniformity of belief enforced in Geneva or in Massachusetts was enforced, partly at
least, on political grounds—to ensure a sufficient amount of
cohesion in small communities struggling for their liberty.
Such communities cannot afford to tolerate those who only ask
for toleration, till they are strong enough to seize the government and refuse toleration to others.[1]

The Federal Constitution of Switzerland may be regarded
as very fairly representing the attitude of a democratic but
prudent people, experienced in the working of institutions,
towards the alleged right of religious liberty. The Swiss Constitution embodies elements derived from the experience (under
which I include the mistakes) of French and American Constitutions; and the Swiss Federal Constitution guarantees
religious liberty in a fuller sense than is done by the Constitution of the United States of America. The American Federal
Congress is forbidden (by the first Amendment to the Constitution) "to make any law respecting an establishment of religion,
or to prohibit the free exercise thereof, or to abridge the freedom of speech, or of the press"; but the several States are left
" free " to restrict the freedom of individuals on these matters.
As a matter of fact, all the State Constitutions do now provide
for religious freedom, and for the equality before the law of
all religious denominations and their members; but several
States, especially in the South, make any one who denies the
existence of God ineligible for office (Arkansas, Maryland, Mississippi, North Carolina, South Carolina, Texas); in two States,
Pennsylvania and Tennessee, another dogma of the "civil religion " is required—the belief in future rewards and punishments. In Arkansas and Maryland a person who does not
accept this belief is incompetent as a witness or juror.[2] "Ne-
vada," we are told, " has recently disfranchised all Mormons
resident within her bounds."[3] Many of the States, especially

---

[1] See Note A at the end of this chapter.
[2] Bryce, *American Commonwealth*, II. pp. 36, 37.
[3] *Ibid.*, III. p. 467 *note*. If it be said that the Mormons are not dis-

in the North, had what were virtually State Churches till some time after the beginning of this century.[1] But "religious equality," as it is called, which simply means the absence of an Established Church, has nothing directly to do with the question I am at present considering, viz., the amount of liberty of expressing opinions on matters of religion, and the amount of liberty in following the precepts of this or that religion guaranteed to the individual. Although in Switzerland every canton has an Established Church or several Established Churches (the Swiss mode of recognising the equality of religious bodies), the Federal Constitution of 1874 lays down (Art. 49) that "freedom of conscience and belief is inviolable," that "no person can be constrained to take part in a religious society, to attend religious instruction, to perform a religious rite, or to incur penalties of any kind whatever on account of religious opinion." Furthermore, "the exercise of civil or political rights shall not be abridged by any provisions or conditions whatever of an ecclesiastical or religious kind." These are provisions which restrict the power of the several cantons as well as of the Federal Government to limit individual liberty, and not, like the provision I have quoted from the American Constitution, restrictions on the action of the Federal Legislature only. But the Swiss Constitution, though thus more favourable than the American to the liberty of the individual in matters of religion,[2] sets very distinct limits to that

franchised on religious grounds, this only furnishes another illustration of what I am urging about a great deal of what is called "religious persecution"—that it is professedly political or social.

[1] Article 3 of the "Declaration of Rights" of Massachusetts, 1780, expressly asserts the right of the people to invest their legislature with the power to require the several towns and parishes "to make suitable provision, at their own expense, for the public worship of God, and for the support and maintenance of public Protestant teachers of piety, religion and morality in all cases where such provision shall not be made voluntarily." This article remained unaltered till 1833.

[2] Professor Vincent, in his admirable work on *State and Federal Government in Switzerland*, thinks that "so long as the cantons maintain established religions, or even attempt to support the ministry of all the chief sects alike, there will be limitations to religious liberty not known in the United States. . . . So far as private belief is concerned, no limitations are set; but as to taxation for religious purposes, complete freedom is yet to be obtained" (p. 98). This passage seems to me to show some confusion between the "liberty" of (*i.e.* the absence of

liberty. In the same Article, 49, it is provided that " No person
shall, on account of a religious belief, release himself from the
accomplishment of a civil duty," which means among other
things that a Quaker's conscientious objection to bear arms
would not be respected by the law.   The 50th Article provides
that "the free exercise of religious worship is guaranteed within
the limits compatible with public order and good morals"; and
on grounds of public order noisy processions have been prohibited, although they constituted the mode of worship of a
religious body.   Article 51 prohibits the reception of the order
of the Jesuits, and of societies affiliated with them, in any part
of Switzerland.   Now the Quaker, the member of the Salvation
Army, and the Jesuit may all declare that they have undergone
"religious persecution" in Switzerland; but in all cases the
ground of action on the part of the Swiss authorities is
political and social, *not* theological.

   In this country, so far as the *law* of the land is concerned,
freedom of discussion on religious matters is not recognised.
It is still possible to prosecute any one who has been educated
in Christianity for denying the authority of the Scriptures.
Practically we know that an anti-orthodox lecturer or writer
is not likely (that is all we can say) to be found guilty by a
jury, if he does not grossly offend the average sentiment of
the community by coarse and offensive attacks on prevalent
beliefs.   The punishment, when nowadays inflicted, is a
punishment for a breach of good manners and decency in

State control over) religious *bodies*, and the liberty of the individual in
matters of religious belief (*i.e.* absence of civil or political disabilities
arising from the opinions of the individual).   Even on the matter of
"taxation for religious purposes," the Swiss Federal Constitution lays
down that "No person is bound to pay taxes of which the proceeds are
specifically appropriated to the actual expenses of the worship of a religious body to which he does not belong.   The details of the carrying
out of this principle are reserved for federal legislation" (Art. 49).   But
let us grant that, through imperfection in such legislation, a small fraction
of the taxes paid by a conscientious "free thinker," who doubts a future
life, is divided among the *four* established churches of Neuchâtel (where
"the liberty of the conscience of the ecclesiastic" in the Protestant
Church is declared inviolable—no test being permissible), has he less
"religious liberty" than he would have in the State of Arkansas, where
his evidence would not be received in a law-court maintained out of
taxes that he cannot escape paying?   To the probable pressure of public
opinion in the way of restricting liberty of thought under the latter
condition, I am not here referring.

controversy rather than a punishment for heresy. And it
would be more in accordance with national honesty, as well as
a necessary security against the possibility of purely "theological" persecution in some time of panic, if legislation
expressly determined the limits of free discussion by considerations of decency alone, and not by any considerations of
doctrine.[1] In all countries, indeed, even in those which guarantee a natural right of liberty to their citizens, the liberty
practically conceded depends on the prevailing sentiment of
the community more than on anything else. The standard of
what is permissible in controversy is in the last resort determined by the prevailing sentiment of the community, and at
the present moment there is probably in this country, at least
in large towns, a greater practical liberty, or license, in the
matter of religious or irreligious eccentricity than is enjoyed,
or dreaded, by the citizens of most of the American States.

At the same time it must be allowed that the existence of
an express declaration in favour of liberty of any kind—however little it is actually guaranteed by the existing laws—has
a certain moral effect in influencing the sentiment of the community, and it may at least supply any one who is struggling
for greater liberty than exists with a convenient rhetorical
premise. On these grounds, as already suggested,[2] Declarations
of Rights have their practical advantages.

I have not attempted to distinguish (4) "social"[3] from
"political" reasons for limiting liberty of expressing opinions,
or of performing what may be considered religious acts. As

---

[1] The Anglo-Indian Penal Code may be taken as representing admirably
the *principle* on which alone most thoughtful persons in this country
would nowadays think it right to limit "liberty" in matters of religion.
Thus chapter xv. sec. 298 makes *insult*, with deliberate intention, to any
religion, penal. The preceding sections forbid injuring or defiling places
of worship with intent, disturbing religious assemblies, trespassing on
burial places, etc. In chapter xiv. sec. 292, under the clause making penal
the printing or exhibiting, etc., of obscene books, paintings, etc., an exception is made in favour of "representations, sculptured, engraved, painted,
or otherwise represented, on or in any temple or on any car used for the
conveyance of idols, or kept or used for any religious purpose." Aristotle
even in his ideal state is similarly complaisant to existing religious prejudices. "Let the rulers take care that there be no image or picture
representing unseemly actions, except in the temples of those gods at
whose festivals the law [*i.e.* custom] permits even ribaldry."—*Pol.*, VII.
17, § 10.

[2] Cf. above, p. 156.   [3] Cf. above, p. 168.

already suggested, I do not think the Tribal, Political and
Social Reasons can be clearly distinguished from one another.
All are different stages of the same principle, and all together
can be distinguished from the "theological" reasons. It might
indeed be said that in the tribal stage of society the political
and theological reasons were simply not yet differentiated.
The cohesion of the tribe and the worship of the tribal god
(who is perhaps thought of as the ancestor of the tribe) were
bound up together. An insult to the god was an insult to the
tribe. In the clearly political stage of thought on the subject,
it is possible to recognise the principle *Deorum injuriæ dis curæ*,
interfering with religion only for reasons of State, for the repression of treason or the maintenance of peace and order.
In the distinctly theological stage, on the other hand, the
purity of doctrine is something to be maintained, even at the
risk of temporal loss and injury to the nation ; purely theological persecution has therefore usually been more an ecclesiastical ideal than a historical fact. In practice, elements of
tribal sentiment or supposed political and social expediency
have generally been among the motives which have induced
the secular magistrate to put his sword at the disposal of the
spiritual power.

We judge past ages very unfairly if we suppose that people
could have been actuated by the same motives which are
predominant now, still more if we suppose that the circumstances in which they had to decide on a course of action presented themselves to their minds as they do to ours now in the
light of subsequent events ; and most of all do we judge unfairly, if we neglect the difference between their circumstances
(as they saw them) and the circumstances with which we are
familiar. In primitive conditions of society—I am using the
term "primitive" in a very wide sense—in a tribal society or
a small Greek city-state living in perpetual fear of attack from
without, a very rigid cohesion is the primary essential of existence, and therefore the most important factor in all moral
judgments. A society of this sort which did not repress dissenters from the worship that held the community together
would have little chance of holding its own in the struggle
for existence. Even the powerful and intelligent city of
Athens suffered, not perhaps from the corruption introduced
by the Sophists, but from the decay of social cohesion and the

growth of individualism, of which the appearance and popularity of the Sophists was only one symptom. We should not blame the average Athenian too severely if he thought the teachings of Socrates socially and politically dangerous; we may be grateful to Athens that the degree of toleration she did allow made the teaching of Socrates possible through so many years. The great empires like the Persian, the Macedonian, the Roman, contained within their limits many tribal religions and many city-state religions, and it is in the co-existence of these differences under the shadow of one ruling power that we get the first form of toleration as a recognised principle.

In the Middle Ages it must be remembered that it was the Church rather than the Holy Roman Empire which really inherited the sovereignty of Rome; and the persecutions of heretics at the suggestion of the Church may be regarded as the endeavour of the Church to maintain its own cohesion—an endeavour greatly checked by the mutual jealousy of the different parts of Christendom. The Reformers certainly did not think of themselves as setting up new Churches alongside of the existing Church. For them also there was only one Universal Church, though there might be considerable permissible differences between its forms in one nation and in another. But the growing varieties of Protestantism and the success of the Catholic reaction made the theory, and even the ideal, of one Universal Church seem, to statesmen at least, more and more impossible; and people became accustomed to the idea of different political societies living alongside of one another, and yet adhering to different religions. *Cujus regio, ejus religio* —that the religion of the people must follow the religion of the prince—seems to us the very reverse of a principle of religious liberty; but there is no doubt that its acceptance as a political necessity marked an important advance in the direction of toleration. It put aside the idea of a crusade for the universal destruction of heresy. That different religious communities might safely be permitted to co-exist within the same political community was an idea that took a much longer time to prevail. In Switzerland, as a whole, it was not recognised till 1848. The efforts of minorities to gain toleration for themselves in the hope of finally prevailing prepared the way for acquiescence in mutual toleration without the hope of uniformity. No religious body as such can claim the merit of having adopted

toleration as its principle, till a certain amount of toleration
had already been forced on them by the practical necessities of
the statesman.   Roman Catholic, Anglican, Presbyterian, Independent have all been persecuted, and have all persecuted
when they had the opportunity.   If the Baptists have never
persecuted, it must be borne in mind that they never had the
opportunity.   The Quakers indeed may claim the honourable
distinction of having been often the victims but never the
agents of religious persecution ; but a nation of Quakers could
never have existed without deserting the principle of non-resistance.   They would have been the easy prey of any enterprising
neighbour.[1]   They could only become a nation by converting
the whole world, and if they did so they would probably
undergo a change like that which makes the difference between
the Christians of the first and those of the fourth century—
between the apostles and the Emperor Constantine.

Apart from a strict application of the principle of non-
resistance, the adoption of toleration as a principle implies
either a statesman's view of religious differences as compatible
with political cohesion—a view only possible when a considerable degree of political and social stability has been attained ;
or it implies the adoption of an attenuated religious creed, so
that the number of non-essential articles increases, while that
of essentials diminishes.   Locke could tolerate diversity of
opinion about the sacraments or about the Trinity : these
seemed non-essential to him.   But, as I have shown, his arguments have no force against those who really think a right
belief about the Trinity, or a due observance of the sacraments, essential to salvation, as Locke thought the belief in a
God essential to social and political stability.   The growth
of charity is greatly due to the decay of faith, *if* "faith" is to
be measured by the number of doctrines in which people

---

[1] Pennsylvania may seem to be a refutation of this statement ; but the
Indians with whom the Quaker settlers in Pennsylvania had to do were
only the Delawares, who were in subjection to the powerful Iroquois, who
were the firm allies of the English against the French (see Fiske, *The
Beginnings of New England*, p. 206).   The Quakers profited here, as elsewhere, by the fighting habits of other people.   In the earlier half of the
eighteenth century, during the struggles between the English and the
French in America, Pennsylvania suffered much from Indian raids, her
Quaker inhabitants not defending the frontiers (Thwaites, *The Colonies*
[in "Epochs of American History"], p. 277).

profess to believe. On the other hand, if faith be taken to mean faith in human nature and in the rationality of the process of evolution, it is only such faith that makes toleration possible ; for to such faith the various beliefs about which men have fought so fiercely are " but broken lights," or partial truths, which are false if taken to be the whole truth. That there should be diversity of belief may even be thought of as an advantage : there is more variety for natural selection to work upon. There is a security against stagnation. There is an educative influence in the substitution of peaceable discussion for forcible repression.

To many, such an attitude towards religious questions may seem incompatible with what they regard as the necessarily dogmatic character of religion. Believing that they possess absolute certainty on some matters at least, they may yet allege that they do not wish to persecute, but only to persuade. Probably nowadays the most bigoted religionist does not really wish to *burn* the worst of heretics, even if he had the power, and was not in fear of reprisals. But suppose him to have the power to control the educational system in a country, and to check the diffusion of what he considers blasphemous and immoral literature ; if a scholar or a scientific man in such a country is prohibited from teaching, and finds that the works of Renan and Strauss, of Darwin and Spencer, which he has ordered from abroad, are seized and destroyed on the frontier, is it wrong to say that he is "persecuted," merely because he is not burned along with the heretical volumes? Undoubtedly a milder tone has spread into the words even of those whose principles lead logically to intolerance. Just as Protestantism has influenced the Catholicism which rejected it, so that tolerant and reverent Rationalism, of which Locke was one of the great initiators, has influenced Protestant and Catholic alike : and the duty of repressing heretics by the secular arm, where it is possible and expedient, is a principle that is kept in the background, from a sort of politeness, or is only treated as an ancient weapon, to be laid up in the museum rather than in the armoury, and to be referred to with a sort of pious regret, like the sigh for the godly discipline of old days at the beginning of the Anglican Commination Service.

Ought we to tolerate those who are bound by their professed

principles not to tolerate us?   On this question of casuistry, the
doctors of "Liberalism" have answered differently ; " No " (as
we have seen) is the answer of Locke and Rousseau; "Yes"
is the answer of Renan, in a passage in his *Lectures on Rome
and Christianity*.   " I have no right to prevent any one from
expressing his opinion, but no one has the right to prevent
me from expressing mine.   That is a theory which will
appear very humble to the transcendental doctors who believe
themselves in possession of absolute truth.   We have a great
advantage over them.   They are obliged in consistency to be
persecutors; as for us, we can be tolerant, tolerant even
towards those who, if they had the power, would not be
tolerant towards us.   Yes, let us go as far as this paradox :—
Liberty is the best weapon against the enemies of liberty.
Certain fanatics say to us with sincerity, ' We take the liberty
you give us, because you owe it to us on your principles; but
you should not receive it from us, because we do not owe it to
you.' Very well, let us give them liberty all the same, and
do not let us imagine we shall be cheated in the bargain. No ;
liberty is the great solvent of all fanaticisms.   In demanding
liberty for my enemy, for him who would suppress me if he
had the power to do so, I give him in reality the worst gift
he could receive. I compel him to drink a strong beverage,
which will turn his head, whilst I shall keep mine steady.
Science can endure the virile rule of liberty : fanaticism and
superstition cannot endure it. . . .   The essential thing
is not to silence a dangerous doctrine, to quench a discordant
voice ; the essential thing is to put the human intellect in a
condition in which the mass may see the uselessness of these
outbursts of anger.   When such a spirit becomes the atmosphere of society, the fanatic cannot find anything more to live
on.   He is himself vanquished by the prevailing gentleness." [1]

    Now, this characteristic passage of the great French writer
contains a profound truth, which rests on facts of ordinary
human nature, and on a large experience of history.   But the
principle of tolerating even the intolerant is asserted in too
general terms.   When we believe that the principle of intolerance has become a mere pious opinion, a mere " counsel of perfection " for a commonwealth that is not likely to be realised,
it is easy enough to give to those who hold the principle and

_____
[1] *Conférences d'Angleterre*, pp. 205-207 (Hibbert Lectures, 1880).

proclaim it the toleration of an easy-going contempt. But when some new belief is still struggling for existence amid hostile surroundings, as was the case with Protestantism in the six-teenth century, a general toleration on the part of those hold-ing the new belief is more doubtful policy, and is certainly less likely to be thought of.   Direct persecution has indeed almost always proved a clumsy and inefficient measure of securing uniformity, unless, as was the case in Spain, it is made so thoroughgoing as to sap the whole intellectual vigour of a people.   But few persons have the opportunities or the special gifts required to make the perfectly unflinching persecutor; and any inconsistent clemency allows some seeds to survive that will spring up again, watered by the tears, if not by the blood, of martyrs.   On the other hand, an absolutely universal toleration is inconsistent with any social cohesion whatever.   It is only on the basis of a firmly established foundation of political and social stability that what are generally understood by liberty of religion, liberty of the press—liberty in the propa-gation of opinions generally—can be granted or are likely to be granted.   Only those who feel themselves secure can afford to tolerate attacks upon themselves; and toleration is then their wisest policy.

The last sentences in the passage I have quoted from Renan suggest that he is assuming what in the eyes of some of the " enemies " he tolerates would seem a very important restric-tion on liberty.   Who is to control education?   Even Lord Burleigh was prepared to tolerate Papists, provided that he might bring up their children as Protestants.[1]   Suppose a country in which complete liberty of the press, complete liberty of religion (and of irreligion), complete liberty of association were all guaranteed by the law, or, if you like, by the absence of all laws on the subject ; suppose, moreover, that in such a country the Government rigidly abstained, in the interests of complete liberty of thought, from instituting any system of public education whatever.   Suppose, in fact, that we had the ideal state of Mr. Auberon Herbert, or at least that of Mr. Herbert Spencer.   But suppose, further, that the best schools in the country were those managed by the Society of Jesus, and that the members of this Society, constantly re-cruited by picked men from other countries as well as from

[1] See note A at the end of this chapter.

that we are considering, gradually obtained, through their
influence as educators, a complete ascendancy over the majority of the population : is it difficult to foresee that ecclesiastical denunciations and excommunications would come to be
more deterrent than any laws in checking the growth of
heresy or free-thought? And it would be only a step farther
to suppose the whole population, with hardly a protest, abolishing the unchristian " Liberalism " of the old constitution (or
we should rather say, of the old Anarchy), and agreeing to
the establishment of a "Christian Commonwealth," which
would burn every copy of Renan's works on the frontier.
With a general system of education in the hands of the
Government, with Universities free from clerical control, or
affected by very diverse theological influences, and with clerical influence largely neutralised by ecclesiastical dissensions,
with the consequent intermingling and intercourse of those
brought up in different religious beliefs ; it is possible to tolerate the advocates of a hypothetical intolerance—possible even
to tolerate the Jesuits, when they are not too numerous, and
when there is a traditional hostility to them well diffused
throughout the community. But it is all a question of time
and place ; and, in the interests of toleration, it would be unwise to adopt any such extreme principles as would be likely
to endanger toleration itself. As to education, that cannot
safely be left alone by the State ; for education left alone
by the State means either a very illiterate and ignorant population, or a population educated by voluntary associations—
that is, mainly, by religious sects. In neither case is there
much likelihood of any considerable amount of freedom of
thought being practically granted.

Many persons sincerely hold that a purely "secular" education, such as the State can ensure, contains grave moral
dangers ; and that some amount of religious teaching must be
given—perhaps some minimum, such as "the Bible." The
policy may be a wise one, but those who advocate it have no
right to allege that they are supporters of complete religious
liberty. If we use language carefully, no one (except Anarchists) does believe in unlimited liberty of thought ; and, on
the other hand, no one allows no liberty of thought whatever.
Even the strictest of sects have drawn their own distinctions
between things essential and things indifferent. Even the

most tolerant of persons would impose some check on the indulgence in personal abuse under the guise of freedom of
opinion. It is easy to tolerate differences of opinion and of
practice in matters which we regard as more or less "indifferent"; it is very difficult to tolerate differences in what we
regard as essentials, and, to some, it may seem questionable
how far it is morally right to do so.

People tolerate differences in matters of religion, but they
are not so willing to tolerate differences of opinion in matters
of morality, except within somewhat narrow limits. A strong
point with the advocates of very strict limits to toleration in
matters of religion has always been that freedom of thought
and expression in religious matters is certain to lead to freedom of thought, and ultimately to license of conduct, in matters of morality. To the average educated person in most
civilised countries, it *seems* easy enough to differentiate religious from moral questions, and especially easy to differentiate theological from moral questions, and consequently to
allow a very wide liberty with regard to the former; while restricting by the pressure of public opinion, and sometimes by
the agency of law, any similar liberty with regard to the
latter. There is indeed one obvious and important difference
between religious and moral tenets : that the truth or falsehood
of religious beliefs cannot be verified by reference to experience; whereas the effect of moral principles on conduct and
the effect of conduct on social well-being seem to admit of such
verification in experience. The effect of religious beliefs or dis-
beliefs on the destiny of individuals in a future life admits of
no test which the ordinary understanding can be expected to
apply ; their effect on the well-being of a society in the present world does admit of such a test, though it is a test which
many ecclesiastics would not regard as satisfactory—they would
refuse to consider *material* well-being, or even *intellectual* progress, a proper measure of the value of religion. While willing
to put down to the credit of Christianity the higher civilisation and worldly success of the Christian nations, and while
ready to put down "the horrors of the French Revolution" to
the discredit of eighteenth century Rationalism, Catholic
controversialists would not allow the greater material pros-
perity and intellectual progress of Protestant countries to be
considered an argument in favour of Protestantism.[1]

[1] "The Church," according to Cardinal Newman, "pronounces the

When appeal is made, however, to moral superiority or
moral progress, it is supposed that the appeal is made to
something on which we are all agreed. Yet is the appeal as
decisive as it might seem at first? There are people who
would measure the morality of a country solely by the paucity
of illegitimate births; yet a neighbouring people, with a less
complete recognition of the virtues that keep the family
together, may be superior in industry and in honesty. Take
the number of suicides, the number of divorces, the number of
convictions for murder, for assaults, for attacks on property,
the prevalence of drunkenness—any of the departments of
conduct that admit of statistical enumeration—and we should
find very conflicting results as to the moral condition of different countries. Moreover, it is useless to take any of these
numbers and consider merely the percentage to population,
without taking account of race, climate, industrial conditions,
the laws of the country at the time, and the success with
which they are enforced. Thus, e.g., in a country where divorce

momentary wish, if conscious and deliberate, that another should be
struck down dead, or suffer any other grievous misfortune, as a blacker
sin than a passionate, unpremeditated attempt on the life of the
Sovereign. She considers direct unequivocal consent, though as quick as
thought, to a single unchaste desire, as indefinitely more heinous than
any lie which can possibly be fancied; that is, when that lie is viewed, of
course, in itself, and apart from its causes, motives, and consequences.
[How a lie can be viewed " in itself," and yet ethically, is not explained.]
Take a mere beggar-woman, lazy, ragged, and filthy, and not over-scrupu-
lous of truth—(I do not say she had arrived at perfection)—but if she is
chaste and sober and cheerful, and goes to her religious duties (and I am
supposing not at all an impossible case), she will, in the eyes of the
Church, have a prospect of heaven which is quite closed and refused to
the State's pattern man, the just, the upright, the generous, the honourable, the conscientious, if he be all this, not from a supernatural power
(I do not determine whether this is likely to be the fact, but I am con-
trasting views and principles),—not from a supernatural power, but from
mere natural virtue " (Anglican Difficulties, p. 205 seq., quoted by
Mr. W. S. Lilly, in his Characteristics from the Writings of J. H. N.).
From the point of view of "the Church," as here explained, social progress would be estimated by a standard incommensurable with that which
the statesman is bound to apply. The forms of Protestantism which
incline to Antinomian views of piety would supply still more startling
differences from the statesman's standard. A Highlander, who considered himself a devout Christian, is reported to have said of an ac-
quaintance: "Donald's a rogue, and a cheat, and a villain, and a liar;
but he's a good, pious man." Probably Donald "kept the Sabbath—and
everything else he could lay his hands on."

is permitted on many grounds, there will be more divorces, but not *necessarily* more frequent violations of the duties of the family, than in countries where divorce is more difficult or impossible to obtain.

Still, in spite of the dispute which may arise about certain parts of morality, there does seem to be a sufficient *consensus* of opinion as to right and wrong, which contrasts markedly with the differences of opinion as to matters of religion. People who would differ from one another in their views as to the nature of God, as to the possibility of miracles, as to the authority of Scripture, as to the definition of a Church, the value of the Sacraments, etc., would recognise a common standard on the leading principles of morality—so far as general statements go. As to the indispensability for human life of certain fundamental virtues, such as justice, fidelity, self-control, there would be no dispute. The differences would show themselves, however, the moment it came to be considered what kind of acts were just ; under what conditions promises were and were not binding, and what degree of self-control was necessary in the different departments of life. As to what people will tolerate in the way of discussion on moral matters, I think we may say that they are generally ready to allow discussion of a serious kind, provided any novel proposals do not go very far beyond what they are accustomed to, or else go so very far that they do not seem likely to bear practical fruit. Thus people who disapprove of all divorce may allow discussion on the subject of divorce, but would certainly disapprove, and might even be inclined to punish an attack on the institution of the family as they understand it. But an advocacy of complete community of wives and children, as in Plato's *Republic*, would seem too alien from their accustomed world to be likely to be of any practical danger to morality. There is, however, a growing feeling that discussion of moral principles is to be tolerated or not very much according to the seriousness of tone with which it is carried on, and the absence of appeals to individual passion or selfishness. This, we may say, is the modern form of the distinction which used to be made between serious discussions among the learned and the dissemination of dangerous and unsettling opinions among the ignorant multitude who are ruled by custom and authority and not by reason. When all are supposed by a convention of demo-

cratic sentiment to be reasonable, and when private judgment
is claimed as a right, or recognised as a duty, the distinction
comes to be drawn differently, the mode of speech being
accounted more important than the class of persons addressed.
The same standard is therefore applied to controversy about
moral, as about religious questions—a standard of decency
rather than a standard of orthodoxy. It should not be forgotten, however, how relative such a standard is; and the wise
maxim is therefore, in doubtful cases, to give the person accused of "indecency," in speech or writing or act, the benefit
of the doubt. Any repression that *seems* to any considerable
number of serious-minded persons to err in the direction of intolerance is certain to be accompanied by clandestine attempts
to evade the law, of which attempts there will not be sufficiently general disapproval.

To those who approach ethical questions with the idea that
everything must have an indisputable and dogmatic basis,
such a position may seem dangerous and unstable. How, it
may be asked, are we to avoid complete moral anarchy if
everything may be questioned, provided the assailant of accepted principles *says* with any plausibility that he is a serious-
minded person? Such an objection ignores the principle on
which scientific ethics rest—the principle of consistency or
coherence—the principle which the Kantian ethics express
in the form of universality. In moral matters, because of the
necessities of education—if for no other reason—the burden of
proof must be laid on the assailant of accepted beliefs. Any
one who simply attacks and insults accepted beliefs about right
or wrong may fairly be regarded as not a serious-minded inno-
vator. He may fairly be asked to show that the principles he
advocates would work out better than the accepted principles.
The thief implies the existence of private property, and
profits by it: his conduct does not belong to a *system* under
which a society could exist at all. No society could exist
by every one stealing from everybody else. On the other
hand, the advocate of communism may be wise or foolish;
but he is advocating a social system, and attacks existing
institutions from the standpoint of an alleged better society.
Similarly, the adulterer presupposes the existence of the
family, and uses it to his own advantage: whereas the advocate of complete promiscuity may be foolish, but he is argu-

ing from the point of view of an alleged better society, not from the point of view of the mere selfish violator of existing institutions.

When we have to deal with works of art, it is more difficult to apply this test of sincerity—the possession of an ideal system ; for the artist as such does not work in a medium of general conceptions, nor has his work any *direct* social aim. Where a work of art (a book or picture) seems to the average person grossly indecent, the artist is bound to prove that his work involves real, thorough, earnest labour. The test of earnest, hard work may be suggested as a help towards distinguishing the serious artist from the manufacturer of mere indecencies ; it is one form of the general ethical test of coherence. The virtue of industry, of honest work, may go along with many defects, but cannot go along with *mere* recklessness and absence of all sense of responsibility.

We may lay down general precepts which seem to us perfectly unexceptionable, and we may expect to escape the mistakes of our predecessors and not to be found persecuting those whom a later age will venerate or at least excuse : nevertheless, we may be certain that similar mistakes will be made again and again. Every new idea with regard to matters of religion, or matters of morality, must offend a great mass of prevalent opinion, and must struggle for existence among the ideas already in possession of the ground. This is inevitable : and it need not be a matter of regret. A great many new ideas are not true or valuable, and it is well that they should not survive. A general willingness to take up every idea, simply because it is new, is not a healthy sign either of a society or of an individual mind. On the other hand, the society which rejects every new idea condemns itself to stagnation and decay. The safest principle is that the fight between ideas should be carried on as fairly, and with as much courtesy as possible. To silence an opponent by burning him, or even by burning his books, is a brutal kind of argument ; but if you really think his ideas nonsense, and mischievous nonsense, there is no reason for hesitating to say so. To go on, however, to suggest that he is an immoral person, or that his motives (about which you know nothing) in publishing his opinions are bad motives, is to overstep the limits of decent controversy. On the other hand, ridicule is a fair weapon on the whole, and is a great improvement on the Inquisition or the censorship.

There is, too, an obvious difference—analogous to that
already referred to — between tolerating the publication of
books which you (whoever the "you" may be) may think
injurious to religion and morality, and tolerating the thrusting
of these books in a cheap form under the notice of young and
inexperienced persons. If a firm of booksellers or the managers of a circulating library "boycott" a certain class of
books, it is perfectly legitimate to ridicule their conduct,
and try to show the inconsistency of countenancing the
works of X, while refusing to supply the works of Y and Z;
but the only way to make the purveyors of innocuous literature alter their conduct is to alter the opinions of the great
reading public: and then the amateur censorship of the press,
exercised by Messrs. Blank and Company, will be sure to
alter its character. If we ask the great reading public, who
are the clients of Messrs. Blank and Company, to abstain from
prohibiting our books altogether, we must not complain if the
private and unofficial "boycott" is substituted for the public
censorship. We must tolerate, in our turn, what we think the
pig-headedness of the great reading public. The case is
different when books are bought, as in a rate-supported
library, out of money to which the whole community contri-
butes; it is then fair to demand that any book likely to be
desired by a sufficient number of readers shall be supplied.
But here, in disputed cases, the only fair resort is to a poll,
and the decision of the majority must be accepted as final—
"until the times do alter." No one, not even if he considers
himself sent direct from heaven to preach a new gospel, can
claim any political or social right to thrust his notions upon
people against their wish—he may consider it a moral duty
to do so, but he must be prepared to face the odium of society.
It would be unreasonable to demand a law compelling Mrs.
Grundy to leave her card on every apostle of every "new spirit":
and the apostle would probably not benefit by such a law in
the long run. The initiator must be prepared to fight his way
to recognition; his ideas may be destructive to the society he
addresses, and need he be astonished if that society is reluctant to hear him? Leave him alone, according to Gamaliel's
wise precept of tolerance; neither give the foolish fanatic
the undeserved honour of martyrdom, nor raise dangerous
obstacles to the peaceable transition of society from one stage

to another. Such tolerance implies a belief in the ultimate
rationality of that struggle between institutions and ideas
which makes the most interesting part of the world's history ;
but, as I have already pointed out, it is a tolerance only likely
to be felt and allowed by those who consider themselves fairly
secure in their position, and who do not fear a violent over-
throw. One of the lessons of experience is that toleration
itself offers a safety-valve, and prevents explosions. There
must be variety of ideas for the selecting process to work
upon ; but in the evolution of ideas and institutions, the less
the lives and welfare of individual human beings are sacrificed,
the higher is the type of evolution.[1]

[1] Since writing the above, I see that, in the *International Journal of
Ethics* for April, 1894, Mr. J. C. Smith, criticising an essay of mine on
"The Rights of Minorities" (republished in *Darwin and Hegel, etc.*), so
completely misunderstands my position as to say that I have been
"exactly anticipated by that arch-Tory, Dr. Johnson : ' In short, sir, I
have got no farther than this ; every man has a right to utter what he
thinks truth, and every other man has a right to knock him down for it.
Martyrdom is the test.'" Now, if natural rights mean merely those
"rights" that exist independently of and prior to organised society, it
is quite true that such a mere struggle for existence is all that we should
find. But if, as I have been urging throughout, natural rights mean, as
they have always *practically* meant to political and social reformers
(amid whatever confusions of thought and language), those rights
which a well-regulated State ought to secure to its citizens, then what I
contend is, that every man ought to have a right secured to him to utter
what he thinks truth, provided that he do so with sufficient decency of
language, and in a manner not calculated to provoke a breach of the
peace ; and that, whether he observes these conditions or not, no other
man shall be permitted to knock him down for it. If he is punished for
indecency or for inciting to violence, it must be by duly constituted
authority. Even the Anarchist, caught in the act of depositing his
infernal machine, must in a well-regulated State be protected by the police
against lynching on his way to prison or the scaffold. "The all-important
right of minorities," I have said more than once, "is the right to turn
themselves into majorities if they can." This principle has been thought
to savour of intolerance, simply because my critics have not realised how
very much that right implies. It means, *at least*, "freedom of the press,
freedom of associations, freedom of public meeting." Mr. Smith thinks
these things are given " wherever there is a fairly representative government and a sound public opinion." Well, I do not know how much he is
prepared to understand by "a sound public opinion" ; there must be a
public opinion *favourable to tolerance*. Representative government, re-
publican institutions, nay, even accumulated Declarations of the Rights
of Man and constitutional guarantees of liberty, are not always sufficient
to secure this so modest right of a minority that I plead for. As I show

When we turn from the more specially political to the more specially ethical aspects of toleration, the matter to be considered is not the right of freedom of thought, but the *duty* of exercising private judgment. The most important question that can be discussed in connection with this duty is the proper attitude of the individual to authority. It is often absurdly alleged that authority in matters of opinion is an antiquated principle, for which the modern democratic spirit can have no further reverence. The man who claims to discard all authority, and to judge everything for himself, if he is quite in earnest, must avoid receiving any education, must avoid even learning a language; and such an one will not be likely to express, or even to form, any opinion of his own whatever. The rejection of authority should, to a reasonable being, who is a social being, mean nothing more than the rejection of authority which refuses to submit to any tests that carefully trained human reason can apply. That the person who accepts any one's authority on any subject should himself be able to test the worth of the authority is a perfectly unreasonable demand. I may accept as accurate the result of a chemical analysis, without myself knowing anything about chemistry; but I may be reasonably suspicious of a person's statement of the value of a food or a medicine, if the person who recommends it refuses to submit it to the analysis of experts at all. I may use a table of logarithms for purposes of calculation without thinking it necessary to test the accuracy with which it has been constructed, but I should have my suspicions of its value aroused, if it were made a penal offence to say anything disrespectful about the manner in which the book had been compiled.

in *Note* B at the end of this chapter, the United States refuse this right to the Mormon community. Whether their action is justifiable or not, on grounds of urgent public safety, I am not prepared to discuss fully: I am not sufficiently acquainted with the particular facts. But their action is certainly inconsistent with this right of minorities, and with the loudly proclaimed right of religious liberty.

What I do strongly hold, however, is that minorities have no "natural right," I mean no reasonable claim, to have their views enforced on other people, and their *actions* in violation of the law of the land (in countries with a fair representative system) safeguarded against legal penalties. But just because of these necessities of public order, the right of striving by peaceable means of persuasion to get the law altered must be the more carefully protected.

Authority in matters of conduct depends on rather more complex considerations than in either of these cases. The cohesion of a society requires in many cases an implicit obedience to commands, though it may no longer require an implicit acceptance of statements about matters of fact. I cannot be allowed, if anarchy is to be avoided, the same license in deciding whether I shall obey a law or not, that I am allowed in expressing an opinion about its justice or expediency. If I am seriously convinced that it is wrong for me to obey the law, it may become my duty to rebel—but it is then also my duty to take the consequences. But this raises a question to which I have to come later—the alleged natural right of resistance. In the meantime it is enough to point out the serious responsibility undertaken by any one who denies the generally accepted principles of right and wrong; he is morally bound to show that the principles he proposes to substitute are workable and compatible with human well-being. But it is a fair demand that the accepted principles shall be capable of justification on some other grounds except their antiquity. The individual may not say: " I have a right to disobey every law and maxim of conduct of whose worth I am not personally convinced "—that is anarchy, which is the *reductio ad absurdum* of any principle of conduct. He may say: "I have a right to discuss in a serious manner, and before an audience that will not be excited to violence by what I say, the justice of this law or this maxim of conduct." That is the toleration which every sufficiently stable and yet progressive society ought to grant. And such toleration imposes on the critic a greater responsibility than can reasonably be demanded of the hunted victim of despotic power. We expect an Englishman to be more sober in his attacks on the institutions of his country than we can expect a Russian exile to be in criticising the authority of the Czar. We excuse a great deal in Voltaire which we should not excuse in a modern free-thinker. We should not be astonished if the man whose soberest criticisms are met by imprisonment or banishment becomes bitter, and turns savagely on his enemies. But neither should we be astonished that any society is apt to be provoked into anger by abusive criticisms of its most cherished institutions. The assailants of time-honoured usages are apt to say of society :—

> "Cet animal est très méchant,
> Quand on l'attaque, il se défend,"

which may be Englished roughly thus :—

> "This animal is very wicked,
> It turns and fights when it is kicked."

Struggle is inevitable ; it rests with us whether it is a brutal or a civilised warfare—a contest of reason on both sides, or a contest of rant on the one side and of cruelty and cant on the other.

NOTE A.

RELIGIOUS PERSECUTION AND TOLERATION : SOME HISTORICAL ILLUSTRATIONS.

HALLAM, in his *Constitutional History*, is justly indignant with such a passage as this of Southey's (from the *Book of the Church*, II p. 285) : "That Church [viz., the Church of England] and the queen [Elizabeth], its re-founder, are clear of persecution as regarding the Catholics. No church, no sect, no individual even, had yet professed the principle of toleration." Hallam points out that the second of these sentences certainly does not help to prove the first of them ; and that, as regards *individuals*, the statement is false. Sir Thomas More, in his *Utopia*, professed a principle of toleration wider even than that of Locke. The dogmas of the "civil religion" of Utopia are only two—a Divine providence and the immortality of the soul, with future rewards and punishments; but those who deny these doctrines, though excluded from all public offices (as at the present day in the law-abiding State of Arkansas), are put to no punishment, and are not banished, as they would be according to Rousseau's "civil religion." In his views on religion, as in several other matters, this Roman Catholic martyr for conscience' sake goes far beyond what many of the champions of religious liberty have dared to dream of.

While Hallam is right in saying that we cannot acquit Elizabeth's government of persecution, I think he does not do full justice to the significance of the contention made by Burleigh : that no one had been *put to death* in Elizabeth's reign for religion, but only for treason. Admit that the interpretation given to treason makes this defence a hypocritical one, is it not significant of a change of sentiment that Burleigh adopts it ? It is the homage paid to a new principle. The pamphlet called *The Executive of Justice in England for Maintenance of Public and Christian Peace*, published in 1583, and ascribed, with every probability, to Lord Burleigh, is included in *The Somers Tracts* (ed. Scott, I. p. 189 *seq.*). The giving up of the punishment of death for heresy as such is indeed only a small step in the direction of religious toleration. In another pamphlet of

1583, *A Declaration of the favourable dealing of her Majesty's Commissioners appointed for the Examination of certain Traitors, and for the Tortures unjustly reported to be done upon them for matters of Religion* (*Somers Tracts*, I. p. 209 seq.), Burleigh asserts that those who applied the rack were specially charged to use it "in so charitable a manner as such a thing might be." It is remarkable, as Hallam points out, that in this same year Burleigh addressed a memorial to the Queen in favour of a lax enforcement of the oath of supremacy on Papists. To pass very stringent laws in order to satisfy the fanatics, and then to allow them to be administered laxly, was a favourite device of statesmen in those days, and is not quite unknown in ours. I have heard an American citizen saying with reference to Prohibitory Liquor Laws (with what amount of exaggeration I cannot judge), "In this country we make laws, but we don't keep them. We pass a strict law about the sale of liquor—that pleases the Prohibitionists; but you can always get a drink, if you know how."[1] It seems to have been much the same with laws against the Papists: it was one thing to pass a stringent law to satisfy the more vehement Protestants, it was another to enforce it rigidly against loyal country gentlemen in the northern counties, where, out of a scanty population, a large proportion were Catholic in sympathies. As to priests, and especially Jesuits—that was another thing.

In this Memorial of Burleigh's (*Somers Tracts*, I. p. 164 seq.), it is noticeable how he argues the inefficacy of persecution *from experience*. "Putting to death," he says, "doth no ways lessen them, since we find by experience that it worketh no such effect, but like Hydra's heads, upon cutting off one, seven grow up, persecution being accounted as the badge of the Church; and therefore they should never have the honour to take any pretence of martyrdom in England, where the fulness of blood and greatness of heart is such, that they will even for shameful things go bravely to death—much more when they think themselves to climb heaven; and this vice of obstinacy seems to the common people a Divine constancy: so that, for my part, I wish no lessening of their number, but by preaching and by education of the younger, under good schoolmasters"—*i.e.*, he proposes to deprive Papists of the control of the education of their children, these children to serve as hostages for their parents' fidelity. In the same Memorial, he advises also against driving out of the Church "the preciser sort" (*i.e.* the Puritans), with whom he had no particular sympathy.

Hallam distinguishes five stages or degrees in restraint on religious liberty. Here is the persecutor's ladder, as one might call it:—

[1] The statement seems, on the whole, to be borne out by Mr. Fanshawe in his *Report* (for Mr. Rathbone) *on Liquor Legislation in the United States and Canada* (Cassell & Co. 1893).

(1) The requisition of a test of conformity to the established religion as a condition of exercising offices of civil trust. (2) Restraint of the free promulgation of opinions, especially through the press. (3) Prohibition of the open exercise of religious worship. (4) Prohibition of even private acts of devotion or private expression of opinion. (5) Enforcement by legal penalties of conformity to the Established Church, or an abjuration of heterodox tenets. "The statutes of Elizabeth's reign," he adds, "comprehend every one of these progressive stages of restraint and persecution."

In the "Declaration of Breda" (1660), Charles II. declares "a liberty to tender consciences, and that no man shall be disquieted or called in question for differences of opinion in matter of religion, *which do not disturb the peace of the kingdom*; and that we shall be ready to consent to such an Act of Parliament, as upon mature deliberation shall be offered to us, for the full granting that indulgence" (Gardiner, *Const. Doc.*, p. 352). We have here the express recognition, in words at least, of what may be called the non-mediaeval principle of interfering with religious liberty solely on political or social grounds. The Parliaments of Charles II. were sufficiently intolerant, but then the words "disturb the peace of the kingdom" may be interpreted in such a way as to justify severe restraints on dissenters.

The Instrument of Government (1653) limits the toleration it concedes to "such as profess faith in God by Jesus Christ," and not only by consideration of the public peace; it also expressly excludes Popery and Prelacy, so that although it implies the giving up of the attempt to enforce uniformity of doctrine and worship, it still maintains the duty of excluding certain kinds of religion, *as such*. On this matter the Instrument of Government, in the main, carries out the provisions of the Agreement of the People (originally drawn up by the army in 1647-8), except that the latter leaves the toleration of Popery and Prelacy so far an open question, *i.e.* a question for Parliament to deal with. "It is not intended to be hereby provided that this liberty shall necessarily extend to Popery or Prelacy." The constitutional Bill of the first Parliament of the Protectorate (Gardiner, p. 353 *seq.*) only provides "that without the consent of the Lord Protector and Parliament, no law or statute be made for the restraining of such tender consciences as shall differ in doctrine, worship, or discipline from the public profession aforesaid, and shall not abuse their liberty to the civil injury of others or the disturbance of the public peace." Bills, however, were without the Protector's consent to become law which restrained "damnable heresies." What are damnable heresies, however, was to be agreed on by Protector and Parliament. This scheme is obviously very far away from what we generally understand by the principle of religious liberty.

If Sir Thomas More in his *Utopia* deserves to be accounted the
first theoretical advocate of religious toleration, Roger Williams, the
founder of Providence (afterwards incorporated in Rhode Island), is
the first person in modern times who actually succeeded in establishing a community on a basis of liberty of conscience (1636); and for
a long time the colony seemed to its more orderly but intolerant
neighbours, Massachusetts and Connecticut, to be a shocking example
of anarchy and confusion. But time justified the bold experiment,
and Charles II. in 1663 granted a charter to Rhode Island, which
remained its written constitution until 1842, and which conceded
a religious liberty such as few could have dared to ask for or to grant
in Great Britain in the seventeenth century. This religious liberty
was granted expressly on the ground that Rhode Island was too
remote to make any breach of "the unity and uniformity established
in this nation."

Mary Fisher, the Quakeress, who was imprisoned in Boston and
half-starved for preaching blasphemous and devilish doctrines, five
years afterwards " went to Adrianople and tried to convert the Grand
Turk, who treated her with grave courtesy and allowed her to
prophesy unmolested. [Did he understand her?] This is one of the
numerous incidents that, on a superficial view of history, might be
cited in support of the opinion that there has been on the whole more
tolerance in the Mussulman than in the Christian world. Rightly
interpreted, however, the fact has no such implication. In Massachusetts the preaching of Quaker doctrines might (and did) lead to a
revolution; in Turkey it was as harmless as the barking of dogs.
Governor Endicott was afraid of Mary Fisher; Mahomet III. was
not" (Fiske, *The Beginnings of New England*, pp. 183, 184).

Roger Williams, in tolerating the Quakers, proved that he adopted
toleration—" soul liberty "—as a principle and not merely as a
policy: for he never concealed his antipathy to their doctrines. He
wrote not only *The Bloody Tenent*, but *George Fox digged out of
his Burrows*. It may be noted that Williams's saying that " A soul
or spiritual rape is more abominable in God's eye than to force and
ravish the bodies of all the women in the world" (*Bloody Tenent*,
1644, p. 94) had been anticipated by the Baptist Busher (*Religion's
Peace*, 1614): " Persecution for religion is to force the conscience.
. . . And herein the bishops commit a greater sin than if they
force the bodies of women and maids against their wills " (Hanserd
Knollys Society's *Tracts on Liberty of Conscience*, 1614–1661, p. 54.
But Williams had to put his principles to the test in the difficult task
of organising a turbulent community. It is true he believed that
toleration would lead the sect of Quakers to dwindle. " They are
likely to gain more followers by the conceit of their patient sufferings
than by consent to their pernicious sayings."

Roger Williams's famous book is entitled, *The Bloody Tenent of*

Persecution for cause of Conscience, discussed in a Conference between Truth and Peace, who, in all tender Affection, present to the High Court of Parliament (as the result of their Discourse) these amongst other Passages) of highest consideration (London : 1644). A reply to Williams's book was made in *The Bloudy Tenent washed and made white in the bloud of the Lambe : being discussed and discharged of bloud-guiltiness by just Defence, etc.   Whereunto is added a Reply to Mr. Williams's Answer to Mr. Cotton's Letter.* By John Cotton, Batchelor in Divinity, and Teacher of the Church of Christ at Boston in New-England (London: 1647). To this a rejoinder was published by Williams: *The Bloody Tenent yet more Bloody by Mr. Cotton's endevour to wash it white in the Blood of the Lambe ; of whose precious Blood, spilt in the Blood of his Servants, and of the Blood of Millions spilt in former and later Wars for Conscience sake, that most Bloody Tenent of Persecution for cause of Conscience upon a second Tryal is found now more apparently and more notoriously guilty.* By R. Williams of Providence in New-England (London : 1652).

From this last work it is worth quoting, in explanation of this quaint title, and for its own sake, the eloquent concluding passage. It comes at the end of "An Appendix" addressed "to the clergy of the four great parties, professing the name of Christ Jesus, in England [the head-line inserts "Old and New" before England], Scotland, and Ireland, viz., the Popish, Prelatical, Presbyterian, and Independent ":—"You know it is the Spirit of Love from Christ Jesus, that turns our feet from the traditions of Fathers, etc., that sets the heart and tongue and pen and hands too (as Paul's) day and night to work rather than the progress and purity and simplicity of the crown of Christ Jesus should be debased or hindered. This Spirit will cause you leave (with joy) benefices and bishoprics, worlds and lives, for His sake, the heights and depths, lengths and breadths of whose love you know doth infinitely pass your most knowing comprehensions and imaginations. There is but little of this Spirit extant—I fear will not be until we see Christ Jesus slain in the slaughter of the witnesses: then Joseph will go boldly unto Pilate for the slaughtered body of most precious Saviour, and Nicodemus will go by day to buy and bestow his sweetest spices on his infinitely sweeter soul's beloved."

NOTE B.

MEASURES FOR SUPPRESSING MORMONISM IN THE UNITED STATES.

It is worth while, in connection with this subject of religious liberty and liberty of opinion, to call attention to the treatment of the Mormons by the Government of the United States, for two reasons especially. In the first place, this is a test case of the extent to which "religious liberty" is really secured to individuals in a country whose constitution is supposed to be strictly limited by the recognition of certain indefeasible natural rights, which Government should protect, but with which it should not interfere.[1] The amount of sympathy, with which the action of the United States Government in its endeavour to suppress Mormonism is regarded in America and in Europe, serves also as a measure of the extent to which people really believe in "religious liberty." Secondly, the action of the United States Government, and the sympathy with which it has been regarded in this matter, help one to realise more accurately the spirit in which Catholics have persecuted Protestants, and Protestants Catholics. Some study of the Mormon question is an important discipline and training for the exercise of the historical spirit in our judgments about the past. You abhor polygamy, you think it a degrading and detestable institution, and the religion of the "Latter Day Saints" which supports it (or did support it) you look on as a tissue of delusions and lies. Transfer these sentiments of yours to the mind of a sincere Protestant of the sixteenth or seventeenth centuries, and you will understand the way in which he regarded toleration of "the idolatrous sacrifice of the mass." You, the enlightened, tolerant, modern Protestant, cannot understand, perhaps, the attitude of the Roman Catholic clergy of the present day to the question of divorce, or the attitude of the bulk of the Anglican clergy to the "Deceased Wife's Sister Bill." On what *general* grounds of respect for individual liberty is there any difference between your attitude and theirs? They abhor and, if they could, would prevent what injures the institution of the family, as they understand the family, and what violates the principles of religion, as they understand religion. You understand the institution of the family and the principles of religion differently from them, and differently from the "Latter Day Saints." The difference is a difference in private judgment; and yet in virtue of an opinion not supported by any infallible court of appeal you interfere with the religious liberty of others; for if "religious liberty" has any meaning, the "religion" must depend on the judgment of the person claiming the liberty, and not on that of the person conceding it. People may glory in not allowing their Government to interfere in matters of religion; but, however much they may disestablish all Churches, they must either concede to their Government the right of

---

[1] As I have pointed out, the Declarations of Rights appear in State Constitutions, but the first amendment to the U.S. Constitution lays down that "Congress shall make no law respecting an establishment of religion, or prohibiting the free exercise thereof; or abridging the freedom of speech, or of the press, etc." This is the constitutional guarantee of the liberties of citizens of the U.S. living in Territories, and is generally understood as a guarantee of " religious liberty."

deciding what *are* matters of religion, or they must bow to the decision of some Church or combination of Churches. By no possible declaration of rights, or constitutional safeguards, can you absolutely distinguish Church and State, the spiritual and the temporal power, for in the last resort *either* Church *or* State must determine the provinces of each.

Now let us admit, not merely that polygamy is a morally defective form of the family, but that its suppression by law is a desirable end, and that the fact of polygamy being practised under the sanction of religion, so far from making it advisable to leave polygamy alone, makes it all the more important to suppress an institution which is more likely to endure and to spread because supported by belief in a religion—however absurd that religion may seem to the majority of persons in the country. How can such suppression of polygamy be reconciled with the maintenance of religious liberty? I think no objection can be taken to the decision of the Supreme Court of the United States in the case of Reynolds *v.* U. S., that "Congress was deprived by the Constitution of all legislative power over mere opinion, but was left free to reach actions which were in violation of social duties and subversive of good order." Who decides, however, what "actions are in violation of social duties and subversive of good order"? The legislature itself,—which means in the last resort the average public opinion of the community, or rather the opinion of those persons who manage to make their will effective at election time. Suppose a strongly Protestant majority united in political sentiment, living alongside of a Roman Catholic minority, whose votes are not an object of importance, as they would be were the majority divided amongst themselves; suppose a great antagonism to the Confessional among the Protestant majority and among a considerable number of husbands of Roman Catholic wives, might not the Confessional be prohibited on the ground that it was "in violation of social duties and subversive of good order"? Would such a law be an infringement of the right of religious liberty? Undoubtedly penitents and priests would have to choose between risking their eternal welfare (as they believe) and breaking the law of the land. Yet, from the point of view of many a legislator, the practice of confession might be regarded as interfering with the duties of family life (as he understands them) in the same sort of way that polygamy seems to do from the point of view of other legislators.

A series of laws passed by Congress between 1862 and 1887 have, with continually increasing severity, sought to stamp out polygamy in the Territories. Lest an ordinary law against bigamy should be insufficient, the Edmunds Law of 1882 makes "cohabitation with more than one woman" a *crime*. To the European who believes in religious liberty, or in what is otherwise described as the secularisation of politics, it must seem astonishing that, in its endeavours to

discourage polygamy, Congress should commit such a direct infringement of religious liberty as is implied in this revival of Puritan
methods of dealing with the voluntary relations of the sexes among
adults, punishing "sins" as "crimes." If in any American State
the Roman Catholic population obtained the control of the legislature,
they might punish as "criminals" persons legally divorced (in other
States) who had married again, or persons who had contracted mixed
marriages, with no more disrespect to the natural rights of liberty,
etc., than that with which the United States Government has made
adultery a crime in Utah. Congress has chosen to proceed on what
may be called mediæval principles of legislation, enforcing by penal
laws certain prohibitions of the Christian Church (though not others).
The Supreme Court, in defending a piece of legislation of which I
have still to speak, lays down that "the primitive power of Government for acts recognised by the general consent of the Christian world
in modern times as proper matters for prohibitory legislation, cannot
be suspended in order that the tenets of a religious sect encouraging
crime may be carried out without hindrance." It is to be noticed
that the appeal is not made, as by the fathers of the Constitution, to
the law of nature or the consent of the human race, but, as it might
have been made by any of the "persecuting" governments of earlier
days, to "the consent of the Christian world in modern times" (*i.e.* at
present). The Christian world, certainly up to the end of the seventeenth century, with trivial exceptions, agreed that "heresy" ought
to be suppressed or at least discouraged by law, though different
parts of the Christian world had (fortunately for the cause of liberty)
different definitions of heresy. The American Supreme Court are
using the very arguments which Lord Burleigh or Archbishop Laud
might have used. You make saying mass a crime, or you make
attending a "conventicle" a crime, and then you say, "No one's
religion shall excuse him from committing a crime against the law
of the land." The method is simple; but is this "religious liberty"?

"But," it will be answered, "the Supreme Court refers only to
the general consent of the Christian world *in modern times.* The
Christian world has come to the opinion that it is wrong to punish
for error in doctrine [Strict Roman Catholics have not come to that
opinion, but only to the opinion that it is sometimes impossible and
sometimes unsafe or inexpedient to do so]. We differ too much about
doctrines, but about morality all Christians are agreed." Are they?
How about divorce? What is the standard of "Christian" ethics?
Is it the opinion of a Church which claims infallibility, or is it
"the Scriptures" to which Protestants appeal? If the former, how
can you sanction divorce? If Christian ethics are to be decided by
the Bible, and the Bible only, it seems specially unreasonable to prohibit polygamy, which is sanctioned by the example of men after
God's own heart in the Old Testament, and is nowhere forbidden in

the New Testament, except in the case of Bishops.[1] But "the
general consent of the Christian world in modern times," it will be
explained, "means the opinion of Catholics and Protestants on those
matters of morality on which they are agreed; the appeal is made
to the actual practice of countries in which Christianity is the predominant religion, though in matters of legislation compromises
between Catholics and Protestants are adopted." Do Great Britain,
France, Germany, Austria, Italy, in all of which Christian Churches
are "established," form a part of the Christian world as well as the
United States of America, in which, professedly in the interests of
"religious liberty," there is no established Church? In none of these
countries is adultery nowadays punished as a *crime*, in the strict
sense of the term—a wrong against the State, to be detected and
punished like theft or murder, quite apart from any initiative of
aggrieved individuals. The tendency of "modern" legislation has
been to give up the attempt to enforce by penal sanctions (I am
not referring to civil remedies) the code of Christian ethics in regard
to sexual morality on adult persons acting voluntarily, and not "contrary to nature." It is a new thing that the United States of America
should be ambitious of being more mediæval than the benighted countries of the old world. Are modern legislators, who profess a belief
in natural rights, and who accept the standard of general happiness
as the test of good legislation, prepared at the bidding of a union
of sects to enact laws which cannot really be enforced without the
introduction of a spy-system that would be far more injurious to the
morality of social life than the laxity such Puritanical laws are
intended to cure? Such laws, one is inclined to suspect, are not
intended to be generally enforced, but are passed (like some liquor
laws) to catch a certain number of votes, and to be used as a weapon
of attack against obnoxious groups, when convenient.

Now, what seems to take away excuse from the Congress and the
Supreme Court of the United States is, that it would have been quite
possible to fight polygamy on the principles which regulate "modern"
legislation in most European countries. The following programme
is what would probably suggest itself to the secularised politicians of
those European countries which have accepted the principles of '89:
First, to recognise no marriage as *legally* binding except a civil
marriage. *Secondly*, to prohibit bigamous or polygamous civil mar-

---

[1] 1 Tim. iii. 2. If the prohibition be of second marriages, this prohibition, binding on *priests* of the "Orthodox" Church, has not been
enforced on the laity by the legislature in any Christian country.
Theologians quote various texts from which they *infer* a prohibition of
polygamy; and some theologians have great powers of inference. They
could more easily find texts deterring from marriage altogether than
from polygamous marriage. Monogamy has come to us as a Roman, not
as a distinctively Christian, institution.

riages—with proper exceptions, of course, for persons legally divorced. *Thirdly*, to make adultery a ground for divorce, in the case of both sexes equally. *Fourthly*, in order to meet the special case of the Mormons, who do not allow a second "marriage" unless the first wife consents, it might be necessary to set a limit to the period of time during which "condonation" or "connivance" is a bar to divorce, so as to allow the legal wife, who repents of a consent, given perhaps under the influence of religious enthusiasm or religious terrorism, full means of escaping from a polygamous husband if she wishes. *Lastly*, instead of *abolishing* female suffrage in the Territory of Utah, as was done by the Edmunds-Tucker Law of 1887,[1] it would have seemed more in accordance with a sincere belief that polygamy was a system of slavery in which women were kept against their will, to have retained female suffrage while ensuring by stringent enactments the inviolable secrecy of the ballot.

Such a series of measures would probably have been very unacceptable to the Mormon community: but they would have been measures for crushing out polygamy without violating, as the existing measures seem to do to the observer from outside, the principle of religious liberty, so loudly professed by the United States. If the devout Mormon were to choose, with the consent of his legal wife, to bind himself by religious ceremonies to support a number of other women for the term of their natural lives, and to put their children on the same footing as to inheritance with his lawful issue, that would doubtless be an unusual manner of violating the duties of the family, and would present a remarkable contrast to the way in which men have been known to treat their wives and their mistresses in other parts of the world—and even of the United States—but it seems hardly so terrible a state of affairs as to call for criminal proceedings on the part of a strong government in a country the vast majority of whose inhabitants are not likely to become converts to the singular revelations of Saint Joseph Smith. The United States Government has not even the excuse of reasonable fear, which may be pleaded for the persecution of Elizabeth's reign. Have the legislators of Congress so little faith in the superiority of monogamy that they can only fight polygamy by the methods which the Puritans used in New England against Catholics and Quakers?

But even supposing it were conceded that there is nothing inconsistent with "religious liberty" in treating as criminal the plural or "celestial" marriages recognised as binding by a religious sect, the "persecution" of the Mormons does not end in the punishment of overt acts which are, or have for the special purpose been made, crimes by the law of the land. The Supreme Court of the United States has decided that it is not unconstitutional to impose on voters a test or abjuration oath, in which they have to swear that they do not

[1] Cf. Bryce, *American Commonwealth*, III. p. 291.

belong to an association which *teaches* polygamy as a religious duty.[1]
Such a test oath is imposed by the statutes of Idaho Territory; that
is to say, a person can be deprived of his political rights simply for
belonging to a religious body which believes in the rightness of
certain conduct which the law of the land has made criminal. Lord
Burleigh has been condemned as hypocritical because, while requiring an abjuration oath from Roman Catholics (which they could not
conscientiously take) denying the papal supremacy in England, he
yet declared that this was not religious persecution. And yet every
Roman Catholic might reasonably be alleged to be a traitor so long
as he acknowledged the power of the Pope to dispense Englishmen
from their allegiance to Queen Elizabeth, and every Jesuit, during a
considerable period, might be reasonably alleged to belong to an
association which taught the rightness and the duty even of assassi-
nating "tyrants" who had been recognised as such by the Pope.
Now no one can argue that polygamy, however detestable, is a
political or social danger of the same kind as rebellion and assassination: and yet the merely belonging to an association that teaches or
encourages the practice of polygamy as a religious duty renders a
citizen of the United States in this Territory of Idaho liable to a loss
of political rights. This kind of "persecution" is indeed but the
first step in the persecutors' ladder, which Hallam has described;
but, as I do not believe that even the Supreme Court of the United
States is infallible, I cannot see how such a test oath is to be reconciled with the decision that "Congress was deprived by the Constitution of all legislative power over mere opinion" (Reynolds *v.* U.S.).

I have said elsewhere that the most valuable right of a minority is
the right to turn itself into a majority if it can: and I have found
myself criticised on the ground that this concedes too much power to
majorities. But the right of a minority to turn itself into a majority
implies the right to free expression of opinion (within the limits of
decency) and the right of association for the purpose of propagating
opinion (limited by respect for the rights of others). So far as I understand the matter, compulsory vaccination is a most valuable measure,
and it seems to me quite right that those who fail to have their children
vaccinated should be subject to penalties: but that Anti-vaccinators
should be deprived of their votes simply because they belong to an
association which teaches and encourages its members to break the
law of the land would be an excessive interference with the right
of a minority to agitate in a constitutional way. I admit that the
teaching or encouraging of such crimes as murder may be very
properly punished, if it can be done; but the punishment should be

---

[1] Davis *v.* Beason. Observe the individual himself need not have
taught or encouraged the practice of polygamy. The Test is clearly intended to exclude the whole sect of Mormons *as such.*

a direct punishment of every individual teaching or encouraging the crime, and not the roundabout method of depriving every one of his vote who does not abjure the membership of Anarchist societies. Such test oaths, though the mildest, are one of the least expedient forms of persecution: they cause irritation without being effectual in doing anything else than making constitutional agitation difficult. They provoke hypocrisy and encourage perjury. It is possible, however, that such legislation as the Edmunds-Tucker Law and the Idaho Test Oath may seem to be effectual (with the help of the Pacific railroad) in destroying those parts of Mormonism to which the majority of people in America object. But to the observer from without it does seem that the institutions objected to might have been attacked in a manner more compatible with the constitutional guarantee of religious liberty. Religious liberty may be thought a good thing or a bad thing; but it is a hypocritical pretence to say you concede religious liberty and yet insist that what *you* do not call "religion" is not religion, or that people who approve of what *you* disapprove of cannot possibly be sincere and conscientious. Religious liberty, whether a good thing or a bad thing, means something very different from a general disestablishment of Churches.

CHAPTER IX

I HAVE treated the subject of toleration and liberty of opinion at considerable length, as a convenient method of getting at some of the principles by which the rights of individuals must be determined. Other aspects of the alleged natural right of liberty may be treated more briefly. A general and unqualified liberty of *action* has never been claimed by any sane or reasonable person. The mere possibility of social existence involves some check upon the liberty of each individual; and, although amiable anarchists may dream of a society in which every one would respect the claims of every one else, without any force, even in the remotest background, to guarantee those claims, and without any body of persons expressly empowered to decide on the merits of rival claims and having the regulated force of the society to back up its decisions, it is clear to all those who have learnt anything from a study of history, or even from a slight reflection on human nature, that without some such available compulsion in the last resort no society can permanently hold together. The less that force needs to be used to compel order, the better on the whole is the condition of the society; but force is not useless in social matters simply because it does not always need to be used.

There are certain particular liberties of action, which are often enumerated as distinct " rights " in popular language and in formal " Declarations." One of these is what we are accustomed to call "the right of public meeting." In the Declaration of Rights of 1793, " the right of assembling peaceably " is mentioned along with the right of free expression of opinion. This right of assembling is not expressly named in the Declaration of 1789, but in the Constitution of 1791, *Titre* i., among the " natural and civil rights," the Constitution guarantees to the citizens " the liberty of assembling themselves peaceably and without arms, provided that they satisfy the police laws "—limitations obviously capable of a very stringent interpretation. The Constitution for the year III. (1795) is, as might be expected, less favourable to the right of public meeting than that of 1793. In *Titre* xiv. § 365, it is laid down that "every armed mob (*attroupement*) is an attack on the constitution and ought to be immediately dispersed by force "; while the following section provides "that every mob without arms should be equally dispersed, at first by way of verbal command, and, if it is necessary, by the use (*développement*) of armed force." I assume that the executive under this constitution reserves to itself the definition of what constitutes an "*attroupement*."

The Belgian Constitution may be taken as a fair specimen of a more modern constitution, which expressly guarantees a right of public meeting under certain restrictions. Its nineteenth article is as follows: "The Belgians have the right of assembling peaceably and without arms, on condition of conforming to the laws which may regulate the exercise of this right, but without having to obtain previous permission. This rule does not apply to meetings in the open air, which remain entirely subjected to the police laws." [1]

This provision in the Belgian Constitution was probably intended, as Professor Dicey suggests, to secure in the main the same liberty of public meeting, which by 1831 at least might be regarded as being recognised in this country. Perhaps we should rather say—which had come *de facto* to establish itself in this country; for, while on the one hand our law makes no distinction between meetings indoors and meetings out of doors, there exists, by the law of the land, no such thing as a right of public meeting at all. "No better instance," says Professor Dicey, "can indeed be found of the way in which in England the constitution is built up upon individual rights than our rules as to public assemblies. The right of assembling is nothing more than the result of the view taken by the Courts as to individual liberty of person and in-

---

[1] " *Les Belges ont le droit de s'assembler paisiblement et sans armes, en se conformant aux lois qui peuvent régler l'exercice de ce droit, sans néanmoins le soumettre à une autorisation préalable. Cette disposition ne s'applique point aux rassemblements en plein air, qui restent entièrement soumis aux lois de police.*" (Quoted by Dicey, *Law of the Constitution*, Ed. 3, p. 251.)

dividual liberty of speech. There is no special law allowing
A. B and C to meet together either in the open air or elsewhere for a lawful purpose, but the right of A to go where he
pleases so that he does not commit a trespass, and to say what
he likes to B, so that his talk is not libellous or seditious, the
right of B to do the like, and the existence of the same rights
of C, D, E and F, and so on *ad infinitum*, leads to the consequence that A, B, C, D and a thousand or ten thousand other
persons may (as a general rule) meet together in any place
where otherwise they each have a right to be for a lawful purpose and in a lawful manner." [1]

Now to ordinary common sense a meeting of a thousand,
or of two or three thousand, persons for a definite and common
purpose is a different fact from an accidental walking and
accidental talking of A, B, C, D, etc., as separate individuals.
The individualist logic, which is taken for granted in our
popular philosophy, may indeed look on even permanent
societies as mere *aggregates* of the individuals who compose
them, and think that the properties of the society can be arrived
at by a summation of the properties of the individuals. But
ordinary common sense, unsophisticated by popular philosophy
(which is a very different thing from ordinary common sense),
can easily see the difference between even a temporary " meeting " and a mere addition of units. If any one were to say that
he happened to be taking a walk in Hyde Park one day, and
that several hundreds of people all happened to be taking a
walk four-abreast in the same direction, and that when they
came to a certain spot, where there happened to be a platform,
first one person, then another, and then more stood up on the
platform, and they all happened to make some remarks, in
rather a loud voice, to the other people, and they all happened
to make remarks of much the same kind and about much the
same subject—we should probably regard such a narrative as a
feeble attempt at humour. [2] But this abstract view of the
facts has sufficed hitherto for English lawyers.

No doubt in this, as in other matters, it has been advantageous for the growth of democracy in England, that the

[1] *Law of the Constitution*, Ed. 3, p. 255.
[2] A great deal of humour, especially the humour of the professional
humourist, consists in abstracting certain aspects of events from their
context, just as caricature in drawing consists in taking certain features

rights of citizens as such were not laid down at too early a date; but it may perhaps be questioned whether the interests of orderly progress are at present best served by this legal ignoring of political facts. On the one hand this habit of regarding a multitude as simply a sum of individuals helps to give countenance to the rather widely spread notion that there is a sort of unlimited right of making processions and holding meetings. A may walk down this street as well as anybody else; B may walk down this street as well as anybody else; and so of C, D, E, etc. Therefore $A + B + C + D + etc.$, may go in procession down this street, when it comes into their joint heads to do so, and the authorities who prevent the procession are interfering with a just and indefeasible right of free Englishmen. In practice the organisers of processions generally recognise a reasonable limitation of their rights by giving sufficient notice of their intention to the police, and consulting with them about the route least likely to cause inconvenience to the rest of the community. But would there not be some gain in making the organisers of processions or meetings more definitely and legally responsible for their orderliness? There would then be better security taken against the presence of those disorderly and ruffianly followers, who have so often brought reasonable and peaceable "agitation" into undeserved discredit. There can obviously be no general right of going in processions or holding meetings at all times and in all places, even if procession and meeting be quite orderly. Even those persons who do not want to make processions or to go to meetings have some "rights" in the public streets and open spaces. On the other hand, the great value of public meetings as expressions, though of a very vague and unsatisfactory kind, of the opinions of certain sections of the community, and still more their great value as safety-valves of feeling which becomes dangerous when pent up, make it very important that no unnecessary obstacles should be thrown in their way, and that no pretext should be given for the supposition that one set of opinions is favoured by the police authorities, while another set is

and exaggerating them to the neglect of the others. This "abstraction" might be illustrated by the story of a man who was asked how his father died, and answered, "He was engaged in serious conversation with a clergyman, when some boards in a platform gave way, and he broke his neck while falling through."

frowned on. Provided that incitements to violence are avoided and a certain decency of language observed, it is generally wise to allow any kind of views to be promulgated, and it would be well if every town and village had its public hall or, failing that, its open space, where all sorts of meetings might be held, provided of course that no one party be allowed to monopolise the use of public property. It is moreover a useful part of a citizen's education to be able to hear the most divergent opinions propounded without a breaking of heads, either by the mutual efforts of the audience or by the guardians of the public peace.

The liberty of association may be regarded as a mere application of the right of public meeting; an association of individuals for any special purpose may be thought of as a public meeting, which is never dissolved, but only adjourned. But an association means more than that; for the body as a whole, by its constitution, comes to acquire definite "rights" over the individuals composing it, in a way to which a public meeting only approximates. An individual who attends a public meeting does indeed thereby become, to some extent, subject to the control of the assemblage as a whole, or of its effective majority, or of those who can control the majority. His right of absolute freedom of speech and action is, for instance, limited far more than it would be were he not present at the meeting. If he makes certain remarks which he might, perhaps, have been allowed to make at his own fireside, or even while walking along a public street, he may incur the risk of being put out of the meeting with necessary or superfluous force, every one recognising the "natural right" of public meetings to maintain such order and harmony as may be necessary for their existence as meetings for hearing speeches or discussions. But the control which an association exercises over the individuals belonging to it is of a wider kind, and of a much more definite kind. As a rule, an individual in joining a more or less permanent association is told something, at least, of the laws and regulations of the association to which he thus becomes subject; membership of other associations than the State is generally supposed to be, and is certainly spoken of as if it were, "voluntary," whereas membership of the State is supposed to be "compulsory." The distinction, however, is not quite so clear and rigid as is often thought. The obvious difference between the State and what is called a voluntary association is, that the State can exercise regulated force in inflicting penalties for disobedience to its commands, whereas a voluntary association is either restricted to the exercise of " moral compulsion," or can only enforce its penalties by making use of the legal machinery which the State itself provides.

The distinction, as thus formulated, does on the whole exist between the *modern* State in all orderly societies, and the greater number of what are called voluntary associations. But the weak States of the middle ages had frequently very much less power of enforcing their commands than was possessed by the Church (which would now-a-days be called a " voluntary association," because it is not the State) in those days when the supernatural and other-worldly penalties of the Church exercised a stronger influence over the mass of people, homogeneous in their beliefs, than the irregularly enforced penalties of the temporal power. At different times and in different places there has been a difference in value between hanging and damning as penalties for the violation of commands or precepts; though, as a rule, the Church, when exercising an effective control over consciences, has also been able and willing to use the secular arm to back up the ghostly terrors which are her own proper weapon. Even if we consider only those times in which the State is strong and can ensure the systematic enforcement of the penalties it threatens, it should be recognised that there is no absolute difference, so far as concerns the effect on the individual's motives, between the pressure of the State and the pressure of other associations. If disobedience to the commands of some powerful association means an effective excommunication, or " boycott," or practical deprivation of the means of obtaining a living, the individual's free choice may be as much limited as by the knowledge that disobedience to the commands of the State will involve death or imprisonment. The fear of starvation for oneself and those dependent on one may be as strong a motive as the fear of the law of the land. Moreover, the belonging, or ceasing to belong, to a " voluntary " association may be as little voluntary as the belonging, or ceasing to belong, to a particular State. In the societies of the ancient world, it is true, citizenship came mostly by birth, and could only be obtained exceptionally, and as a special favour,

by an outsider. But in the modern world, to a considerable
extent, citizenship depends on the will of the individual.
Thus it is more easy for an able-bodied person, or a person
with sufficient personal property, to exchange a country and a
nationality, that he finds disagreeable, for one more to his
liking, than it is for a barrister or a doctor, who is dependent
on his earnings, to violate the etiquette of his profession.
Again, a great many persons are born into, or brought up
into (if we may say so), a "voluntary" association, or are
made to feel it necessary to join one. Most persons are "born"
in this or that religious body, quite as much as they are born
of this or that nationality. To belong to a trade-union may
be an almost indispensable condition of obtaining a living by
the occupation to which one has been brought up. It may
need a strength of will and power of defying the opinion of
one's neighbour, very much above the average, to refuse to
pay certain "voluntary" subscriptions.

This ultimate similarity between the State and other associations is overlooked in that very naïve proposal of certain
"Individualists" to make taxation voluntary. I shall not
discuss the spectacle of a First Lord of the Admiralty sending
the hat round (a cocked hat, I suppose it would be—very
soon, if not at the outset), with a polite request : "Your contributions are respectfully solicited for the maintenance of the
British Navy." Of course such an idea is not necessarily
absurd, though it belongs to a stage of society which in some
matters has become unfamiliar to us. It is only custom that
makes us see no incongruity in keeping up lighthouses at the
public expense, while lifeboats are dependent on private subscriptions, or in keeping up poorhouses out of the rates, while
hospitals are private charities; in many such matters we progress only by degrees from the voluntary, *i.e.* the haphazard,
to the political, *i.e.* the more systematic method of meeting general needs. But let me leave the question of external
defences out of sight. Suppose a model town on the voluntary
system. Instead of a police force maintained out of the rates,
we should have a private association maintained by voluntary
subscriptions for the defence of person and property. Possibly
some of the wealthier inhabitants might not care to join, but
would provide their own staff of guards, and protect their
houses or factories or shops in the good old fashion of the

mediæval baron. Humbler persons would have to combine, as they could each only afford the expense of a fraction of a six-foot policeman. Now suppose that a certain citizen, in the full exercise of the freedom he enjoys under this reign of liberty, refuses to subscribe to the defence-fund, his name would be conspicuously absent from the subscription list, and of this absence the burgling profession would keep itself informed. To most people subscriptions of this sort would only differ in name from rates and taxes, and might be even more troublesome and vexatious. The tax-gatherer is an unpopular person ; but the blackmailer would be a greater nuisance.

The State differs from other associations in having the common good professedly as its end, and therefore—(1) in not being limited *a priori* to certain particular aspects of life,[1] and (2) in including all the inhabitants (except resident aliens) of the national territory, in some sense or other, in its membership. If we hold that the liberty of individuals in any real and positive sense[2] is one of the principal objects which the State ought to secure, then it is indispensable that the State should claim the right of interfering, where necessary, with the actions of voluntary associations. To concede a general " liberty of association " is to turn the liberty of the individual into a mere empty and meaningless form. The progress of individual liberty, in any real and positive sense, has meant to a great extent the emancipation of the individual from the absolute control of various associations, natural and artificial, against which the individual in many cases needs to be protected by the State. The family, the Church, the joint-stock company, the trade-union, the political club are all " associations," whose " liberties " often conflict with those of one another, and with the liberty of individuals who are and who are not their members. The abolition of slavery, and the legislative protection of children and of wives, are interferences with " the family " as that used to be understood. If heads of households are no longer allowed the same control over other members of the household which they exercised when the

---

[1] My meaning is that, prior to discussion and to an investigation of the teachings of experience, we must not assume (*a*) that the State ought only to concern itself with certain matters, nor (*b*) that it ought to concern itself with all ; for experience may show that some matters cannot conveniently be dealt with by any State, or by this or that particular State.

[2] See above, pp. 138, 139.

family was itself a little State—a State in germ—the independence of the family has certainly been diminished, but
in the interest of the liberty of individuals. Compulsory
education, compulsory vaccination, compulsory notification of
infectious diseases, etc., are infringements of the independence
of the family, but in the interest of the liberty—the real,
positive liberty—of the individuals who belong to the family,
and of others. If an individual has a certain minimum of
education and of protection from gross neglect and from
infectious disease secured to him, he is to that extent more
"free" to make what he can of his natural powers and of his
opportunities, than if he is entirely at the mercy of ignorant
parents, and of dirty, diseased, or fanatical neighbours.

The "liberty of the Church" has in past times meant that
churches, *i.e.* those in authority in them, have had a free hand
to rule over individuals as they chose. Such liberties restrict the
freedom of individuals in many ways, notably in respect of the
free expression of opinion, and in respect of such matters as
marriage and divorce. There is, however, an obvious difference between "the liberty of *the* Church," *i.e.* the power of
one great international organisation, whose system of ecclesiastical discipline is supported here and there by the organised
force of States, and the tolerated existence of what are called
different denominations, *i.e.* religious associations which do not
claim, or have been practically obliged to give up the claim, to
dictate *directly* the policy of the State in any matter. Such
associations may, of course, influence their own members and
others to use their rights as citizens in such a way as to further
the religious interests and the opinions of a particular sect in
matters of education, of prohibition of work and amusement
on certain days, and of various other legislative interferences
with the liberties of individuals in the interests, or supposed
interests, of morality ;[1] but such political influence of religious

---

[1] Those who argue against established churches on the ground that
the Christian religion should never be supported by the force of the
State are guilty of inconsistency, if they support the prohibition, *e.g.* of
trade or of theatrical performances on Sundays. Such prohibitions do
mean the State-establishment of Puritanic Christianity, and are an
infringement of the religious liberty of Jews, who observe their Sabbath
without State-help, and likewise of all non-Sabbatarians, whether
Christians or not. To provide by law that every one should have one
holiday in every seven, or any other number of, days, without specifying

bodies is of the same kind with the political influence of professedly political clubs, and of other associations for organising
and controlling the votes of electors.   I do not think it can be
laid down absolutely that the State ought never in any way to
interfere with "free churches," any more than that it ought
never to interfere with political clubs or humanitarian societies.
A charitable institution, for instance, might conceivably fill a
district with semi-criminal, semi-lunatic paupers, to the injury
of the community as a whole ; a so-called political club might
become a gang of conspirators to promote assassination ; and a
church might use an assumed power of inflicting supernatural
penalties in such a way as dangerously to control the political
and civil liberty of its members.[1]   No political society can
safely recognise any absolute right of private association among
its members ; for such private associations may conceivably
grow into what are practically separate States waging war,
from a vantage-ground, against the national existence.   It is
in this as in the general question of toleration : time, and
place, and experience of the past must decide what is best to
be done.   What will actually in any case be done will depend
mainly on the extent to which those, who happen to exercise
effective sovereignty, *fear* disturbance, or feel strong enough to
concede the toleration of contempt, or confident enough in the
general reasonableness of their fellow-citizens to recognise the
educative value of diverse associations for the promotion of
different and conflicting kinds of restraints on individual
liberty.

The name "Free Church," as already indicated,[2] is an interesting example of the ambiguities and contradictory suggestions

the day, would be a different matter, and would be the only consistent
course for those persons (probably very few in number) who *really* disapprove of all State-establishment and State-enforcement of any religion
whatever.   The *endowment* of churches is a separate question from the
establishment of religion.   But those who would take ancient endowments from churches, and use them for the support of schools, in which
religious doctrines of *any* kind are taught, are using the power of the
State to endow a certain kind of religion.

[1] To refuse to give legal recognition to religious vows (*French Constitution* of 1791) is to interfere with complete liberty of association, as well
as indirectly with complete freedom of contract ; monks or nuns who
repent of their vows will be protected against the associations to which
they have bound themselves.

[2] See above, p. 138.

in the word "free." In its most famous historical use, as the
official designation of the vigorous, militant, and in many ways
heroic religious body which originated in the Scottish Ecclesiastical Disruption of 1843, it represented a renewal of the same
claim which is asserted in the phrase "liberty of the Church,"
—a claim to be supported by the State, without recognising
any mutual obligation on the part of the ecclesiastical power
to obey the State, except in those matters which the ecclesiastical power itself decides to be the concern of the civil power.
It represented a renewal of the claim of the older Puritans,
not to be "tolerated," but to dictate directly to the State as
to what might be tolerated, and what might not.[1] Such
proud assertions tend to become meaningless when they are
made by a body which finds itself a minority of the population,
and by a body, however important, of dissenters, dissenting
from other dissenters. And so in course of time "free church,"
and even "Free" with a capital, may come to connote nothing
more than absence of direct connection with the State. In
French-speaking Protestant Switzerland, where there is a
tendency to that multiplication of sects which is often supposed to be a special characteristic of the English-speaking
peoples, there is a considerable religious body known as the
"Free" Church. It "sprang," says Mr. Vincent, in his
valuable work on *State and Federal Government in Switzerland*, "from an endeavour to gain freedom from State interference, and at the same time to maintain a stricter confession
of faith. It was, in reality, a protest within the Protestant
Church, and in Geneva and Vaud goes back to the time of the
abolition of the Helvetic Confession. In Neuchâtel it was a result of the ecclesiastical law of 1873, which made every citizen,
ipso facto, a member of the Church, and abolished all theological
tests for ministers."[2] In Neuchâtel and Geneva the liberty
of the conscience of the minister is declared inviolable by the
constitution,[3] and against this liberty the "Free" Church is a

[1] Hallam, *Const. Hist.* p. 142 ("World Library" edition), has pointed
out the striking resemblance between the demand of Cartwright, that the
civil magistrate should, "as the prophet speaketh, lick the dust of the feet
of the church," and the ecclesiastical theory of Pope Gregory VII. The
original position of the Scotch "Free Church" has been similarly described by its critics as that of Protestant Ultramontanism (with an interesting oblivion of the *original* sense of the latter word).

[2] *Ibid.*, p. 176.   [3] *Ibid.*, p. 180.

protest. A similar dislike to the liberty of the conscience of the minister may, occasionally, be found as a motive in the making and continuance of " free " churches elsewhere than in Switzerland.

Commercial companies have generally grown up to some extent under the protection of the State. Great trading or industrial enterprises, as a rule, require the interference of the State on their behalf, *e.g.* in order to enforce contracts, to secure protection in foreign countries, to obtain compulsory power of purchase of land, etc. ; and the State has thus an easy means of restricting the liberty of companies, in return for the advantages it confers on them. As has been generally recognised, there is a much stronger case for the State to interfere on behalf of employees with the " liberty " of companies on which it has conferred special privileges, than with the " liberty " of private individuals whose commercial or industrial enterprises are not aided by the State in any special way. The right of the State to regulate the hours of railway servants —apart from reasons of public safety—has been recognised by those who still feel doubtful about the expediency or justice of any general attempt to fix a maximum working-day by law. In protecting shareholders against fraud or culpable neglect on the part of directors and promoters, in protecting the general public against the tyranny of companies which have, whether by law or by the operation of economic causes, a monopoly in the supply of any particular commodity or service, and in bringing under more direct State-control, or even under immediate State management (I include administration by municipalities or other local bodies invested with power by the Central Government), enterprises which it has become sufficiently convenient for the State to undertake—in such extensions of State control over joint-enterprises, for the sake of individual liberty, and in the interests of the general wellbeing, lies much work for political energy in the immediate future.

Trade-Unions have fought their way through persecution to toleration. From an evil to be suppressed, they have become, in the eyes of politicians, a necessary evil, or even a beneficial institution. As benefit societies, as teachers of a spirit of co-operation, however limited and narrow, their value is generally admitted. Even as instruments of industrial warfare, their advantages are widely acknowledged; it is always easier to deal with an organised body of men than with an unorganised mass. Trade-unionism, still, means warfare; but it is the civilised warfare of disciplined armies, not of irregulars, banditti, or savages. But what of the attitude of the militant Unionist towards the "free labourer"? The State has the obvious duty of protecting even those whom the Unionist calls "blacklegs" against anything like physical compulsion on the part of the Unionist—by the use of military force where necessary. Unless or until Trade-Unions have become absorbed by government departments (in which case a strike would be punishable as a mutiny by military law), the Trade-Unionist can make no legitimate claim to use any weapon but persuasion against the non-Unionist; and if it is in the public interest that some particular industry should be carried on, the State has the duty imposed upon it of protecting by all the necessary force those engaged in carrying on that industry against the interference of Unionist strikers. If the State cannot successfully protect individuals against any Union or combination of Unions, regular government has broken down, and the country is at the mercy of a revolutionary usurpation, ruling by terrorism. In any given case, one may sympathise with the Unionist striker, or with the "blackleg"; but, as I have said, so long as the Unions are not directly responsible to national control, the State as such is bound to be impartial. The assumption, too readily sanctioned even by some responsible statesmen, that military force is not justifiably used in repressing *disorder*, is an unfortunate inheritance from the time when military force was freely used by despotical governments to prevent the free expression of *opinion*.

Some Trade-Unionists seem to take for granted that because Trade-Unions have undoubtedly improved the conditions of life, and raised the standard of living among a large portion of the population, an extension of Unionism, and a greater support of Unions in case of strikes by public opinion, constitute the true or, at least, the chief solution of our economic and social difficulties. There is this fatal objection to such an idea:— A Trade-Union must either include all the workers of a given trade, or only some; and all the Trade-Unions of the country must either include all the workers or only some. At present the unions exclude a great number of the workers,[1] and it is against these excluded workmen far more than against the employers that the struggle in a strike or lock-out is really carried on. By using persuasion (accompanied or not by threats of violence) towards non-unionists, or by refusing to work along with them, unionists seek to compel employers to accept their terms, *i.e.* they artificially produce the same effect as would be produced by the death or emigration of the workmen competing with them for employment. It is true that in such struggles it is " the fittest " (in the biologist's sense) who survive, and in this case " the fittest " generally means those who have most skill and most steadiness of character, though not necessarily so in every instance. The effect of a successful strike for higher and steadier wages is often to supplant a larger body of irregularly employed and unorganised workmen by a smaller body, more regularly employed. The diminution of casual employment is undoubtedly a gain in many ways, but it increases the number of the unemployed. Suppose, on the other hand, that the unions include all the workers in all the industries of a country—I pass over the obvious difficulty of unemployed and casual labourers paying their subscriptions regularly—and that the unions are federated together into one vast industrial association, it will follow that, for many purposes, such an industrial association will have become practically the State itself. But this association will acquire the responsibilities along with the advantages of the State. Is every one born in the country (even if foreign immigrants are rigorously excluded) to be, by the mere fact of his existence, entitled to have work and subsistence found for him, however incapable he may be? A continually increasing population does increase to some extent the demand for commodities, but will, in course of time, press more heavily on the resources of the country. And if immigrants are excluded, other countries will probably

---

[1] According to the best calculations, the Trade-Unionists of England and Wales number only 20 per cent. of the adult male manual-working population, only 4 per cent. of the total population. Even in the exceptional counties of Northumberland and Durham, where Trade-Unionism flourishes most, the Trade-Unionists number only 11·23 and 11·24 per cent. of the population, whereas adult male manual-workers are reckoned at 18 per cent. of the population; so that even there more than one-third of the working men are non-unionists (see Mr. and Mrs. Sidney Webb's *History of Trade-Unionism*, pp. 409–413).

retaliate and prevent the relief hitherto obtained by emigration. The Industrial Federation of united unions will thus be
face to face with the population difficulty, but such an Industrial Federation will not be able to deal with that difficulty,
nor with any of the problems of production and distribution
that will arise, unless it ceases to be a mere congeries of " voluntary" associations, and becomes openly a State able to enforce
and maintain a rigid discipline and a sacrifice of individual
aims and likings, such as hitherto has only existed in the army
and the navy, and in some of the strictest of monastic orders.

Very many Trade-Unionists do not yet sufficiently recognise
that the ultimate outcome of their policy is a Socialistic State;
and I doubt if any of them recognise at all the absolute necessity for a very severe discipline in the industrial armies of the
future. Such a transformation of Trade-Unions from associations of particular groups of producers into a highly organised
State is, however, not likely to take place by a one-sided development. If on the one side Trade-Unions approximate more to the
conditions of political organisations, with responsibilities to the
common good of all, on the other side the State will probably
meet them half-way. If a social re-organisation is to take
place without violence, and in such a way as to be fairly
stable, it must come about gradually; a sudden change would
probably mean gross mismanagement, corruption, disorder—
possibly civil war, and a terrible reaction. The State which is
to undertake responsibilities such as no State has yet attempted
to undertake, must be free from jobbery or the suspicion of
jobbery, and its citizens must possess sufficient enlightenment
and a sufficient spirit of obedience for the sake of the common
good to subordinate personal or sectional ambitions and pre-
ferences to the decision of experts—responsible indeed to the
community, but allowed a tolerably free hand, like generals
in command of an army in the field. Trade-Unionism, with
all its defects, its narrowness of outlook and disregard for
interests outside the material well-being of special sections of
producers as such, does supply part, though a small part, of
the necessary training in obedience and discipline which alone
can make anything like a Socialistic State possible.

It is a delusion to suppose that shorter hours, whether obtained by the efforts of Trade-Unions, or by legislation, or by
a combination of both means, will lead to a solution of the diffi-

culty of the unemployed. Higher wages and shorter hours—
if the wages are to be *really* higher, *i.e.* capable of purchasing
more commodities—will lead to the use of more machinery,
and not, directly at least, to the employment of more men;
and a greater demand for machinery can only to a small extent, if at all, increase the demand for labour. The present
system of Trade-Unions supplemented by legislative restric-
tion of hours of labour cannot do away with the difficulty of
obtaining employment, but may even increase it. But though
not solving the problem, Trade-Unionism may help to put it
in a form more capable of solution. Anything that diminishes
casual and irregular employment makes the class of the unemployed a more definite body, with which the State may more
easily hope to deal; and the more sharply defined line between
the more capable and the more incapable portion of the population may prepare public opinion for those stringent, though
beneficent, measures by which alone the pauper class can be
prevented from injuring the more vigorous section of the race.
If subsistence is to be guaranteed by the State to all its
members, the unemployed must, if capable of it, be set to work;
but this work must not compete in the labour market with
that of those already in employment, else the suffering is only
shifted from one set of individuals to another. The unemployed, if cared for by the State, must be treated as, for industrial purposes, a separate and isolated community, whose more
capable members may, when occasion arises, be drafted into
the ranks of the regular and organised workers;[1] and, as
already argued, there must be some check on the increase of
the population by State-pensioners. If such powers of control
are refused to the State by the moral sentiments or prejudices
of the community, the State may reasonably refuse to deal with
these economic difficulties.

I have ventured to refer thus briefly to one of the most
difficult of social questions—what is very often called *the* social

Cf. Charles Booth, *Life and Labour of the People*, Ed. 2, Vol. 1, pp.
165-168. Mr. Booth does not shrink from using the word "State-slavery"
as a name for the only form in which the problem can be dealt with.
One thinks of Fletcher of Saltoun's proposal to dispose of paupers as
slaves in the "plantations and at home." See his *Second Discourse on
the Affairs of Scotland* (*Works*, p. 146-149, Ed. of 1737). The moral
objections to slavery, where slaves were private property, are not applicable to State-slavery in Mr. Booth's sense.

question—in order to illustrate the impossibility of dealing
with "the rights of associations" without considering the
general question of the relation of the State to individuals;
and to show how an unlimited liberty of association is incompatible with the very existence of the State. The State itself
is the only association whose liberty cannot be limited by the
State.

ONE of the most important rights of individuals is generally supposed to be the right to enter into contracts with other individuals, and the most important function of the State, according to the theories of those who most seek to minimise its functions, is supposed to be the enforcement by law courts of obligations arising out of contract. The famous theory which explains political obligation as dependent on *the* social contract is, in one aspect of it, an illogical generalisation of this notion about the functions of government—illogical, because contracts are the product of political society, which cannot therefore be based upon a contract. To try to escape this argument by substituting the term social pact, or compact, for the legal term contract, is a mere evasion; for the social pact is assumed to be as binding as if it were a contract that could be enforced, or rather it is assumed to be much more binding than any particular contract depending on it. An alleged natural right of freedom of contract is meaningless, if it be implied that a State ought to recognise a right in its members to enter into contracts of every possible kind, and should undertake to enforce these contracts. Such an absolute right to freedom of contract would require the State to enforce an obligation to commit crimes and to rebel against itself; but this is anarchical and absurd. It is generally recognised, even by the staunchest upholders of the sanctity of contracts, that the State may prohibit or refuse to recognise contracts of certain kinds. Such an admission implies of course that the State exists for other purposes than simply for the enforcement of contracts: it implies that the State has the right of restricting individual liberty in various ways, even where no contract has been broken, and of discouraging certain kinds of contract by the refusal of legal remedies. If the State may prohibit or dis-

courage certain kinds of contracts, it is admitted (though it
may be unconsciously) that the State has a moral function,
and may rightly endeavour to bias its members in favour of
certain kinds of conduct and against others, which is, after all,
the only way in which the State ever can be said to try "to
make people moral."

But if a State has not prohibited a contract of a certain
kind, may the State never by any legislative or judicial or
executive proceedings interfere with and impair the obligations
to which that contract has given rise? If it may not, great
hardships may undoubtedly be inflicted on individuals, and
the disastrous result follows that courts of justice will be
obliged to enforce what public sentiment may consider to be
injustice; law may come into conflict with what is approved
of by the average conscience of the community, and the habit
of respect for law and of obedience to it may be seriously
weakened. If, on the other hand, the State may interfere with
the enforcement of contract-obligations, which the State itself
has sanctioned, is not the feeling of security which is one of the
primary benefits derived from good government, and which we
are told is one of the natural rights of man, very seriously im-
paired, and a bad example of dishonesty set to the community?
Now, it is obvious that to interfere with the obligation arising
out of a contract already made under public sanction is, on these
grounds of honesty and general security, a much more disput-
able policy than the prohibition of certain kinds of contract.
But an absolute respect for all contracts, not previously prohibited, may be a sacrifice of public well-being, and even of
the very existence of the community, to the letter of formal
legality. Circumstances may have changed so that the enforcement of a contract undertaken with full deliberation and
on equal terms becomes a practical injustice; or it may come
to be recognised that the contract, though in appearance a
contract freely entered into, was practically a compulsory
submission of the weaker to the stronger, and that its strict
enforcement would do more harm, not merely because of the
material suffering it may cause, but because of the detestation
of law and order which it may excite, than a departure from
the general rule of holding people to their legal obligations.
No cut and dried rule can be laid down: time, place, and circumstances must determine the manner and degree in which

the State may wisely and safely impair the obligation of contracts.

The Constitution of the United States of America is often held up as an example in contrast to recent legislation in this country, because of the greater sanctity which it recognises in contract obligations. Our critics, especially our American critics, are perhaps apt to forget the difference of circumstances between an old country, with a very complex society and a very chaos of ancient customs and institutions, on the one hand, and a new country, with, until recently, free space for individual enterprise—a country which made a fresh start after a revolution only a little over a hundred years ago. The time may come when social needs and changing ideals may compel the people of the United States to impair some contract obligations, which are enforced at present. And to do this, they need not delete the section (Art. I. § 10) which prohibits laws impairing the obligation of contracts: for that prohibition only applies to the States. The Federal Congress is not prohibited from infringing vested interests or violating the obligation of contracts in regard to any of those matters in which the constitution empowers it to legislate ; *e.g.* the Federal Congress may make laws releasing debtors from their obligations, whereas the States are (wisely perhaps) prohibited from doing so.[1] If equity or public security seemed to require an infringement of legal obligation in some matter over which Congress has not control (*e.g.* the land laws of a State), it might be safer to extend the powers of Congress by an amendment to the constitution in that respect, than to give State legislatures too free a hand. The difficulty of amending the Federal Constitution at all may, indeed, put serious delays in the way of necessary legislation.

The "free labourer," who is the object of dislike to the militant Trade-Unionist, may be regarded as a person who asserts the natural right to dispose of his labour as he chooses, *i.e.* who demands the protection of the State in order that he may have this freedom. This right of freedom in the disposal of labour is expressly asserted in the French Declaration of 1793. In article 18 it is provided that " Every man may engage his services and his time, but he cannot sell himself, or be sold ; his person is not an alienable property. The law does not

---

[1] *Desty's Federal Constitution,* p. 81.

recognise the condition of servitude (*domesticité*) ";[1] while personal bondage is excluded, the right of perfectly free contract between employer and employed is recognised. Such a principle, if strictly carried out, would of course prevent any legislative interference with the hours or the conditions of labour, and would certainly require the State to put a considerable check on the freedom of Trade-Unions in boycotting blacklegs, or in doing anything beyond endeavouring to persuade free labourers, by logical or rhetorical arguments, not to undertake work on conditions unfavourable to themselves or to other workers in the same trade. The evident purpose of this and some other articles in the French Declaration was to get rid of restrictions, whether due to legislation or to the customary privileges of guilds, etc., on the free movement of labour. The ideal was "a career open to talents"—complete negative liberty. This is the *droit du travail*: the *droit au travail* is the positive right to get work found for one.

A subsequent article (21) in the same Declaration recognises the right of citizens to subsistence in the following form: "Public relief (*les secours publics*) is a sacred debt. Society owes subsistence to *unfortunate* citizens, either by procuring work for them, or by assuring the means of existence to those who are not capable of working." In the Jacobin draft this principle is expressed in somewhat stronger language: "Society is obliged to provide for the subsistence of *all* its members, either by procuring work for them, or etc."—as before. The form adopted was apparently a compromise between the Jacobin form and the draft of Condorcet, which says nothing about the procuring of work, though recognising that "Public relief is a sacred debt."

In the Declaration of 1848, it is asserted (art. 8) that the Republic "ought by fraternal help to assure the existence of necessitous citizens, either by procuring work for them, within the limits of its resources, or by giving, where the family cannot (or does not?) do so [the words are *à défaut de la famille*], assistance to those who are incapable of working." The wording is somewhat vague. What is to be done with those who *will* not work, though able to do so? And what is to limit the power of the government to find work for the unem-

---

[1] Practically identical in Condorcet's draft. Cf. Lord Halsbury's words quoted in Chap. I. p. 15.

ployed? May it increase taxation, for instance, in order to provide unremunerative work, or does "the limits of its resources" imply that taxation should not be increased for this reason alone, and that the work ought to be remunerative? If the work is to be remunerative, how is competition to be avoided in a market which is proved to be already overcrowded by the mere existence of unemployed labourers?

It may be necessary to repeat what has often been pointed out, but is still generally ignored, that the experiment of national workshops in 1848 was an experiment tried under most unfair conditions and managed by persons who did not wish it to succeed: the failure of this experiment is of itself no argument against the State undertaking the responsibility of providing work. But a careful consideration of those questions, which are suggested by the cautious but ambiguous wording of the Declaration, calls attention to some of the difficulties involved. In the long run, we always come face to face with the ultimate problem: Can a State, without the certain prospect of ultimate disaster, undertake to provide work and a satisfactory subsistence (judged by the average standard of living at present) for *all* its members, without taking some security against an indefinite increase of population, and against a disproportionate increase of the less capable part of the population?[1]

[1] Charles Mackay sings:—

> "There's a good time coming, boys,
>   A good time coming;
> And a poor man's family
> Shall not be his misery
>   In the good time coming.
> Every child shall be a help,
>   To make his right arm stronger;
> The happier he the more he has;—
>   Wait a little longer."

Such a sentiment is meaningless and foolish except under the conditions of a new and thinly peopled country. If the resource of emigration be largely diminished, through the filling up of new countries, and through the policy dictated by the wage-receivers there, and if the right of every one to subsistence and, if he *can* work, and will work, or has worked as long as he could, to a *comfortable* subsistence, be legally conceded,—a continuous increase in population must mean a continuous, not necessarily an exactly proportionate, lowering of the standard of comfort.

A "free country," or a "free people," may mean that the government is of a more or less democratic kind, but it may only mean that the country is not under the rule of any foreign power. Wordsworth lamented the extinction of the Venetian Republic and the conquest of Switzerland by the French; but the Venetian Republic was a close and tyrannical oligarchy, and the establishment of the Helvetian Republic by the help of French arms was a liberation of the people of Vaud and Ticino from the oppression of the German cantons. Those Poles who have come under the sway of Russia have gained nothing and lost a great deal; but the liberty of Poland meant the liberties of an aristocratic caste who showed particularly little capacity for governing—to say nothing about governing well. A people may often prefer to be ill-governed by rulers of their own race, to whom they are accustomed, rather than to be governed much better by aliens. The resistance of Spain to Napoleon is a typical example. And in the long run it is generally best that a people who have too strong sentiments of nationality to be readily assimilated even by a higher form of civilisation, should work out their political and social problems for themselves. Progress may be very much slower, but it is likely to be more steady and more secure.

The question, however, arises: In what sense has a nation, a country—that is to say, a particular group of people—a right to freedom, in the sense of independence? In other words, how far can we suppose that other nations are morally bound (of any other obligation it is superfluous to speak) to respect the independence of a particular nation? Suppose this nation is in a chronic state of disorder, that laws are not enforced, or that there is so much oppression that discontented and persecuted persons are always endeavouring to cross the frontier, may not neighbouring nations have "a right" to interfere—even on behalf of the inhabitants of the country itself? Or suppose that the territory possessed by a particular race or nation is fertile and full of natural resources, but that owing to misgovernment or backwardness in civilisation these natural resources are left undeveloped; may not neighbouring nations with an overflowing population capable of utilising these natural resources be thought to have a right to seize such of this territory as is convenient for them?

I do not think there is much profit in discussing the morality of aggression without taking account of the fact that, under such circumstances as I have supposed, neighbouring nations are certain to avail themselves of convenient opportunities for enlarging their territory and increasing the advantages of their members. And where aggression is undertaken because of disorderliness or great misgovernment, which makes a neighbouring country a breeding ground of criminals haunting the frontier, or a breeding ground of pestilences, aggression may very reasonably be held to be a kind of police-measure and a legitimate form of self-defence.

Professor Lorimer, in his interpretation of the Law of Nature, speaks of a "natural right of aggression." "Aggression," he says, "is a Natural Right, the extent of which is measured by the power which God has bestowed on the aggressor or permitted him to develop."[1] This seems to me a very much more logical and consistent application of the idea of nature, than is to be found in most theories of natural rights. Natural right is here determined simply by might or power, as in the theory of Spinoza. It should of course be carefully noted that "power" does not mean simply what is called "brute force," but all those intellectual and moral qualities which are implied in greater strategic skill, greater discipline, and, above all, in the power of keeping possession of territory seized by war and of turning a conquered population into orderly and peaceable subjects or fellow-citizens. Such a recognition of a natural right of aggression is often strongly objected to by those who see nothing wrong in a trade-union striking to secure better terms for its own members, when a favourable opportunity occurs, even though a strike necessarily involves much suffering to many individuals other than the strikers themselves. But the principle in either case is the same—the action, so far as it is justified, can be justified only on the grounds of its success and on the better condition of some very considerable number of human beings which results from that success.

It is important to note that such a right of aggression depends on the superiority in civilisation of the conquering power—that is to say, it is assumed that the nations concerned are not treated as equals. Where it has become convenient

---

[1] *Institutes of Law.* I quote from the "Contents" of Book II., chap. 5.

and customary, as it has among the civilised powers of
Christendom, to assume the diplomatic equality of powers
whose military and other resources are very unequal, there is
also the feeling that aggression as such is not justifiable, and
that war is only justifiable if entered upon for what may
plausibly be considered the purpose of self-defence. But it is
of course very easy to give "defence" a wide interpretation.
For a nation under all circumstances to wait until it is attacked
may mean to give such an advantage in carrying on war to
the assailant, that the nation may lose its independence, or that
some portion of it may be annexed by a less scrupulous neighbour.[1]

As to instances of the use of force by civilised over barbarous
or savage peoples, it is cheap virtue to call them "international burglaries," and a very misleading use of language.
The word burglary can only be used metaphorically in cases
where there is no common criminal law to which both parties
are subject; and the use of the term involves a naïve acceptance of the *status quo*, analogous to what is implied in calling
any legislative interference with ancient rights of property
"confiscation" or "theft." People who are ready to advocate
the disendowment of an Established Church have very little
right to call the conquest of India or the invasion of Egypt
acts of burglary. They ought to leave that language to those
who call any readjustment of the ancient endowments of corporations a "robbery of God." A savage or barbarous people,
misgoverned by some ferocious or incapable tyrant, cannot be
regarded, except conventionally, for some special purpose of
international convenience, as an independent nation in the
same sense as one of the great powers of Europe. In the
interests of humanity we can recognise no absolute right in
all governments, however bad, never to be interfered with.
We laugh at the Divine Right of Kings, claimed by Stuarts

Did the French Republic, in 1792, enter on a war of aggression, or
of self-defence? Did Prussia, in 1870, enter on a war of aggression, or of
self-defence? Even the peace-loving Mr. Herbert Spencer speaks of
territories taken from the French "in punishment for their aggressive-
ness" (*Principles of Ethics*, Vol. I. p. 318). He assumes apparently
that nothing can be said against the view that Germany in taking Alsace
and Lorraine was simply recovering stolen goods. How far a province
may have been assimilated by a conqueror is a matter your abstract
thinker does not dream of considering.

or Bourbons; but the natural right of a king of Dahomey, or of every robber chief or murderous pasha, to be left undisturbed by all civilised nations, is at least quite as absurd. There would be more reason for arguing that there is a natural right inherent in all men to be governed well—an idea suggested by the language of the French Declarations, which are Declarations of the rights of *men* as well as of citizens. And it is good government that alone legitimises conquest; but it does legitimise it in the minds of those who are prepared to think out questions of right and wrong in the light of actual human experience and not of arbitrary and *a priori* principles or prejudices.

I do not mean to suggest that the dealings of civilised nations with uncivilised or less civilised races present no difficult moral problems. All that I mean to insist on is, that a general principle of non-intervention, based on an assumed inalienable natural right of every group of human beings that may call itself an independent tribe or people, is of no use whatever for practical guidance. It is an unworkable principle, and it is a wrong principle. A nation acts unwisely, and therefore wrongly, if it undertakes responsibilities which it cannot properly fulfil and which it could have avoided. It is wrong to interfere, if we cannot reasonably hope to leave things in a better condition than that in which we found them—a better condition for the *individuals* whose national or tribal independence has been interfered with. But it is absurd and misleading to class all interferences under the same general condemnation; it is a transference to foreign affairs of the abstract belief in *laissez faire*. The contact of higher and lower races, especially where the gap between them is great, often forms one of the most unpleasant and saddest parts of history; but the contact is likely to be more disastrous in its consequences where it comes simply through the irresponsible action of private adventurers, than where a certain measure of order and security and systematic administration of justice is bestowed on a people in lieu of the right of being left a prey to native despots and slave-raiders. Lovers of peace ought to show due gratitude to the *pax Romana*,[1] which gave Europe a time of quiet such as it has never enjoyed since the Empire fell to pieces, and to the *pax Britannica*, which would come to a speedy end were India left to the Indians. "India for the Indians," indeed, may serve as a good specimen of those cant phrases which are used so freely as rhetorical substitutes for argument. There may be an Indian nationality some day; if there is, its existence will be due to British rule and its language will, in all probability, be the English tongue.

Closely connected with this subject of national or tribal independence or liberty is the "right" by which a State may claim to reserve the territory it possesses for the exclusive use of the present inhabitants and their descendants—the right to prevent or restrict immigration. It is clear that there is no sense in talking about a general natural right on the part of every human being to go and settle in any part of the world he chooses; the right will depend on whether other nations wish to have him or, if they do not, on whether they can manage to keep him out. In the past, when facilities for movement were much less than they are now, countries which served as an asylum for the persecuted have generally profited greatly by the folly of their neighbours in weeding out many of the most vigorous minds and characters in the nation. When a country, however, is fairly well filled and has a sufficiently mixed stock already, it may reasonably refuse to help to solve the problem of pauperism for other lands.[1] The country which excludes desirable immigrants, on the other hand, will suffer for it in the long run. And the need of an outlet for a vigorous and overflowing population may become so urgent as to break down barriers against immigration defended by too scanty hands.

Here indeed we come upon the other side of the population

only along with this change has the sentiment of justice become more pronounced." A fighting people is not necessarily a legislating people; but does Mr. Spencer know of any great governing people which has not shown its capacity for conquest *and for retaining its conquests?*

[1] The United States of America have already given up their right to the once famous boast that their—

"Free latch-string never was drawed in
Against the poorest child of Adam's kin."

The rights of the existing citizens are now asserted against any general rights of man.

question. It may be argued that, if the more civilised races were to become stationary in numbers, the world might be overrun by the lower races. Those who use this argument are apt to forget two things—first, that the quality of a race is more important than mere numbers. A swarming population of hereditary paupers is no gain to the country that is burdened with their support. Secondly, a *race* may even dwindle, and yet its type of civilisation may be successfully imposed on immigrants of other races, so that the *nation* increases. France attracts numerous immigrants from neighbouring countries, but the Frenchman need not be despondent about the future of his country so long as he turns them all into Frenchmen, as he has hitherto always succeeded in doing.

Exclusion of immigrants, if allowed to be in some cases a justifiable policy, is, it should be clearly recognised, quite inconsistent with any sincere admission of the equality of all human beings, or with any natural right of all to share in the gifts of nature. It is inconsistent also when those, who object to the immigration of labourers who will lower the standard of living, object to the endeavour of trade-unions to exclude from employment free labourers of their own country who will lower the standard in a similar way. There is indeed this difference in favour of the former policy over the latter, that a nation *may*, with an honest government, decide the question at least in the light of the whole nation, taking into account the probable effects of its policy on the treatment of its own citizens in foreign countries affected by this policy, while a trade-union is very unlikely to consider anything except the obvious and apparent interests of its own members, and may even leave out of sight the effects of its policy on the price of commodities and consequently on the ultimate *real* wage even of its own members. Both endeavours, however, that of a nation and that of a trade-union, to keep up the standard of living are irreconcilable with any doctrine of natural rights, except such as frankly recognises the connection between natural right and the power of getting one's own way.

THE French Declaration of 1789 names among "the natural and imprescriptible rights of man," whose maintenance is the end of all political society, not only the rights of liberty, of property, of security, but the right of resistance to oppression. The Declaration of 1793 asserts that "Resistance to oppression is the consequence of the other rights of man" (art. 33). The following article gives what appears to be intended for a definition of "oppression," but it is somewhat more epigrammatic than lucid. "There is oppression of the social body when any single member of it is oppressed : there is oppression of every member when the social body is oppressed." This statement really implies a theory of the relations of society to the individual that is fundamentally inconsistent with the individualistic view of society implied in the whole doctrine of natural rights. The 35th and last article of the Declaration is as follows: "When the government violates the rights of the people, insurrection is for the people and for every portion of the people the most sacred of rights and the most indispensable of duties." "Resistance to oppression" might indeed be used to mean simply legal remedies against illegal or arbitrary action on the part of officials; and doubtless that was part of what the framers of these Declarations were thinking of. And it is a reasonable demand that a Constitution should provide individuals with legal means of defending those rights which the Constitution professes to guarantee to them. But the last article of the Declaration of 1793 gives a wider meaning to the term "resistance." That a Constitution should provide means for its own amendment is essential, if it is not by claiming eternity to provoke revolution; and it is expedient that the delays and difficulties of the amending process should not be such as to make amendment seem practically impossible. Some of the American Declarations indeed assert that the people "have *at all times* an inalienable and indefeasible right to alter, reform, or abolish [Query, without substituting anything in its place?] their form of government in such manner as they may think expedient."[1]   Between "at all times" and "never," or "at very long intervals," a mean is often deemed expedient.   But such a right of constitutional amendment by constitutional means is a very different thing from a constitutional guarantee of the right of overthrowing the government by the use of force.   Such a constitutional right of insurrection is the most anarchical and contradictory notion that it ever entered into the heart of man to conceive.   Even the vaguer right of resistance to oppression is left out of the Declaration of 1795, for obvious reasons of historical experience.   As Bentham remarks, " Between 1791 and 1795 Citizen Resistance-against-Oppression had been playing strange tricks."[2]

It would be very unjust, however, to suppose, as is frequently done, that this notion of a right of resistance was the outcome merely of French political inexperience.   As asserted in the Declaration of 1789, it may be regarded as only a repetition of the right which is asserted in the American Declaration of Independence, and the right there claimed is nothing more than had been recognised and defended by Locke in his *Treatise of Civil Government*—the theoretical defence of the English Revolution of 1688.   The American Declaration of Independence is, however, a Declaration of war, and is hardly therefore the best model for a Declaration of those Rights which are to be guaranteed by a Constitution.   To find a genuine parallel to the constitutional recognition of a right of resistance we must go back to times when the idea of the State was in a very rudimentary stage—to such documents as the "Golden Bull" of King Andrew (A.D. 1222), which concedes, while like *Magna Charta* only professing to confirm, the special privileges of the Hungarian nobility.   "Should we," it is written, "or any of our successors, at any time be disposed to infringe upon any of these our orders, the bishops, as well as the other lords and the nobles of the realm, shall be at liberty, jointly or singly, by virtue of this letter, to oppose and contradict us and our successors, for ever, without incurring the penalty of

---

[1] "Declaration of Rights," in Constitution of Alabama, 1809.
[2] *Anarchical Fallacies*, in *Works* (1843), II. p. 525.

treason."[1]   Such a method of imposing a check on oppression
is only a degree less primitive than the letter of King Ahasu-
erus, in which he permits the Jews to massacre those whom he
had previously permitted to massacre them[2]—violence checked
by counter-violence.   In a written constitution of the modern
type, it is, however, an anomaly and an absurdity to recognise
a right which, strictly interpreted, would make government
impossible, a right which contradicts the fundamental notion
of sovereignty.   Rousseau's teaching about the sovereignty of
the people is often made responsible for the anarchical theories
of some of the French revolutionary leaders, but those who
thought they derived a right of insurrection from Rousseau
proved themselves unintelligent disciples; for on Rousseau's
theory there is no sense in claiming the right of insurrection.
If a people throw off a tyrannical government it is an act of
sovereignty; and to call it an "insurrection" involves the
assumption that the government is the sovereign, which it
never can be, on Rousseau's theory, except by usurpation.
Such a usurping government should be called a "rebel," and
punished as such.   This theory may seem strange; but at least
it is logical, which the guarantee of a right of insurrection is
not.   It is, indeed, only a Constitution like the present Federal
Constitution of Switzerland, with its *referendum* on all constitutional changes, and potentially on all laws, that gives any
security for the smooth and quiet working of a *legal* sovereignty
of the people.[3]

Those, indeed, who accepted what may be called the Hilde-
brandine theory of the Papal power, may be said to have made
the Church, *i.e.*, for convenience, or in explicit theory, the
Pope, the only true sovereign over all Christian peoples.   The
justification of resistance to tyrants (even of assassination of
tyrants, when necessary) by many mediæval theologians and
by some Jesuit casuists (in reference to Protestant rulers, of
course) always rests on the assumption that the Pope can decide
who is and who is not a "tyrant."   When allegiance to the
Pope is thrown off, every one is left to decide for himself what
constitutes the "tyranny" or "oppression" that justifies resist-

[1] Vambéry, *Hungary* ("Story of the Nations" Series), p. 130.
[2] See *The Book of Esther*.
[3] On this subject I may be allowed to refer to an Essay on "The Conception of Sovereignty," in my *Darwin and Hegel, etc.*

ance, and thus, although morally resistance may seem perfectly justifiable and necessary, the appearance of legality, that might seem to cling to it in the minds of those who accepted the Pope's deposing power, has altogether disappeared.

If indeed a Constitution be thought of as a Compact, there is considerable plausibility in regarding the "insurrection" of one of the parties to the compact as constitutionally justified by the failure of the other party to perform his (or its) part of the compact—the party that considers itself aggrieved claiming the right to judge when the compact is broken. It was by appealing to this notion of a contract between King and People that the English Convention Parliament justified the Revolution of 1688.[1] The idea of a contract between King and People was very widely held in the middle ages, and frequently received a sort of express recognition in the form of the coronation oath. The theory, like many other illogical theories, has been practically very useful in helping the cause of political liberty; but the very fact that it gives a quasi-constitutional sanction to rebellion is a refutation of its claims to represent the true legal theory of a Constitution.

There is no doubt that the theory of the United States Constitution of 1787 as a Compact between Sovereign States was widely held at the time the Constitution was framed; and if it had not been a plausible interpretation of the Constitution, several of the States might have been more reluctant than they were to give up the more independent position which they held under the original Confederation. And I think it must be granted that there is a greater appearance of constitutional *legality* in the South Carolina Declaration of Independence of 1860 than there is in the Declaration of Independence of the Thirteen Colonies in 1776. The Thirteen Colonies could only appeal to natural rights and to abstract principles, inherited from the theories of Locke and others: South Carolina appealed, in addition, to a definite written agreement actually formed between sovereign States—the terms of which agree-

---

[1] Even Grotius, who rejects the idea that there is any general natural right of resistance, allows a right of resistance when a prince has abdicated, or when he is manifestly bearing himself as the enemy of his whole people.—*De Jure Belli et Pacis*, I., c. iv. §§ 8 *seq.* The English Revolution of 1688 might fairly be brought under the sanction of his principles.

ment had, it was alleged, been broken.[1] Furthermore, whereas the majority of the Colonies, when they renounced their allegiance to the British Crown, had to frame for themselves new Constitutions and all of them had to make themselves from dependencies into States which previously had no legal existence as such, South Carolina, in seceding, was simply retaining her existing constitution and resuming the position she actually had occupied in 1787. The better legal theory of the United States Constitution undoubtedly rejects the view that it is a Compact: it is not made by the " United States," but by "the *People* of the United States"—a sovereign body that had no existence in the Confederation of 1777. The fortune of war confirmed the interpretation adopted by the Supreme Court; and events revealed that an American Nation had grown up in a sense which the particularism of the South had not realised. But, still, there was a very plausible case for the *constitutional* right of secession—more plausible than could be alleged for many rebellions where the moral duty of rebellion seems clear and where the appeal court of history has condoned the want of legal right. For legality and morality, legal rights and political or historical facts, are often very different things. And the gravest objection to the whole theory of natural rights is, that it is always tending to confuse the two sets of notions, by representing what may on occasion be moral duties as legal or quasi-legal rights, and by concealing under such ambiguous terms as "can" and "cannot" the difference between "ought" and "is," or between "wish" and

---

[1] The South Carolina Declaration of Independence, after referring to the Declaration of Independence of the Colonies, which asserted their existence as sovereign and independent States, to the recognition of the United States as sovereign and independent States by Great Britain in 1783, and to the formation of the Constitution of 1787 by the sovereign States, proceeds as follows: " We hold that the government thus established is subject to the two great principles asserted in the Declaration of Independence [viz. the right of a State to govern itself and the right of a people to abolish a government when it becomes destructive of the ends for which it was instituted], and we hold further that the mode of its formation subjects it to a third fundamental principle, namely, the law of compact. We maintain that in every compact between two or more parties the obligation is mutual—that the failure of one of the contracting parties to perform a material part of the agreement entirely releases the obligation of the other, and that, where no arbiter is appointed, each party is remitted to its own judgment to determine the fact of failure with all its consequences."

"power."[1] Much is lost in logical clearness, and nothing is gained in practical politics, by endeavours to shirk the necessarily unlimited character of sovereignty—the legal despotism of the legal sovereign. Disobedience to the law of the land—if it is the law of the land—can never be a legal or constitutional right; it may be morally excused, or it may be a moral duty. If there is this conflict between law and morals, that is a reason for changing the law if possible—peaceably and constitutionally if possible; but it is no reason for pretending that the law is what we think it ought to be, or that what we think ought to be is law.

When people think about a "right of resistance" they are really concerned with a moral, not a constitutional, question. When, if ever, is it right to use force against a *de facto* government? This is an important question of political casuistry. It is said that a bishop, in a country that I need not specify, was once consulted as to whether a rebellion of a certain kind would be justifiable: he answered, "There are reasons on both sides. For the negative there is, *first*, that you have no cannon——"[2] It was unnecessary to proceed with the argument. The worthy ecclesiastic laid stress on a very important element in determining the rightness of resistance—a reasonable chance of success. But success ought to be taken to mean, not merely overthrowing and destroying the existing government or constitution, but substituting something better that is likely to last fairly well. Another most important consideration is this: Have all peaceable and constitutional means of reform been tried in vain, or does the government make it impossible to have recourse to them? And the last question, the question which should really be asked first, is this: Are the evils under which we are suffering such that they are worse than the risk of disorder and bloodshed?[3] This last question is likely to be answered very differently by persons and races of different temperament.

---

[1] Cf. Bentham, *Anarchical Fallacies*, *Works*, II. pp. 494, 495, 499, 500, etc.

[2] Cf. the story of the answer of Bishop Lesley to the Earl of Southampton, p. 177, *note*.

[3] On the ethics of resistance see T. H. Green, *Philosophical Works*, II. pp. 455 *seq*.

CHAPTER XII

EQUALITY [1]

AMONG the natural rights of man which a Constitution ought
to guarantee, equality is not named in the French Declaration
of 1789, although in article 6 the equality of citizens before
the law is expressly asserted. "The law should be the same
for all, both in protecting and in punishing. All citizens being
equal in the eye of the law, are equally admissible to all
dignities and public places and employments, according to
their capacity, and without other distinction than that of their
virtues and their talents." In the Declaration of 1793,
"equality" is named along with liberty, security, and property, as one of the natural and imprescriptible rights to
guarantee which government has been instituted (arts. 1 and
2. A separate article asserts that "all men are equal by
nature and before the law." This more extreme position of
the Declaration of 1793 comes nearer to the words of the
American Declaration of Independence. In the Declaration
of Independence it is said, "We hold those truths to be self-
evident, that all men are created equal, that they are endowed
by the Creator with certain unalienable Rights, that among
these are Life, Liberty, and the pursuit of Happiness." The
equality of mankind is asserted to be a self-evident truth, and
equality is not regarded as the creation of the law, but as
something which exists independently of any human law.
Some of the State Constitutions contain similar assertions in
their Declarations of Rights. Thus in the Connecticut Declaration (1818) we read, "That all men, when they form a social
compact, are equal in rights, and that no man or set of men
are entitled to exclusive public emoluments or privileges from

[1] A short article of mine on this subject appeared in the *Contemporary
Review* for October, 1892. The present chapter, though written from
quite the same point of view, is an independent treatment of the question.

the community." It is instructive to put alongside of this the
parallel passage in two Southern Constitutions formed about
the same time. In the Mississippi Declaration of Rights of
1817 and in the Alabama Declaration of 1819, it is declared
" that all *freemen*, when they form a social compact, are equal
in rights," etc.—a significant amendment of the phraseology
that was common at the time of the War of Independence.

Now, what is meant by the *natural* equality of men? The
meaning may be only this: that distinctions in rank, in wealth,
in political and social status, etc., are due entirely to social
arrangements, and apart from society would not exist. This
is a principle which may be accepted, not perhaps as self-
evident, but as a consequence of a process of abstraction, by
which we eliminate all that history and experience prove to be
due to human institution, deliberate or unconscious. In this
sense the natural equality of mankind means the same sort of
thing as the freedom of mankind by the *jus naturale* which
Ulpian recognises. In this sense the equality of mankind is
accepted equally by Hobbes and Locke. Hobbes, indeed, goes
farther than this, and makes the natural equality of men mean,
not merely the absence of those inequalities which are due to
institutions and conventions, but an approximate positive
equality in faculties of mind and body. "Nature," he says
(*Leviathan*, ch. xiii.), " hath made men so equal in the faculties
of body and mind, as that, though there be found one man
sometimes manifestly stronger in body, or of quicker mind
than another, yet when all is reckoned together the difference
between man and man is not so considerable, as that one man
can thereupon claim to himself any benefit to which another
may not pretend as well as he. For as to the strength of body,
the weakest has strength enough to kill the strongest, either
by secret machination, or by confederacy with others that
are in the same danger with himself. [The need of secret
machination and of confederacy with others is an odd reason
to give for equality!] And as to the faculties of mind   .   .   .
I find a yet greater equality amongst men than that of
strength. For Prudence is but Experience, which equal time
equally bestows on all men in those things they equally apply
themselves unto. That which may, perhaps, make such
equality incredible, is but a vain conceit of one's own wisdom,
which almost all men think they have in a greater degree

than the vulgar; that is, than all men but themselves, and a
few others, whom, by fame or for concurring with themselves,
they approve." Hobbes seems to adopt an unnecessarily wide
premise for taking down the pride of those who think themselves superior persons. Locke, who cites "the judicious
Hooker" in support of the self-evident character of the equality
of men by nature,[1] does not venture to assert the actual positive
equality of men in the same way as Hobbes does. Children,
he confesses, are not born *in* this full state of equality, though
they are born *to* it,[2] a distinction which implies a recognition,
however slight, of difference between nature as the original
condition, and nature as an ideal of what ought to be. And
in speaking of the "State of Nature," he argues that the state
is one of equality, "there being nothing more evident than
that creatures of the same species and rank, promiscuously
born to all the same advantages of Nature and the use of the
same faculties, should also be equal one amongst another,
without subordination or subjection, unless the Lord and
Master of them all should, by any manifest declaration of His
will, set one above another, and confer on him, by an evident
and clear appointment, an undoubted right to dominion and
sovereignty"[3]—a passage which suggests that it cannot be self-
evident that the Creator has made all men equal, if the Creator
could, without contradicting Himself, make some superior: the
positive Divine law is usually supposed to be limited by the
law of nature. Locke makes equality consist in the being
born *to* the same advantages of Nature, as if it were not
self-evident that all were born *with* the same advantages.
Furthermore, he limits equality to those of "the same species
and rank." But what determines sameness of *rank* (it must
be *natural* rank, of course)? and what if it were held that
different human races were *naturally* different in rank?

The natural equality of all mankind in the sense of a
positive equality of *inherited* bodily and mental powers
(acquired powers being obviously due to institutions) is not so
likely to be dogmatically asserted now-a-days as it was in the
days when biology did not exist as a science, and when it was
still possible for the inhabitants of civilised countries to idealise
the noble savage. Let it be admitted as fully as possible that

---

[1] *Treatise of Civil Government*, II. § 5.
[2] *Ibid.*, § 55.   [3] *Ibid.*, § 4.

the *natural* gulf which separates the lowest savage from the
highest extant ape is greater than that which separates the
lowest savage from the highest civilised race ; that is to say,
let it be admitted that the brain of the savage differs more
from the brain of the ape than it does from the brain of the
civilised man, while the actual mental furniture of the savage
is nearer to that of the ape than to that of the civilised man,
this proves indeed the enormous extent to which inequalities
are due to differences in training and in social environment—
i.e. to human institutions ; but no careful or thoughtful person
can now-a-days deny the very great differences in mental and
moral capacities, even among persons of the same race, nay,
even of the same family, and with equal opportunities of cultivating their natural powers. Differences in bodily health,
strength, etc.(prior to training), are too obvious to need remark;
some persons *inherit* better constitutions and more capacity for
physical development than others. It is perfectly unscientific,
and, therefore, perfectly useless, now-a-days to discuss the
political and social aspects of equality, except on the basis of
admitting the great natural inequalities among human beings.
But suppose these admitted ; it does not follow that in respect
of legal and political rights persons who may be naturally unequal ought in no case to be treated as legally and politically
equal. In the first place, natural inequalities, especially mental
and moral inequalities, are not always easy to discover ; they
take time to show themselves. Even Aristotle, while basing
his defence of slavery on the natural inequalities of human
beings, admits that it is not always easy to tell who is by
nature a slave, and who is by nature fit for freedom, and contents himself with the rough practical rule that the Greek
race is superior to barbarians, and that therefore Greeks
ought not to be enslaved.[1] Thus laws and institutions may
often treat unequals as equals, simply because of the difficulty
of deciding degrees of inequality by any sufficiently certain
standard. Secondly, because Nature has made human beings
unequal, it does not follow that human laws and institutions
should attempt to follow Nature in this matter, even if it
were possible to do so. It may often be considered best to endeavour to remedy the inequalities which Nature has inflicted
on her children. "It is precisely," says Rousseau, "because

[1] *Pol.*, I. 4-6.

the force of circumstances tends always to destroy equality,
that the force of legislation ought always to tend to maintain
it."[1] There are, of course, obvious limits to the extent to
which this ought to be done ; *e.g.* it would not be safe to make
every citizen in turn commander of the navy or the army on
grounds of equality. Even in Athens, where the lot was used
in order to secure a rotation of official experience among the
citizens the dominant caste of free men—be it understood),
the principle was not applied in electing generals. How far
equality should practically be applied in determining the rights
of citizens is a matter that cannot be decided *a priori* by any
reference to Nature, but must be settled in every case by some
compromise, based on a consideration of what is safe, when
the maintenance of security against external enemies and the
avoidance of discontent at home are both considered. The
existence of the ideal of equality in the minds of a people is,
of course, an important factor in determining what can be
done, what ought to be done, and what is likely to be done.

This ideal of equality is an inheritance from the inequalities
of ancient societies ; it is the idea of a peerage—an order or
caste of nobles who recognise each other as in some respects
and for some purposes equals, while asserting their superiority
to the rest of the nation or the rest of the human race.[2] The
idea of equality has grown out of the idea of privilege ; the
same is the case with the idea of freedom. Both ideas are the
outgrowth of aristocratic and slave-holding communities. It
was in *contrast* with the subject and the slave that men first
felt themselves equal and free. The ancient democracies were
slave-holding aristocracies; but the ideas of liberty and equality
once started go farther. Even in the modern democratic ideal,
there is no doubt that the equality of mankind is connected
with the superiority of man as such to all the lower animals.
Those who would assert the equality of all sentient beings
would put an end to the equality of mankind as such. For
it is the recognition that there is something in man which
distinguishes him as such from all other animals that alone
justifies one in speaking of the equality of men as men.

[1] *Contr. Soc.*, II. c. xi.
[2] Cf. G. Tarde, *Les Lois de l'Imitation*, p. 257: "Le véritable travail
préparatoire de l'égalitarisme actuel a été exécuté dans le passé par la
noblesse et non par la bourgeoisie;" and ideas spread downwards.

When Bentham uttered his dictum, " Everybody to count
for one, nobody for more than one,"[1] and assumed it as a
principle by which to interpret his formula of Greatest Happiness as the ethical end, he uttered a dictum which has been
extremely serviceable in aiding legislative reform by putting
a check on arbitrary appeals to the law of Nature ; but it is
a dictum which itself involves the assumption of that natural
right of equality, against which he himself protests.[2] We
are not entitled to assume the equal claims of all men to
happiness if our ethical principle is based solely on the fact
that all sentient beings naturally pursue pleasure. If the
greater sum of pleasures be always to be preferred, and be our
sole ultimate criterion of right and wrong, it is quite illegitimate to prefer a smaller sum of pleasures distributed among
a larger number of persons to a larger sum of pleasures though
shared among a smaller number of persons. For the purpose
of this moral arithmetic we must, of course, assume that pains
may be simply reckoned as a set-off against pleasures, so that
m units of pleasure would be exactly cancelled by m units of
pain. We must also assume that our hedometer (a desirable
instrument that no Greatest Happiness moralist has yet
invented) will enable us to measure intensity against duration. We *must* make these assumptions, strange or ridiculous
as they may seem, if the hedonist ethical standard is to be
saved from the caprice of every individual, and to be put on
an objective and "scientific" basis by the introduction of
quantitative measurement.

J. S. Mill, although he quotes the dictum about everybody
and nobody to which I have just referred, denies the quite
sound criticism of Mr. H. Spencer, that " the principle of utility
[in Bentham's sense] presupposes the anterior principle, that
everybody has an equal right to happiness."   According to
Mill, Bentham's principle only supposes " that equal amounts
of happiness are equally desirable, *whether felt by the same or
by different persons*," and, he adds, " if there is any anterior
principle implied, it can be no other than this, that the truths
of arithmetic are applicable to the valuation of happiness, as of

[1] Quoted by J. S. Mill, *Utilitarianism*, p. 93. This maxim seems to
belong to the unwritten doctrine of the Utilitarian master. Cf. Bonar,
Philosophy and Political Economy, p. 231, *note*.
[2] *Anarchical Fallacies*, in *Works*, II. pp. 498, 499.

all other measurable quantities."[1]   If this be so, there must be
many cases where Bentham's dictum about equality of persons
cannot possibly apply.   Suppose that some one presents a dish
of olives to five persons, of whom two are passionately fond of
olives, while three detest them, the greatest happiness of the
company will obviously be attained by dividing the olives
among the two who like them, and giving none to the others.
Suppose that there are only two concert tickets available for
five persons, and the two who enjoy music most get hold of
them and deprive their less musical friends of what to them
would be a very inferior pleasure, or even a positive pain, is not
this the plan which produces the greatest sum of happiness,
although equality is quite neglected?   Now, suppose that in
a political community there is a small, but able and powerful
and wealthy and well-armed ruling caste, with a subject
population of greatly inferior intellectual type, placid, ac-
quiescent and careless of liberty and equality, so long as they
are sufficiently well-fed, and not treated with positive cruelty,
will not the greatest sum of happiness be attained by the
ruling caste keeping to themselves the pleasures and excite-
ments of a splendid life of political activity and intellectual
and æsthetic enjoyment, unfettered by the drudgery of manual
toil, and subsisting on the labour of their slaves and depend-
ants?   To introduce equality into such a community means a
curtailment of the pleasures of the higher caste with no com-
mensurate increase of the pleasures of the lower, who will
undoubtedly be made more discontented, and therefore more
miserable, by having new ideals of life put before their minds,
and new wants created.   The ideal of a modern democracy is
an ideal far more difficult of attainment than the ideal of what
the Greeks understood by democracy; and for that very reason it seems true, that the Greatest Happiness moralist ought,
if he is consistent, to prefer the Greek ideal wherever and so
long as it is possible.   We know that Bentham and John
Stuart Mill would not prefer it; but that is just because the
one introduces a principle of equality, and the other a distinction of qualities of pleasure—criteria of right and wrong
which are fatal to the purely quantitative and objective
weighing of lots of pleasure against one another—the arith-
metical method by which it was proposed to bring ethics under

[1] *Utilitarianism*, p. 93, *note*.

the exact sciences. Undoubtedly there are many cases in which a Benthamite might quite consistently come to the practical *conclusion* that it is best to treat people as equal; he may do so simply because the problem of adjusting things to persons in such a way as to promote the really greatest sum of happiness is too difficult of solution; and so, giving up the problem, he may settle the matter by bestowing equal shares on persons with admittedly unequal capacities of enjoyment— that is the same sort of thing as settling a difficulty by "tossing up," which is, of course, not to decide rationally, but to leave the decision to chance. Further, if the ideal of equality (however absurd such an ideal might seem to a thoroughly scientific quantitative hedonist with a well-constructed hedometer) has once got possession of a large number of persons, it may be dangerous to attempt anything but such a rough-and-ready way of solving ethical and political problems; and the pains of discontent may, to some extent, be allayed (though probably new pains of discontent will be created) by professing to reckon everybody as one, and nobody as more than one. But in all such cases equality must be adopted as a conclusion from considerations of what is socially expedient, and not taken for granted as a premise.[1]

With regard to equality, an ethical system which starts from the fact of man's rationality is on a somewhat different footing from a system which starts from the fact of man's sentience. Man's rationality is what separates him from the lower animals, and connects him with his fellow-men. His sentience connects him with all other animals, but, as such, gives him no *special* link (apart from his rationality) with his fellow-men. It is not necessary to the assertion that man is rational to assume that the gap between him and the animals is absolute: it is enough to recognise that the barrier of communication and interchange of ideas is less between any human beings, however far separated in degree of civilisation, than between man and the lower animals. We must not be misled by such facts as the amount of sympathy a man feels with his dog. The dog, as I have already pointed out, is an

<hr/>

[1] In the foregoing passage, and some of what follows, I have found myself unable to avoid some repetition of what has already been said in Chapter V. (pp. 95, 96). To repeat has seemed to me in this case a less evil than merely to refer the reader to what was said in a different context.

artificial animal—a parasite that man, by artificial selection through long generations, has adapted to his own convenience or fancies. Even the most fanatical dog-lover, in his saner moments, will admit that he could carry on a more elaborate, even if a less agreeable, conversation with a negro than with a creature that can only bark and whine and wag its tail. In all human beings we recognise, not merely the participation in the same general physical structure as in ourselves, and consequently in the same general life-history, but we recognise also a participation in the same idea of self—a power of reflecting on one's place in the universe which, however little developed, is there in germ in every human being. What kind of consciousness the lower animals have we can only guess, and we can never verify our hypothesis in any direct manner. Our belief in the consciousness of other human beings, and in the likeness of their consciousness to ours, is a hypothesis also; but it is a hypothesis that we can verify by comparing our mental experience with theirs. Thus human beings are not only linked together as members of the same animal species, but as the sharers in the same type of mental life, and therefore *potentially* in the same ideals of conduct. We find that each of us—each human being—is a centre of a universe of his own, from which, in one sense, each of us can never escape.

When Kant enunciates the moral law in the form that " we should so act as to treat humanity in ourselves and others in every case as an end, never as a means only," he asserts a certain equality of all men; but he does so with better logical justification than Bentham, for he starts from the rationality and not from the sentience of human nature. Kant's ethical thinking is, indeed, pervaded by the individualism which lies at the basis of the whole theory of natural rights, and I think it must be admitted that in this formula he is guilty of a one-sided exaggeration in his way of expressing the idea of humanity as an end-in-itself. That " we should *never* treat any human being as a means only " cannot be a part of the moral law, unless the moral law is by its very nature incapable of being obeyed—so that we should have to say, "I ought, therefore I cannot." Is it necessarily wrong to climb up on another person's shoulder for a lawful purpose, when there is no ladder at hand, or to employ a human model instead of a lay-figure, or to ask a policeman to show one the way? It is a curious comment on Kant's language about humanity being always an end, that in his *Philosophy of Law* he allows the rightness of impressing men for military service.[1] Interpreted in a rigid way, the idea of never using a human being as a means is unworkable. What Kant really intends is, that no human being should be regarded as being altogether only a means; that every human being, however much he may serve as a means for the satisfaction of the needs of others, has still a life of his own that ought to be respected. A human being may be a "living tool," as Aristotle defines the slave, but in a well-regulated society no one should be a "living tool" only. Kant, that is to say, has a social ideal which excludes such institutions as slavery; but the fact that he is judging conduct from the point of view of such a society only comes dimly to the front, when, *e.g.*, he speaks of human beings as being members of "a kingdom of ends."

The "equality" of human beings as such, which alone is necessarily implied in an idealist system of ethics, would be

[1] *Rechtslehre*, § 55 (*Werke*, IX. pp. 197, 198, ed. Rosenkranz: VII. p. 163, ed. Hartenstein). Mr. Bonar, in his *Philosophy and Political Economy*, p. 273, curiously misrepresents Kant's own view in saying simply, "The right of the State to impress soldiers is deduced from its *creation* of them." What Kant really says is, that the right of the State to compel its subjects to fight for it *appears* to be easily deducible from the principle that what one has substantially made for one's self is one's own property, and that one may do what one will with one's own property. Now population could not grow up without the protection of government; therefore, etc. Such a principle may be accepted by the mere jurist, "and may be supposed to float dimly before the mind of monarchs; but, though applicable to animals, it will not apply to man at all, especially when he is viewed as a citizen, who must be regarded as a member of the State with a share in legislation—*not merely as a means, but at the same time as also an end-in-himself*. As such, he must give his free consent, through his representatives, not only to the carrying on of war in general, but to every separate declaration of war; and it is only under this limiting condition that the State has a right to require of him such dangerous services. We must, therefore, perhaps deduce this right from the duty of the sovereign to the people, not conversely [from the duty of the people to the sovereign, as on the theory first suggested]. The people having the right of voting may be considered, though passive, to be also active and to represent the Sovereign himself." The passage is not very lucid; but it avoids the exaggeration of Mr. Bonar's interpretation, as well as of a too literal application of the "end-in-himself" notion. The necessity of the "consent" of the people to *every* declaration of war would, however, if strictly taken (which Kant does not seem to mean), prove an unworkable principle.

more correctly expressed as their potential membership of a
common society. It is only in so far as we can think of
humanity as a possible society that we can regard human
beings as equal moral units. They are persons potentially, because they are potentially members of a society. As a matter
of historical development, it is only in smaller societies that
the idea of moral personality has grown up. The idea of
humanity as a possible society has been of gradual growth,
and therefore also the idea of every human being as a person
—the idea, as it is sometimes phrased, of "the infinite worth
of every human soul." The idea of *one* God, as the God of all
races of mankind, is an essential element in this conception.

Such metaphysical notions may seem far away from practical
politics, but it is only in the light of them that we can put any
tenable meaning into the political dogma, or, let me rather say,
the political ideal of equality. The historical connection between religious and political ideas is easily seen, and it is
usually through religion that metaphysical ideas first grow up
or become popularised. When a religion ceases to be the
affair of a particular race or a particular nation, we have the
first step in the proclamation of the right of equality. When
it is declared that God is no respecter of persons, but accepts
all, irrespective of race, sex, or outward condition, we are still
a long way from the democratic formula; but the most
formidable barriers of caste, the religious barriers, have been
broken down. The hierarchical Church of the Middle Ages
may indeed seem far removed, not merely in its actual condition but in its ideals, from the doctrine of equality. But in
its priesthood, which was no hereditary caste, but recruited
from all classes, even the lowest, it suggested the idea of "a
career open to talent" at a time when the whole structure of
secular society suggested rather a rigid system of caste.[1]
When Protestantism, especially in its extremer forms, revolted
against the monarchical and aristocratic character of the
Mediæval Church, the way was prepared for the revolutionary
doctrine of equality.

[1] Relatively to lay society the clerical order was a separate, and, in a
sense, a superior caste—a spiritual aristocracy. The idea of equality—
in the negative sense of an absence of permanent barriers, even to the
highest offices—spread down from this spiritual aristocracy to the lay
community. (Cf. above, p. 248, *note* 2.) Protestantism tended to recognise the potential priesthood of all men, and their potential kingship also.

"Equality before the law" is the first and most essential kind of equality. And *this* equality is transferred from the Declaration of 1789 even into the Constitutional Charter of the restored Bourbons, of which the first article runs: "Frenchmen are equal before the law, whatever otherwise their titles and ranks may be." The significance of this equality is to be found by considering that it means the abolition of the special privileges and immunities of the clergy and the nobility —it means an increasing unification and integration in the national life, the disappearance of various quasi-States before the one State. As with the idea of equality in ethics and in religion, equality before the law means the membership of a great whole.

Equality in political rights—in the suffrage and in eligibility to office—is a different matter. Many champions of the idea of natural rights do not assert the natural right of every one to have a vote. The suffrage, by all thoughtful persons at least, is regarded as a means to the working of the constitution; and the right of voting is obviously a right created by the law (whether special constitutional law or ordinary law), and cannot intelligibly be represented as a right prior to and independent of law. A constitution may be thought of as existing in order that individuals may have security and liberty ; but cannot logically be regarded as existing in order that certain persons may have votes. On whom the suffrage should be conferred is a matter not to be settled *a priori*, but by reference to the particular circumstances of the country. In this, as before, we have to consider what is safe, regard being had both to external and internal dangers—the latter including the discontent that is apt to arise from the refusal of political rights that are enjoyed by others.

A high property qualification, or, at least, some property qualification, is often urged as a necessary safeguard against the political instability that is likely to follow from political power passing into the hands of the more ignorant or the more reckless part of the population. The revolutionary Ireton,[1] who appealed to the Law of Nature and of Nations in justification of the right of resistance, thought it unwise to give votes except to persons owning land ;[2] but then

[1] *Cf.* Chap. I., p. 10.
[2] Mr. Firth (*Clarke Papers*, p. lxx.) compares Ireton's attitude to the

Ireton objected to the theory that a man had by "birthright" any claim to a voice in the government of his country. To him the claim of an equal right in all men to a vote seemed no more reasonable than "an equal right in any goods he sees, meat, drink, clothes, to take and use for his sustenance." When, indeed, it is urged that representation should go along with taxation, it is reasonable that no one should have a vote who does not pay some taxes. In our local government a rate-paying qualification is considered a reasonable limit.

But to make the voting power of different classes depend on a ratio to the amount of direct taxes which they pay—as is done in the Prussian "Three-Class System"—is open to the objection that it conspicuously confers political privileges on the wealthy, *as such:* it is thus a provocation of discontent. Elaborate systems of "proportional representation" are open to a similar objection; they *seem* difficult to understand to the ordinary person, and suggest an element of trickery, which *seems* absent from an apparently simple phrase such as "one man one vote." To introduce a property qualification where there has been "universal suffrage," or to raise the property qualification to one higher than before, are likewise dangerous devices, because they would certainly create a sense of injustice. On the other hand, the abolition of any provision for illiterate voters, or the introduction of an educational test—after compulsory and gratuitous education has been in operation for some time—seems unobjectionable. To require "every voter to be able to write his name, and to read any section of the Constitution in the English language"—a proposition which has been carried by popular vote in the State of California [1]—seems a wise and reasonable method of checking the negro and foreign

proposals of the Levellers of 1647 (see pp. 307, 308), with that of Lord Braxfield to the Reformers of 1794. The latter, in his charge to the jury in the trial of Thomas Muir, said: "A government in every country should be just like a corporation, and in this country it is made up of the landed interest, which alone has a right to be represented. As for the rabble, who have nothing but personal property, what hold has the nation of them? They may pack up their property on their backs and leave the country in the twinkling of an eye, but landed property cannot be removed."

[1] Oberholzer, *The Referendum in America* (Philadelphia, 1893), p. 18. This provision appeared in the Massachusetts Constitution of 1857, with the qualification that it was not to apply to voters already on the register, nor to persons over 60 years of age.

vote. If with free education citizens do not qualify themselves for a vote by learning a little of the language in which the government of the country is carried on, it is their own fault, and it might be possible even to require more than "reading a section of the Constitution" from those who are called upon to have a voice even indirectly in the government of their country, without creating discontent, except among a portion of the population who would be least likely to find supporters elsewhere, save, indeed, from motives of faction. The partisan use which can always, unfortunately, be made of the grievance of an excluded class, is indeed one argument for universal suffrage.

When the suffrage is claimed for some hitherto excluded class—*e.g.* for women—far too little is usually made of the argument that the exercise of political rights has an educational value: there is too much appeal to the ambiguous claim of "rights," and too little is said about the exercise of such rights as the State bestows being the imposition of a public duty on the individual citizen. To accentuate this aspect of the suffrage, it would be very reasonable to impose a fine on any elector who did not vote at an election, except for such reasons as would be held to excuse a person liable to serve on a jury absenting himself when summoned. Of course the voter, coming to the poll under penalties, could not be prevented from leaving his ballot-paper empty, or from filling it up with opprobrious language; but, even so, it would be very important for the political statistician to find out what proportion of the electors were unable to make up their minds, or really despised and disliked their political rights.

Compulsory voting is not unknown in the history of English-speaking communities. In the colony of Virginia, it was enacted in 1646 that all freemen absent from an election without lawful cause should be fined one hundred pounds of tobacco. "After 1662 the amount of the penalty was increased to two hundred pounds of the same staple. The law of compulsory voting was re-enacted in 1705, and again in 1763."[1] In the colony of Plymouth voting was also made compulsory as early as 1636. The arguments for compulsory voting become especially strong where the electors have the

[1] Cortlandt F. Bishop, *History of Elections in the American Colonies* (Columbia College Studies, Vol. III., No. 1), New York, 1893, p. 191.

right and duty of voting directly on laws or on constitutional amendments. Compulsion would be the best security against the excessive preponderance of cliques, and against the very fluctuating interest most people are apt to take in politics, and would have the permanent merit of bringing before every citizen his political responsibilities.

The claim of equality, in its widest sense, means the demand for equal opportunity—the *carrière ouverte aux talents*. The result of such equality of opportunity will clearly be the very reverse of equality of social condition, if the law allows the transmission of property from parent to child, or even the accumulation of wealth by individuals. And thus, as has often been pointed out, the effect of the nearly complete triumph of the principles of 1789—the abolition of legal restrictions on free competition—has been to accentuate the difference between wealth and poverty. Equality in political rights, along with great inequalities in social condition, has laid bare "the social question"; which is no longer concealed, as it formerly was, behind the struggle for equality before the law and for equality in political rights. As in the case of liberty, our attention is called to the difference between "formal" or "negative" and "real" or "positive" equality. The abolition of legal restrictions on free competition allows the natural inequalities of human beings, in vigour of body and mind, to assert themselves. Even under a socialistic *régime*, which fell short of a complete communism penetrating to every detail of every individual's life, there would be inequalities of condition which, though they might seem slight when looked at from the standpoint of all civilised societies with which we are familiar, might prove extremely galling to persons who were strongly possessed with the passion of levelling. That a society should have attained such stability of economic conditions, and should be permeated by such a spirit of discipline and of zeal for the common good that it was able to provide work and comfortable subsistence for all its members who were fit to work, with comfortable subsistence also for all those physically unfit to work, and severe penalties, rigidly carried out, for the idle and rebellious—such a society may seem a satisfactory ideal to those who seek a remedy for the most pressing of present discontents, and who believe that the orderly and sympathetic instincts of mankind are capable of development; but it would prove unsatisfactory alike to the enthusiast for individual liberty and to the dogmatic believer in absolute equality.

Most of the advocates of the natural rights of liberty and equality have not proposed to interfere legally with the institution of the family; some of them, indeed, have protested against legislation which has diminished the customary rights of parents over their children. But no real or positive equality in social conditions can be secured so long as individuals are looked at in any respect as members of families, and not in every respect as members of the State alone. Suppose two workmen receive equal wages, but the one has no children and the other has six, all too young to earn anything, where is the equality in the social condition of the individuals supported out of these equal wages? Even under the system of a compulsory minimum of education, has the child of incapable or vicious parents—quite apart from his hereditary disadvantages—an equal opportunity given him, in any true sense, with the child who has grown up in a careful and regular household? For a great many purposes still, in spite of individualistic sentiment and socialistic legislation, the unit of society is the family and not the individual. And we cannot think out any social problem fairly without taking that fact into account. Society is not yet at least, and possibly never will be, so atomist as professed individualists and most of those who call themselves Socialists imagine it to be. Even supposing very great changes to take place in the character of the family —changes of which the diminished control of husbands over wives, of parents over children, may be taken as specimens— the physical conditions of infancy and maternity will always throw some difficulty in the way of the State regarding every human being simply as an individual. The patriarchal family, in its literal sense, as the family in which the father rules over his wife or wives and children—and possibly over household slaves also—is the social unit, which, however late it may come (according to some theories) in the social evolution of the human race, is the chief bond of cohesion that we find within the historical period, in all those peoples that have developed a high civilisation. The growth of the power of the State has everywhere tended to diminish the power of the house-father over his subjects, and has made possible the social existence of individuals owning no allegiance to any household monarch. But the individualism, which asserts itself in the reaction against the old social system, seems to be too chaotic for humanity to rest in it; and the State can only secure the real well-being—I may add, the real liberty and equality (so far as these are socially useful ends)—of its citizens, by taking over the functions of which it deprives the family and performing them in a higher and better way. Is any State that yet exists anywhere prepared to do that, or fit to attempt it? Yet all modern States are consciously or unconsciously moving in that direction.

The modern assertion of the equality of the sexes brings the special difficulties of the problem more prominently before us than anything else. The demand of women for equal political rights with men is only a small part of the problem. It may be noted, by the way, that this demand, though it had been put forward by isolated thinkers, such as Thomas Paine, Condorcet, and Mary Wollstonecraft, who applied the idea of natural rights a little more logically than most of their contemporaries, did not become prominent in practical politics till after the American civil war had put an end to the disabilities of the blacks—in constitutional theory at least. The feeling of racial superiority to the negro-voter was certainly an important factor in suggesting the absurdity of enfranchising any black man while excluding every white woman. Similarly, in this country, the enfranchisement of the agricultural labourer has undoubtedly made the anomaly of the unenfranchised woman taxpayer of the upper and middle classes more conspicuous. Though the idea of female suffrage once started may be more readily taken up among the women of the poorer classes, the idea originated only among the men and women of the middle classes.[1] New ideas almost always begin among the class that at the time is dominant, and work downwards. As already said, the idea of equality seems pri-

---

[1] It is sometimes urged—as with other rights that are claimed—that the right of women to the suffrage once existed, but has been put an end to by the selfishness of men. Mr. Ostrogorski has shown that where women in feudal times, as in Austria still, had an indirect right of voting, the vote was really attached to property and not to persons. The first effect of the modern democratic idea of the suffrage as a right belonging to persons has been to abolish this apparent voting power of women. See his *Rights of Women.*

marily to be the outgrowth of an aristocratic sentiment; it is
aristocracy passing over by a logical process to its own negation.

But the equality of the sexes implies much more than
equality in political rights and duties. As the opponents of
female suffrage and its more thoughtful advocates alike recognise, the franchise would be chiefly valuable as a symbol of social
equality. The economic independence of women, even of those
who have become wives and mothers, is what the more logical
advocates of the equality of the sexes see to be necessary for
the real social equality of the woman with the man. This
leads many of them to object to all legislative interference
with the work of women. And yet, as things are, it is only
too clear that the competition of women in the labour-market
with men and with one another lowers the wages of men, so
that, as Mr. Charles Booth has shown, the characteristic of a
poorer class is the wage-earning of the women belonging to
it.[1] The work of married women away from home is, moreover,
the source of great injury to their children: their work in
their homes is a principal cause of "sweating." But even if
the wage-earning of married women were entirely abolished,
in all old countries there are a vast number of unmarried
women and widows who are compelled to work for a living;
and to them it is simple irony to say that women's proper
place is in the household, unless polygamy were made compulsory on all men having more than a certain income.
Household industries, moreover, have disappeared, the word
"spinster" has lost its meaning, and the male head of the
household, in losing his ancient privileges, can no longer be
expected to make himself responsible for all the women of the
family, when he is not able to marry them off by compulsion.
The modern widow cannot so easily adopt the methods of
Naomi and Ruth without reproach. Trade-unions among
women workers may help to raise some of them to a better
economic level; but a large number must always be excluded,
and if married women who are mothers become to any great
extent economically independent of their husbands, this can
only lead to a general lowering of wages, diminution of comfort, and decay of physique. Women who are mothers can, as
a general rule, only attain economic independence by receiving

[1] *Life and Labour of the People* (2nd edit.), Vol. I. p. 50.

State-support. But, as I have already pointed out,[1] the State cannot safely undertake the legal responsibilities of the husband without having a choice in its wives.

The Socialistic ideal of the State must still be Plato's ideal, *i.e.* the State must be regarded as one family, in which all shall work according to their capacity and receive according to their needs—an ideal which requires a very high level of sympathy, but which has no connection with any abstract principle of equality. In saying this, I do not mean that the State need make any regulations about the relations of the sexes in violation of the religious and moral sentiments of the community. The Platonic ideal may be impossible of realisation, but a very considerable legal limitation of the right of parentage would be quite compatible with the continued recognition of monogamy as a moral, though no longer as an economic, institution. It might even be argued that only under such conditions would monogamy as a moral institution be fairly tried. In the absence of difficulties about property and about the proper maintenance of children, the attachment of women as well as of men to monogamy would be experimentally tested in a manner at present impossible. Whether any such very great economic change would not tend to alter many moral ideas may very well be asked. Of this, however, we may be certain, that no community can hold together for any length of time unless its institutions and customs are in harmony with the moral sentiments of its members and the ideas of religious duty which they have come to hold.

[1] Cf. above, pp. 129–134.

CHAPTER XIII

THE confusions which permeate the theory of natural rights come out most conspicuously of all in the case of the right of property. With regard to property there are three questions which should be carefully distinguished from one another: (1) How does the right of property originate? This is a purely historical question, and does not directly and for its own sake concern us here. In discussing rights which are alleged to be natural, we are dealing with a different question, viz.—(2) What is the justification of the right of property? But we cannot discuss that question fairly, unless we consider also the question—(3) What does the right of property at any given time and place imply? This question involves a whole series of different questions, such as:—What objects may be held as property? How far does the right of property over these objects extend? Does the right of property imply only the right of using, or also the right of using up (*jus abutendi*)? Does it involve the right of destroying in the case of things that can be used without being destroyed, as well as in the case of things that perish in the using? Does it include the right of alienating? And does the right of alienation include the right of bequest? And, if bequest, with or without limitation? Further, in what sense is there any right of individual property against the State? In the discussion of such questions we should be compelled to consider the actual historical origin and development of property, public and private, in its different forms (*i.e.* our first question is really only a part of our third). Now, I cannot attempt to write a history of property. That can only be satisfactorily done by the combined labours of many anthropologists, historians and lawyers. I only wish to point out that "the right of property," which has been said to be a natural right in many Declarations, is a very ambiguous phrase.

People are too ready to dispute about the good or evil of property, or of "private property," as if every one was agreed on what it means.

In the Constitution framed for the State of Kansas, and adopted by the pro-slavery party in 1857, the 7th article contains these words: "The right of property is before and higher than any constitutional sanction [Locke's theory, it will be noted, as distinct from Hobbes's], and the right of the owner of a slave to such slave and its [*sic*] increase is the same and as inviolable as the right of the owner of any property whatever."[1] This seems to most of us, probably, a very startling claim, but I cannot see that there is any greater *a priori* objection to it than to any other alleged natural right—so long as we simply appeal to "Nature," and do not consider social expediency. In the Bill of Rights which forms part of the constitution which was adopted by the anti-slavery party in Kansas, in 1858, it is declared that "All men are by nature equally free and independent," etc., and then that "the right of all men to the control of their persons exists prior to law, and is inalienable." I assume that the framers of this phrase did not really mean that the right is so inalienable that a convicted felon has a claim to the control of his own person ; but, like their opponents, they were only constructing a major premise from which to deduce a conclusion favourable to their side in the controversy about negro slavery, and were not very careful about its literal truth.

Now, here is "a very pretty quarrel " among the believers in inalienable natural rights ; and it has needed a civil war to settle the dispute. Most Americans think that in their declarations of natural rights they have a security against those socialistic interferences with liberty and property to which our carelessness on the question of natural rights and our unlimited sovereign legislature leave us exposed. But supposing that public opinion, and it is to be hoped without a civil war, were to be convinced that certain other forms of private property, besides property in human beings, were incompatible with the equal freedom and independence of all men, no amount of declarations of natural rights could bar the way to a torrent of socialistic legislation, nor could a multitude of constitutional

[1] This clause is taken word for word from the Kentucky Constitution of 1850, and was still there in 1890.

checks do anything except render the conflict of old and new ideas more dangerous to the public peace. Sooner or later the constitutional lawyers would have to put a different interpretation on the word "property" from that which their predecessors put upon it. A declaration of rights can never have more than a moral force, and may come to lose that.

The French Declaration of Rights of 1791 (*i.e.* the Declaration framed in 1789) lays down that "the right of property being inviolable and sacred, no one ought to be deprived of it, except in cases of evident public necessity, legally ascertained, and on conditions of previous just indemnity." The Declaration of 1793 lays down that "the right of property is that which belongs to every citizen to enjoy and to dispose at his will of his goods, his revenues, the fruit of his toil and industry." This is the formula framed under Girondist influence. In the Declaration put forward by Robespierre and his followers in the Jacobin Club, the corresponding clause is worded in a manner that would, I think, commend itself better to an English lawyer. "Property is the right which every citizen has to enjoy and to dispose of that portion of his goods which is guaranteed to him by the law." But even the Girondist Declaration does not make the right of property absolute as against the State; for a subsequent clause recognises, in almost the same phrases as are used in the Declaration of 1791, the right of the State to take property from the individual, under conditions. "No one can be deprived of the least portion of his property without his consent, unless when public necessity, legally ascertained, demands it, and under the condition of a previous just indemnity." And the right of taxation for purposes of general utility, and under popular control, is recognised in the following section.

The fifth Amendment to the Constitution of the United States of America declares that private property shall not be taken for public use "without just compensation." None of these written constitutions define the term "just." None of them are so rash as to attempt to answer the question of Socrates: "What is Justice?" So that what is "just compensation" must ultimately depend on public opinion at the time when the compensation comes to be given, as much as in Great Britain, where there is no written constitution, and where we have hitherto got on somehow without declaring our natural rights. It may also be pointed out that "legally ascertained" or "due process of law" is a phrase to which different ages and countries would give a very different meaning.

The attempts to base the right of property on the Law of Nature take two principal forms: in both of these we see the influence of that sense of "nature" in which the natural means what is least affected by human institutions. There is the theory which bases property on *occupation*, and there is the theory which bases it on *labour*.

The theory which bases property on the occupation of what is previously unoccupied represents the facts of the most primitive condition of human society. We may go lower even than *human* society. When a cat catches a mouse, and there is no stronger or cleverer animal about to dispute possession, the mouse, in a very intelligible sense, becomes that cat's property; and of course the cat can make her title under the Law of Nature quite secure by depositing the mouse in the internal safe with which Nature has provided her. Similarly, when a bird has taken an unoccupied site for her nest, we may consider that the bird has at least a temporary right of property in that site. So it is with human beings in the hunting and fishing stage. As a matter of fact, whoever can catch may keep, unless a stronger deprives him of his prey. We may call that the Law of Nature if we like. Possession, as we say, is nine points of the law, and it is so even among the animals; because, unless food is scarce, as a rule it is less trouble to go and find for one's self than to have the trouble and risk of fighting. Only a very pugnacious sparrow will fight for another sparrow's crumb instead of looking out for an unoccupied crumb.

But when reflective human beings wish to find a good reason for the right of the first occupier, they are not content to base it simply on force and on the convenience to the individual. They seek a social reason for it. And, obviously, unless the right of the first occupier had some good utilitarian justification, it would not in the long run have been recognised by flourishing societies. The first occupier, it is said—by Locke [1] for instance—has a right to keep and use, so long as there is enough and as good left over for others. This, it may

---

[1] *Treatise of Civil Government*, II. ch. v. §§ 32, 33.

be noted, is the principle of "equal liberty" in that modified
form in which "similar" is substituted for "same."[1]   But this
is a justification of the right of the first occupier which must
perpetually diminish with the growth of population. The best
land, not necessarily the most fertile, but the most conveniently situated, will be first taken up, and the later comers as
a rule have to content themselves with what is inferior. Yet,
if they were to plead this law of nature—the law of equal
rights—they might all claim to get equally good land; and
these natural rights would have to be decided by a vast amount
of natural litigation, *i.e.* fighting. As a matter of fact, people
take what they can get, and are content with the inferior,
unless they are very pugnacious, in which case they act like
the pugnacious sparrow aforementioned, but at a vastly greater
risk, because they have not merely other individuals against
them, but individuals who are holding together in some sort of
society.[2]   If I go to borrow a book from a circulating library,
and the most desirable books are out already, I do not, if I am
a fairly reasonable person, make a row because according to
the law of nature no one has a right to any books unless equally
good books are left for all.   I am content to abide by the rules
of the library, whatever they may be.   If I do not like them, I
may try to get them altered.   But the rights, in any case, are
determined by a society, and do not exist prior to the society.
Thus, so far as the right of the first occupier is still recognised
as a basis for the valid holding of property, it is because the
society in question recognises the rule as socially convenient, or
at least has not yet come to feel it specially inconvenient.   It
is only "natural," either in the sense of being socially expedient,
or in the sense of being a survival of the primitive prevalence
of force, tempered by fear and by laziness.

In the dealings of nations with one another we have clear
survivals of this state of nature.   International law recognises
the right of the first occupier: that is to say, nations generally

---

[1] Cf. above, p. 143.

[2] Cf. Prof. Huxley, *Evolution and Ethics* (Romanes Lecture). p. 10.
" Wolves could not hunt in packs except for the real, though unexpressed,
understanding that they should not attack one another during the chase.
The most rudimentary polity is a pack of men living under the like tacit
or expressed convention, and having made the very important advance
upon wolf society, that they agree to use the force of the whole body
against individuals who violate it, and in favour of those who observe it."

acquiesce in the seizure of unoccupied territory by other nations, because it is usually more convenient to seize for one's self than to fight with other nations, unless a specially favourable opportunity arises. It need hardly be said that unoccupied territory means practically, for this purpose, territory unoccupied by other civilised or by other powerful nations, though the formal consent or the supposed benefit of the natives may be needed to satisfy the conqueror's conscience.[1] Reflection on what is beneficial to humanity as a whole gradually—very gradually—begins to mitigate the primitive law of nature, which, as I have said, is simply the law of force tempered by fear and by laziness.

The theory which bases the right of property upon labour represents likewise what we find among animals and among savages. A pair of birds build a nest, and the nest then becomes the nest of these birds. The savage builds a hut for himself and his mate, and it becomes his hut until a stronger tribe comes and seizes or destroys it. He may be said to own the materials and the site by the right of first occupation, and the finished hut by the right of labour. Grotius, in criticising the Roman Jurist Paulus, who had already anticipated Locke's theory and made labour a justification of property, points out that, since nothing can be made except out of pre-existing matter, acquisition by means of labour depends ultimately on possession by means of occupation.[2] So far as any such rights, whether based on labour or on occupation, are recognised in a more complicated society, this only means that the society recognises them as advantageous to itself, or has not yet come to feel them disadvantageous. In a complicated society there is no such thing as individual labour, unless a person were purposely to isolate himself and live like a savage; and even then it would only be by the recognised law and custom of the society that he could maintain his isolation

---

[1] The conversion of the Indians to Christianity was, no doubt quite sincerely, alleged as a justification of the Spanish conquests in America. The Puritans in New England, like the Dutch settlers at the Cape, were sometimes influenced by the Scriptural example of the utter destruction of the Canaanites. Now-a-days, the consent of the native community or of their chiefs is generally thought necessary to a good title in International Law. See Maine, *International Law*, pp. 71—75.

[2] Grotius, *De Jure Belli et Pacis*, II. iii. § 3.

unmolested. Mr. Edward Carpenter,[1] in his polemic against
civilisation, calls the policeman a "parasite." In a crowded
country the policeman is only a part of the orderly organisation
which makes it possible for the peaceable citizen to abuse
civilisation at his ease. Locke, in propounding his theory of
property, recognises fully that to the making of a loaf of bread
in a civilised community there go an immense number of
industries besides that of the baker; but he does not recognise,
as he should have done, that those who keep the peace within
the society, those who defend it from attack from without, and
those who in any way advance the orderliness and the intelligence of the society and its power over nature, all contribute
their share to the making even of a loaf of bread. So that
when we come to consider fairly the question, "Whose is the
loaf?"[2] not merely the miller, the farmer, the ironworker, the
miner may put in their claim for a portion, but the magistrate,
the policeman, the soldier, the man of science, the schoolmaster.
All labour in a civilised society is social and not individual
labour; and therefore no law of nature helps us to determine
a priori how the produce of labour ought to be distributed.

To some persons, indeed, a great part of the highly paid work
of the world, the work of the lawyer or the merchant, for instance, or the work of the general and of the officials of the War
Office, may seem useless or even mischievous work, while the
work of the "labouring man" seems honest in comparison. To
this it need only be answered that the mere fact of work being
manual does not make it socially beneficial. The enterprising
capitalist who puts adulterated or deleterious goods in the
market may be more morally blameworthy than the workmen
he employs to execute his nefarious plot upon the community;
but it cannot be pretended that these workmen are conferring
any benefit upon society. And, if they deserve credit simply
because they are busy—no matter at what—the same plea
must serve for many of those whom the "labourer," or the
labourer's advocate, calls "parasites." What industries should
be permitted at all, and how the product of industry is to be
divided among the community, must in all cases be determined
by social arrangements which the State tolerates or brings into
being; and every society in the long run seeks to discover what

---

[1] *Civilisation—Its Cause and its Cure*, p. 16.

[2] Not the loafer's!—unless society thinks it expedient to maintain him.

social arrangements are the best for its well-being as a whole. We can only allow natural rights to be talked about in the sense in which natural rights mean those legal or customary rights which we have come to think or may come to think it most advantageous to recognise. Of course, in this question of what is advantageous, it is very important to consider how any change, if a change is considered desirable, can be brought about with the least amount of friction. Thus, if it has come to be thought that any particular form of private property is inexpedient, it would be disadvantageous to a society to take away that right of private property without what the community at large would consider "just compensation," unless the community at large, and not merely some fanatical section of it, came to consider that form of property so immoral, *i.e.* so socially inexpedient, that it held "just compensation" to mean " no compensation at all," and the mere absence of a criminal prosecution to be the extreme of charity. But, as has been iterated throughout these pages, all such questions are best discussed without dragging in those vague and rhetorical appeals to the Law of Nature.

As a final example of the ambiguities in these theories of natural rights, let me take the dispute between those two scholastic theologians, Mr. Henry George and Pope Leo XIII. Both of them adopt the theory which bases private property on labour. The Pope justifies private ownership of land on the same ground as Locke, that man has mixed his labour with it (*Encyclical* of May, 1891), and also on the ground that a man with his honestly-earned savings may buy land. To the latter argument Mr. George very pertinently replies that it would justify slavery, wherever savings had been invested in human flesh.[1] To the former he might have answered that the legitimate occupation of the land is presupposed. Mr. George himself argues that the right of property, since it originates in the right of the individual to himself, " attaches only to things produced by labour, but cannot attach to things created by God." " Thus," he continues, " if a man take a fish from the ocean he acquires a right of property in that fish, which exclusive right he may transfer by sale or gift. But he cannot obtain a similar right of property in the ocean, so that he may sell *it* or give *it*, or forbid others to use

[1] *The Condition of Labour*, p. 35.

it." Mr. George apparently thinks that man produces the fish by his labour; but surely much land in the world is more man's product than any fishes in the open sea. How Mr. George expects His Holiness the Pope to believe that God did not create the fish, in the same sense as that in which He created the land, I may leave as a problem to those persons who care for that casuistry of natural rights, of which I have given a quite sufficient number of specimens.[1]

---

[1] I have discussed Locke's theory of property somewhat more fully in an essay, under that title, included in *Darwin and Hegel*, etc.

CHAPTER XIV

THE right, not merely of pursuing but of obtaining happiness, which is named as one of the natural rights of man in most American State Constitutions, may seem, in this world of ours, to be a very large order on the bank of Providence. The right of pursuing happiness is clearly only a generalised form in which is asserted the right of the individual to be left alone in his conduct. The right to pursue happiness may be quite compatible with the right to be left to suffer the effects of one's own folly, though it might also suggest a right to be protected against the folly, as well as against the wilful malice, of other people. But a right to obtain happiness—if it means anything more than the right to pursue happiness—when such a right is guaranteed by the State to its citizens, involves a recognition, however implicit and unconscious, that the function of the State is not merely the negative function of securing to the individual certain rights as against other individuals, but the positive function of aiding him in the attainment of his desires, so far as these are compatible with the general well-being. If the guarantee of a right of obtaining happiness has any definite and specific meaning, it means the same thing as the assertion in the first Article of the French Declaration of 1793, that "the end of society is the common happiness (le bonheur commun)." No such Article occurs in the Declaration of 1789, and many of those who have defended "the principles of '89" have pointed to this article in the forefront of the Constitution of 1793 as a proof of falling away from the sane and sober doctrines of the earlier creed of the Revolution.

There is no doubt that the recognition of happiness as the end of government—still more the recognition of the *common* happiness as the end—involves a departure from the strict individualism with which, as we have seen, the doctrine of natural rights is most properly connected. It is true, also, that the term "happiness" may be interpreted in such a way that the making of it the direct end of government would justify tyranny, and would logically lead to a refusal of those other rights of liberty and of the *pursuit* of happiness which were chiefly in the minds of those who began the American and the French Revolutions. If happiness meant, as the Hedonist Utilitarian professes to make it mean, simply a sum of pleasures and absence of pains, then undoubtedly such happiness might be best secured by a powerful and skilful ruling caste keeping the mass of the people, if possible, in comfortable and contented ignorance, taking care that they were fed and amused, saved from the anxiety and misery of the struggle for existence and of the struggle for intellectual and moral progress. We have seen already in Chapters V. and XII. that this is not *practically* what the great Utilitarian reformers have meant by "happiness," whatever logical consistency might have obliged them to admit. Nor is it what the mass of mankind have commonly meant by happiness; for the contrast between "real and true happiness" on the one side, and "pleasure" on the other, is a commonplace of popular moralising. Still less can any such conception of "happiness" —as a sum of pleasures—be retained as a conception of the ethical end by the Evolutionist Utilitarian. Since, on the confession of John Stuart Mill himself, happiness is something that can only be attained by not being pursued,[1]—since, according to Clifford, the individual's happiness is irrelevant to the welfare of the social organism, except in so far as it makes him a more efficient member,[2] it would be better in ethics to give up the use of the term altogether as a designation of the moral end, adopting some vaguer but less misleading term, such as "welfare" or "well-being."[3] Such a term would suggest the two elements both of which must enter into any conception of the ethical end that avoids the onesidedness alike of Asceticism and of Hedonism—the element of right conduct, virtuous action, *well-doing*, and the element of favour-

---

[1] *Autobiography*, p. 142.

[2] *Lectures and Essays*, II. pp. 122, 175. Cf. above, p. 99.

[3] Suggested in Prof. Fowler's *Progressive Morality*, pp. 99, 100, as corresponding best to Aristotle's εὐδαιμονία. Kant's use of the term "Eudaemonism" has led to much misunderstanding of Aristotle.

able environment, pleasure, or, as we can say in English, of *doing well* in the sense of faring well. Furthermore, the idea of welfare is more applicable to a community than the idea of happiness. Nevertheless, popular usage allows us to speak of a nation being "happy," and popular usage may make it convenient and permissible in *politics* to retain the term "happiness" as expressive of the end. For ethics happiness appears rather the external and accidental element in the end—the word has never entirely lost its association with "hap";—it depends on favourable circumstances[1] whether right conduct is unimpeded[2] or not. But since politics is concerned with the providing of these favourable circumstances, and can only indirectly affect the right conduct of the individual, happiness may be said to be the end for politics.

With due qualifications as to the meaning of the term, nearly every one, except the most rigid sticklers for the "principles of '89" in their most narrowly individualist form, would now-a-days allow that the happiness of the citizens ought to be included among the ends of government. How far this end can be attained by leaving people alone, and how far it can be attained by interference—on this the great practical differences of opinion would begin. Where some would lay more stress on the need of directly removing obstacles to physical health, to intellectual and moral development, others would lay more stress on the need of "freedom,"—on the need of letting people learn even by mistakes and failures, in order that their ultimate progress may be more secure. The desire to see "England free rather than *compulsorily* sober" meant the fear that compulsory abstinence from vice, and even from morally neutral actions, might make virtue impossible. And so if any one would rather see his country free than happy, it is because he fears that happiness obtained at the cost of freedom would mean a lower kind of happiness, and an impediment to the pursuit of any higher kind. On the other hand, those who argue for compulsion are

---

[1] Aristotle's εὐτυχία, τὰ ἐκτὸς ἀγαθά.

[2] Pleasure is ἐνέργεια ἀνεμπόδιστος, *Eth. Nic.*, VII. 12, § 3 (not, in any way, inconsistent with X. 4, § 8). In *Pol.*, IV. 11, § 3, and VII. 13, § 5, the teaching of *Eth. Nic.*, I. 7, §§ 14–16, is combined with the accounts of Pleasure in Books VII. and X.: the chief good (εὐδαιμονία) is "the unimpeded realisation of excellence." I do not think these Aristotelian definitions have been superseded or surpassed. We are only getting back to his sane and scientific way of regarding the ethical end.

bound to show that it will do more than produce an immediate
absence of certain evils: they are bound to show that it will
set free energies for good which are at present impeded; and
those who wish to make people "happy" by legislation must
prove that the happiness will help and not hinder their progress. You could make a great many people "happy" for a
short time by making them drunk; but the wise legislator
will prefer more roundabout methods, even methods such as
education and political liberty, which may make people more
acutely sensible of their misery. The general aspects of such
discussions I have already had to deal with in connection with
the alleged natural right of liberty: and it has been my chief
endeavour to show that particular practical solutions cannot
be given *a priori*, but must depend on time, place, and circumstances.

The reader may complain that after all these tedious and
intricate discussions on matters that closely concern political
practice, I give no practical help; I do not tell him "what to
do." In answer, I might say, in the first place, that my object
has not been to preach, to exhort, to rouse to enthusiastic
action: there are plenty of people engaged in doing that, more
or less effectively, more or less wisely. However I may have
failed of my object, my object has been scientific, to expose
confusions, to set those people thinking who can be induced to
think. For science does not only consist in accumulating facts,
in arranging statistics; it involves a criticism of terms, an
examination of phrases, which are apt to deceive, it, though
worthless or worn out, they are accepted as good sound coin.
"We shall never think rightly in politics until we have cleared
our minds of delusions," Professor Huxley has admirably said;
and this "clearing our minds" in regard to a certain set of
famous political phrases is all that I have set myself to do.
If any one thinks such merely critical work to be unworthy
the name of Political Science, I shall not quarrel with him.
For myself I prefer to call it by the really more modest, though
seemingly more high-sounding name of "philosophy"—not
wisdom or "systematic knowledge," but the effort after knowledge. "Philosophy" has been well defined as "a criticism of
categories," *i.e.* of fundamental conceptions.

¹ *Collected Essays.* Vol. I. *Method and Results*, p. 424.

But, though my procedure has been professedly critical, I do not think that the result is entirely negative. Any one who chose could pick out of the foregoing pages considerable fragments of a constructive creed : whether he would then accept this creed is another matter. The demand, that if one criticises, one must construct, is a just demand to this extent only—that criticisms in order to be listened to, and to be intelligible, must proceed from a fairly consistent standpoint : but they do not need to be made on the basis of a completed dogmatic system. It would not be legitimate criticism, for instance, to use strictly individualist arguments in criticising socialism, and then to use the assumptions of dogmatic socialism in criticising individualism. But in order to see the weakness in the logic of individualism one need not be a dogmatic and uncompromising socialist : and in order to see the weakness in the practical schemes supported by socialists one need not be an advocate of universal *laissez-faire*. It is possible to believe that political and social development is proceeding in a certain direction and must proceed in that direction, if violent revolution is to be averted ; and yet to feel very uncertain as to the precise form which society is likely to assume in fifty years' time, or in the remote future, and to be rather sceptical about the value of certain remedies which are commonly advocated as if they were panaceas.

It seems to me perfectly certain that in all civilised countries there is an unconscious, as well as a conscious, tendency in what can be most conveniently described as a socialistic or "collectivist" direction. The economic tendency is, on the whole, towards the concentration and depersonalisation of capital : the company with salaried officials replaces the "capitalist," of whom old-fashioned economists and popular agitators continue to speak. The older questions of political liberty and of national independence are settled, or approach settlement, only to make way for the "social question." In philosophy, in ethical theories, in religious movements, in popular sentiment there is a tendency, more rapid and pronounced in some quarters than in others, away from the individualism which we have come to think of as characteristic of the last century and not of this. The reaction against the French Revolution, the Romantic movement in literature, with its return to mediaeval ideals, the Catholic revival bringing

back the religious value of the idea of an actual community or
corporate body, the truer understanding of the Hellenic spirit
with its idealisation of the State, the biological conceptions
of evolution and organism supplanting in social theory the
older conceptions of a mechanical aggregate and of the merely
external relation of contract—all these movements and tendencies in thought, some of them connected with one another,
others working separately and in seeming antagonism, have
contributed to produce a new way of dealing with practical
social problems, unlike that which commended itself to the
political thinkers of the last century, and of the earlier part
of this.[1] The enormous growth of town populations, due to
"the industrial revolution," has made the suffering and the
uncertain conditions of life, if not always greater, certainly
more conspicuous than they were before. Social problems
stare every one in the face, and socialistic instead of individualistic solutions are now the more frequently proposed.
But along with a great deal of socialistic talk there goes the
old individualist logic of the ethics of Bentham or even of
Hobbes, and theories of natural rights in their crudest forms
survive alongside of new political ideals, which appeal
to sentiment without having been fully thought out. The
phrases "social organism" and "evolution" are on everybody's lips, but those who use them most frequently have
often grasped their significance the least.

Believing that a transformation of society is in process,
more far-reaching perhaps in its ultimate effects than the
break-up of mediaeval society which culminated in the great
French Revolution, I believe also that this transformation cannot take place safely or without much loss and much suffering
in any country, unless there is a corresponding transformation
in ideas, in sentiments, in ideals of life—a transformation at
least as great as those changes which we call the Renaissance
and the Reformation combined. For this reason I do not
shrink from saying that I hope the transformation will not
take place rapidly. Those who have pictured their full-blown
Collectivist society are very apt to be impatient for its

---

[1] Note, for instance, the difference between the older religious "revival-
ism" and the "Salvation Army," which is an *organisation* to begin with,
and which does not shrink from schemes of bettering the *material* conditions of human souls.

realisation, and, amid the social misery and dissatisfaction of
which we have become acutely conscious, their impatience is
excusable. Those who venture to hint at doubts and difficulties, and to point out that the existing structure of society
cannot be altogether evil if it really contains the germs out of
which a better society is to be evolved, are apt to be re-
proached with selfishness or to be scoffed at as *bourgeois* persons—"*bourgeois*" having rather an ugly sound in the English
language, and having for the purposes of abuse the additional
and indisputable advantage of beginning with the letter *b*.
The reproach of possessing a "middle-class" mind may not
seem to every one a reproach: the so-called middle-class and
the upper-class have hitherto provided the leaders and champions of the "proletariat," and the severest attacks on the
middle-class are all of middle-class origin. Nor is this to be
wondered at: for it is only those who have had the opportunities of contact with varied ideas who are likely to initiate
new movements, and it is decidedly to the credit of a class
that it can produce and tolerate hostile criticism. The term
bourgeois ought to carry the opposite of reproach: it is the
burgher, the *citizen*, who has kept up those institutions of
orderly and responsible government, which only in modern
times have been extended to large numbers previously excluded. And our ideals for the future must, at the least, not
be placed lower in the scale of civilisation than the civic
institutions of the best sort in the past. If we look at human
history as a whole, we see how recent and how rare civilisation has been; and, in striving after an extension of its benefits
to larger numbers, we must be very careful that, if possible,
none of the hardly accumulated gains of humanity be lost in
the process. To prevent such loss we must be content, we
must even be glad, if the transition to a new form of society
takes place more slowly than some enthusiasts desire. Any
attempt to transform institutions suddenly is certain to bring
disaster, to involve loss, and to provoke reaction. We may
envy the feelings of exhilaration with which the earlier stages
of the French Revolution were greeted by generous spirits in
other lands as well as in France; but the bitter disillusions
and the dreary years of reaction and oppression which followed
remain as a salutary warning, if only we can learn by it.

Another reason why progress must be gradual is that no one

nation can solve *social* problems apart from other nations.
The solidarity of the interests of the working classes throughout the world is recognised by socialists in words; but in their
practical proposals there lurks the same confusion between the
rights of the citizen and the rights of man which Bentham
pointed out long ago in criticising the French Declarations of
Rights. What becomes of this solidarity of interests between
the workers of the world, when land nationalisation is taken to
imply the absolute right of the existing inhabitants of a
country, however they may originally have come there, to
shut the door in the face of all the rest of mankind? On the
other hand, where is the consistency between approving the
trade-unionist's indignation at "blacklegs" and yet permitting
the immigration of aliens? And if aliens are to be excluded
because they may lower the rate of wages, how does that
policy differ *in principle* from a policy of protective tariffs?
(That it may differ very much in its actual effect on the
majority of the population there is not much doubt. A work-
man who perhaps calls himself a Socialist, and who may even
boast that he has outgrown patriotic prejudice, may be heard
complaining that the British consumer buys articles "made in
Germany"; he does not reflect that he is living on wheat
grown in America or in Russia. Starvation or exile for a large
number would be the speedy consequence of protection all
round, whether enforced by law or by boycotting. We have
not yet got beyond the Nationalist stage of regarding our
social questions, and there is no use in talking as if patriotism,
even in its narrower and meaner aspects, was likely to be an
extinct sentiment for a long time to come. We must work up
from the good elements in patriotism towards a wider tie.
And we cannot get to a federation of the world all at once.
Our citizens cannot yet be citizens of the world; we cannot
afford to sink the citizen in the man. The difference between
civilised and uncivilised races is a real barrier; and to try to
ignore it, as Socialists and philanthropic Radicals almost
habitually do, is only to fall a prey to false and mischievous
abstractions.

Short cuts over unknown country are generally a mistaken
policy. And here we must give the Socialists every credit for
pointing out the errors of old-fashioned Radicals and of many
eager social reformers, who wish to strike at symptoms of

disease without removing the causes. To increase the number
of small landowners, to pass Puritanical laws which cannot be
enforced without creating fresh evils, to disendow ancient corporations which are serving professedly at least some social
function—measures of that sort which till lately formed the
most conspicuous part of every "advanced" programme—are
seen by the Socialist to be moves in a wrong direction or un-
important changes. But the Socialist himself is too apt to
overlook the problem of population—not merely of over-popu-
lation, of excessive quantity, but the less considered problem
of degeneration in quality—which at every point confronts the
reformer who in any way combats the cruelty of natural
selection. And, as I have had occasion to argue, the Socialist
is generally too oblivious of the need of discipline, of the virtues
of what he detests as "militarism," and too apt to be infected
by Anarchist views of society, which are logically antithetic to
his own professed creed.

Eagerness for social legislation is apt to make the reformer
neglect the importance of political machinery. There is
noticeable in many quarters a growing impatience of representative government, a dislike of discussion of what are con-
temptuously called "constitutional conundrums," a certain
craving even for the despot, the strong man, who will carry
out great schemes promptly and ruthlessly. All these symptoms contain elements of danger. It is something, indeed,
to recognise the secondary character of all merely political
changes; it is something to see that what is called "free government" is not everything; it is something even to give the lie
explicitly to false notions of equality, and to feel the need of
superior skill and superior force. But while admitting that
machinery is only a means to an end, we must not suppose
that any means will do equally well. Great changes in
political institutions have probably yet to come : we are only
beginning to see the problems of the proper working of democratic government. The stability of parliamentary institutions and their usefulness is threatened by the break-up of the
old system of two parties and two parties only. Those who
are fond of denouncing party-government seem to forget that,
so far as experience goes, there is something worse than party-
government, and that is the absence of definite and responsible
parties altogether, and the predominance in politics of hap-

hazard combinations of fluctuating groups. The supporters of "independent" parties say, Why not introduce in Great Britain the Second Ballot, which most European countries already have? It is a most desirable reform—in the interests of political honesty; but it would undoubtedly hasten the formation and the increase of independent groups and the consequent diminution of parliamentary stability.

Possibly the Referendum, if worked as well or no worse than it has been worked on the whole in Switzerland, might compensate for many of the losses which the decay of the old party system would bring. We might, conceivably, get an Executive, like the Swiss, not based on party at all, and administering the business of the country on purely business principles. But the advantages are not all on one side. And the eager social reformer, if he is wise, must tolerate many discussions on the Referendum, on Federation, on the relations between Executive and Legislature, which may seem to him uninteresting and purely academic. The academic study of political questions is indeed sorely needed, and the academic temper in dealing with them.

No change in political machinery and no change in social institutions will lead to social stability and to the "obtaining of happiness" on the part of the citizen, unless the moral feelings of the community are adapted to the new institutions. This is the most important reason of all why successful reforms must be brought about gradually. Here we come upon the antinomy which is always recurring in discussions on social progress. On the one side, "No progress is possible without a moral improvement in the individual;" and so it is often inferred that no external or material change is of any use. On the other, "Change the circumstances which mould men's characters, and the characters will change;" and so it is often inferred that external or material changes are the sole thing needed. Each premise is true, but not the whole truth: and therefore both inferences are fallacious. Human beings are dependent on circumstances, but they have also natures of their own, natures inherited from their ancestors, and modified by reflection and sentiment; so that for social progress there must be harmony between character and circumstances. Progress takes place through some individuals being in advance of the average of their neighbours in their ideals and sentiments; a certain diffusion of these ideals and sentiments among others is necessary under any form of government, most of all under a democratic, in order to bring about legislative changes. A law or institution once established, if it is backed by a fair amount of approving sentiment, fixes and makes definite the ideals to which it corresponds. If it is not backed by such approving sentiment, it remains more or less a dead-letter, or it provokes active opposition : in either case it fails to produce its proper effect, and no real progress has been effected by its means.

Laws and institutions to be progressive must furthermore be educative: they must be such as prepare people to go beyond them, in quiet and orderly fashion. When some evils are specially prominent, the changes that promise a relief from these evils are thought of as if they were final changes, could they only be obtained. Reformers are always apt to look forward to " living happily ever afterwards " when once the great crisis is over. But it is only in old-fashioned stories that trouble ends with the wedding bells ; and it is a very crude and inexperienced kind of political thinking which ex-pects even the biggest of Collectivist schemes to leave no social problems for the future. It is wiser, though a rare wisdom, frankly to disclaim finality. It may destroy the opportunity for much moving rhetoric, but it will save a good deal of painful disillusion. A plan which offers opportunities for alteration, even for moving back again if necessary, is preferable to one which admits of no return, and leaves amendment out of the question.[1] Too great completeness is not a merit in a political or social programme.

Two different kinds of objections are likely to be made to such a political creed as is indicated in the foregoing words. The first, to which I have already referred, is that of the eager socialist, who is wearied with wandering in the wilderness, and wishes to rush impetuously into the promised land he has pictured to himself, who wants his millennium to begin by act of parliament, or by plebiscite, on the first of January next. The other objection is that put forward by the pessimist, who is keenly alive to the vanity of human wishes and the weakness of human nature, and who is very sceptical

---

[1] The opportunity of experimental legislation is a strong argument for decentralisation of power and centralisation of information.

about any amelioration in the intellects or the characters of
the mass of mankind, and who sees too clearly that every
advance in external comfort only brings new cravings
and new pains, more vividly realised than the old dumb,
hopeless suffering or apathy ; to such an one resignation is
the supreme virtue, and what is called political and social
progress a matter of indifference.   After all, is not a despotism
the best form of government for the Stoic or the Buddhist, or
other ascetic individualist, to live under, since his ideal life is a
life of protest and of withdrawal into the inward peace that
he can find only in the spiritual calm of his own passion-
freed soul ?   At the best, supposing the dream of a perfected
society to be accomplished on this earth, the remedy would be
very transitory ; and all the results of long tedious effort
must perish, as our planet gradually becomes incapable of
supporting life.   Such pessimism about the worth of human
society may go along with an intense belief in the certain
bliss of another world, in comparison with which every other
aim is empty ; or it may exist in the more bitter form that
has no hope to outweigh its despair.

Let me take this second objection before returning to the
first.   Suppose we admit the impossibility of any final or
complete happiness for beings such as we are in any future,
either here or elsewhere, it is surely a piece of "abstract
thinking" to ignore the difference between a worse and a
better—or, let us say, a less bad—condition in human affairs.
Before the pessimist obtains our votes as to the worthlessness
of all social effort, it is surely reasonable to try whether life
cannot be made more tolerable, more worth living, to the mass
of human beings than it has been hitherto.   Moreover, as
already said, pessimism will always meet with a practical
refutation through the operation of natural selection.   Those
who sincerely resign "the will to live" must inevitably give
place to those who assert it.   Pessimism never can be anything else except a bye-product of the reflective consciousness,
relatively useful if it quickens sympathy with suffering, and
thus stimulates the effort to relieve it.   Pessimism then
becomes an element in that very striving after social progress which, if taken as a final creed, it seemed logically to
condemn.   And to this practical self-refutation of pessimism
may be added the philosophical consideration, that the mere

judgment that human life or human society is evil implies an
ideal of goodness and perfection by which as standard the
existing world is judged. Such a contrast between the ideal
and the actual is explicitly recognised in the pessimism of
Christian ascetics. And the sense of the contrast leads the
more courageous spirits to seek to overcome it. The fanatical
hermits of the Thebaid were replaced by the Benedictine
monks, who became to barbarous races the missionaries of
ancient learning and civilisation, and by the Franciscan
friars, who, after their lights, fought with disease and want
and ignorance in crowded cities, and beginning without ornaments and without books, trained some of the boldest of mediæval philosophers and kindled the fire of Italian art. In the
modern movement for diffusing the benefits of civilisation and
improving all the conditions of human life, amid all the errors
and absurdities and narrowness of outlook that inevitably
accompany any great movement, can we not still recognise
the same aspiration as is expressed in the one prayer in which
all sections of divided Christendom unite,—the aspiration
that the heavenly kingdom, the reign of peace and righteous-
ness and love, should not remain a far-off vision, but should be
realised here, in the actual human world: "Thy kingdom
come: Thy will be done in earth as it is in heaven"?

However unconsciously, the effort for social amelioration
implies what we can only call a religious faith. In words the
social reformer may disclaim any religious belief, and may
argue that one of the main causes of the growth of socialism
and kindred tendencies is that decay in religious belief
which is often said to be one of the prominent features of our
time: in particular it is often said that the disappearance of
belief in the compensations of another life is one of the principal sources of the eagerness with which immediate and
earthly justice is demanded. But, in the first place, it is
important to recognise that, as Professor Wallace has expressed it, "The religion of a time is not its nominal creed,
but its dominant conviction of the meaning of reality, the
principle which animates all its being and all its striving, the
faith it has in the laws of nature and the purpose of life." [1]
In the second place, the diminished importance of "other-
worldly" considerations is only one aspect of a change which

---

[1] *Hegel's Philosophy of Mind*, p. xxxvii.

has been going on within, as well as without, the visible
Churches. Few moralists nowadays venture to stake the obligation to morality upon the sanctions of future reward and
punishment. Like Plato in the *Republic*, they would rather
put aside such sanctions altogether, aware of the demoralising
manner in which they have often been conceived, until the
superiority of justice to injustice has been shown through considerations of social well-being; and the hope of continued
existence is based mainly, if not solely, upon the independently
established facts of morality. Not only in Kant and those whom
he has influenced, but in the poets who have taught our age a
great deal of its theology—in Tennyson and Browning—we find
"the hope of immortality" based mainly on the inadequacy
between man's ideal and what he can accomplish in his short
span of earthly life. The hope of immortality has become one
aspect of the desire for progress. And those who believe and
those who doubt the persistence of the individual consciousness after death alike agree that strenuous well-doing in this
life would be the best preparation for another. "Whatsoever
thy hand findeth to do, do it with thy might; for there is no
work, nor device, nor knowledge, nor wisdom, in the grave
whither thou goest."[1] "Thou hast been faithful over a few
things; I will make thee ruler over many things."[2] The implied belief may seem to be different : the practical moral lesson is the same. To neglect social duties in order to save one's
own soul is, happily, a dwindling type of religion.

Now what is implied in saying that effort for social progress implies a religious faith? It may be said by the pessimist that such faith is entirely irrational. An irrational faith,
i.e. a blind instinct, may induce people to seek to preserve
their own lives and to continue their species. Such irrational
"egoism" and "altruism" cannot lead them to plan and think
out schemes of social reorganisation. To do so implies a belief
(however little recognised) that the evolution of the world is a
rational process; else how could we ever hope by our reasoning
to hit upon any scheme that would work in harmony with
the laws of nature and of human nature? But when such a

[1] *Eccl.* ix. 10. Is not this echoed in John ix. 4: "I must work the
works of him that sent me, while it is day: the night cometh, wherein
no man can work"?
[2] *Matt.* xxv. 21.

belief in the ultimate rationality of nature, and especially of human history, becomes explicit, it is no longer logically possible to turn our back upon all the past, and to disdain all the present. Our trust in the possibility of a better future must be based on a belief in the rationality of past and present also. And thus the impatience of the social reformer—intelligible and excusable as it may be—is due to an imperfect recognition of the rational basis of the faith which stimulates his efforts. Even those who talk freely about " development " often show very little appreciation of what is meant by the growth of institutions, and of the ideas which may lead to their reconstruction; and the use of the phrase " social evolution " may go along with a great disrespect for history.

The truth in the theory of Natural Rights—what gave the theory its practical value—was the belief in " Nature " as an ideal, the belief in a Divine purpose determining the ends which man should set before him, and the belief that this ideal, this Divine purpose, could be discovered by the use of human reason. The defect of the theory lay, as we have seen, in the tendency to set this ideal in abstract antithesis over against the actual and the historical. In the light of the conception of evolution applied to human society—*i.e.* using an historical method in the study of institutions, and being influenced by an historical spirit in dealing with all human problems—we must think of this ideal, this Divine purpose, as something not existing definitely formed in the mind of any one man however inspired, of any set of legislators however honest and however enthusiastic, but as something gradually revealing itself in the education of the human race. In other words, an adequate theory of rights and an adequate theory of the State must rest upon a philosophy of history; and steady progress in political and social reform cannot be made unless there is a willingness to learn the lessons of experience, and a reasonable reverence for the long toil of the human spirit in that past from which we inherit not only our problems, but the hope and the means of their solution.

APPENDIX.

A DECLARATION OF RIGHTS,

Made by the Representatives of the good People of Virginia, assembled in full and free Convention, which rights do pertain to them and their posterity as the basis and foundation of government.

I. That all men are by nature equally free and independent, and have certain inherent rights, of which, when they enter into a state of society, they cannot by any compact deprive or divest their posterity; namely, the enjoyment of life and liberty, with the means of acquiring and possessing property, and pursuing and obtaining happiness and safety.

II. That all power is vested in, and consequently derived from, the people; that magistrates are their trustees and servants, and at all times amenable to them.

III. That government is, or ought to be, instituted for the common benefit, protection, and security of the people, nation or community; of all the various modes and forms of government, that is best which is capable of producing the greatest degree of happiness and safety, and is most effectually secured against the danger of maladministration; and that, when a government shall be found inadequate or contrary to these purposes, a majority of the community hath an indubitable, unalienable, and indefeasible right to reform, alter or abolish it, in such manner as shall be judged most conducive to the public weal.

IV. That no man, or set of men, are entitled to exclusive or separate emoluments or privileges from the community but in consideration of public services, which not being descendible, neither ought the offices of magistrate, legislator or judge to be hereditary.

V. That the legislative, executive and judicial powers should be separate and distinct; and that the members thereof may be restrained from oppression, by feeling and participating the burthens of the people, they should, at fixed periods, be reduced to a private station, return into that body from which they were originally taken, and the vacancies be supplied by frequent, certain and regular elections, in which all, or any part of the former members to be again eligible or ineligible, as the laws shall direct.

VI. That all elections ought to be free, and that all men having sufficient evidence of permanent common interest with, and attachment to the community, have the right of suffrage, and cannot be taxed, or deprived of their property for public uses, without their own consent, or that of their representatives so elected, nor bound by any law to which they have not in like manner assented, for the public good.

VII. That all power of suspending laws, or the execution of laws, by any authority, without consent of the representatives of the people, is injurious to their rights, and ought not to be exercised.

VIII. That in all capital or criminal prosecutions a man hath a right to demand the cause and nature of his accusation, to be confronted with the accusers and witnesses, to call for evidence in his favour, and to a speedy trial by an impartial jury of twelve men of his vicinage, without whose unanimous consent he cannot be found guilty; nor can he be compelled to give evidence against himself; that no man be deprived of his liberty, except by the law of the land, or the judgment of his peers.

IX. That excessive bail ought not to be required, nor excessive fines imposed, nor cruel and unusual punishments inflicted.

X. That general warrants, whereby an officer or messenger may be commanded to search suspected places without evidence of a fact committed, or to seize any person or persons not named, or whose offence is not particularly described and supported by evidence, are grievous and oppressive, and ought not to be granted.

XI. That in controversies respecting property, and in suits between man and man, the ancient trial by jury of twelve men is preferable to any other, and ought to be held sacred.

XII. That the freedom of the press is one of the great bulwarks of liberty, and can never be restrained but by despotic governments.

XIII. That a well-regulated militia, composed of the body of the people, trained to arms, is the proper, natural and safe defence of a free State; that standing armies in time of peace should be avoided as dangerous to liberty; and that in all cases the military should be under strict subordination to, and governed by, the civil power.

XIV. That the people have a right to uniform government; and therefore that no government separate from or independent of the government of Virginia ought to be erected or established within the limits thereof.

XV. That no free government, or the blessing of liberty, can be preserved to any people, but by a firm adherence to justice, moderation, temperance, frugality and virtue, and by a frequent recurrence to fundamental principles.

XVI. That religion, or the duty which we owe to our Creator, and the manner of discharging it, can be directed only by reason and conviction, not by force or violence; and therefore all men are equally entitled to the free exercise of religion, according to the dictates of conscience ; and that it is the duty of all to practice Christian forbearance, love and charity towards each other.

Extract from the Declaration of Independence of the United States of America—July 4, 1776.

The unanimous Declaration of the thirteen united States of America.

When in the Course of human events, it becomes necessary for one people to dissolve the political bands which have connected them with another, and to assume among the Powers of the earth, the separate and equal station to which the Laws of Nature and of Nature's God entitle them, a decent respect to the opinions of mankind requires that they should declare the causes which impel them to the separation.

We hold these truths to be self-evident, that all men are created equal, that they are endowed by their Creator with certain unalienable Rights, that among these are Life, Liberty and the pursuit of Happiness. That to secure these rights, Governments are instituted among Men, deriving their just powers from the consent of the governed, That whenever any Form of Government becomes destructive of these ends, it is the Right of the People to alter or to abolish it, and to institute new Government, laying its foundation on such principles and organizing its powers in such form, as to them shall seem most likely to effect their Safety and Happiness. Prudence, indeed, will dictate that Governments long established should not be changed for light and transient causes ; and accordingly all experience hath shown, that mankind are more disposed to suffer, while evils are sufferable, than to right themselves by abolishing the forms to which they are accustomed. But when a long train of abuses and usurpations, pursuing invariably the same Object, evinces a design to reduce them under absolute Despotism, it is their right, it is their duty, to throw off such Government, and to provide new Guards for their future security.—Such has been the patient sufferance of these Colonies ; and such is now the necessity which constrains them to alter their former Systems of Government. The history of the present King of Great Britain is a history of repeated injuries and usurpations, all having in direct object the establishment of an absolute Tyranny over these States. To prove this, let facts be submitted to a candid world.

[Then follow statements of particular grievances.]

N.R.   U

In every stage of these Oppressions We have Petitioned for Redress in the most humble terms: Our repeated Petitions have been answered only by repeated injury. A Prince, whose character is thus marked by every act which may define a Tyrant, is unfit to be the ruler of a free People.

Nor have We been wanting in attention to our British brethren. We have warned them from time to time of attempts by their legislature to extend an unwarrantable jurisdiction over us. We have reminded them of the circumstances of our emigration and settlement here. We have appealed to their native justice and magnanimity, and we have conjured them by the ties of our common kindred to disavow these usurpations, which would inevitably interrupt our connections and correspondence. They too have been deaf to the voice of justice and of consanguinity. We must, therefore, acquiesce in the necessity which denounces our Separation, and hold them, as we hold the rest of mankind, Enemies in War, in Peace Friends.

We, therefore, the Representatives of the united States of America, in General Congress, Assembled, appealing to the Supreme Judge of the world for the rectitude of our intentions, do, in the Name, and by Authority of the good People of these Colonies, solemnly publish and declare, That these United Colonies are, and of Right ought to be Free and Independent States; that they are Absolved from all Allegiance to the British Crown, and that all political connection between them and the State of Great Britain, is and ought to be totally dissolved; and that as Free and Independent States, they have full Power to levy War, conclude Peace, contract Alliances, establish Commerce, and to do all other Acts and Things which Independent States may of right do. And for the support of this Declaration, with a firm reliance on the Protection of Divine Providence, we mutually pledge to each other our Lives, our Fortunes and our sacred Honor.

DECLARATION DES DROITS DE L'HOMME ET DU CITOYEN (1789). (PREFIXED TO CONSTITUTION FRANÇAISE DU 3-14 SEPT., 1791).

Les représentans du peuple français, constitués en assemblée nationale, considérant que l'ignorance l'oubli ou le mépris des

Translation given in Thomas Paine's "Rights of Man." DECLARATION OF THE RIGHTS OF MAN AND OF CITIZENS, BY THE NATIONAL ASSEMBLY OF FRANCE.

The representatives of the people of France, formed into a National Assembly, considering that ignorance, neglect, or con-

droits de l'homme sont les seules causes des malheurs publics et de la corruption des gouvernemens, ont résolu d'exposer, dans une déclaration solennelle, les droits naturels, inaliénables et sacrés de l'homme, afin que cette déclaration, constamment présente à tous les membres du corps social, leur rappelle sans cesse leurs droits et leurs devoirs ; afin que les actes du pouvoir législatif et ceux du pouvoir exécutif, pouvant être à chaque instant comparés avec le but de toute institution politique, en soient plus respectés, afin que les réclamations des citoyens, fondées désormais sur des principes simples et incontestables tournent toujours au maintien de la constitution et au bonheur de tous.

En conséquence, l'assemblée nationale reconnait et déclare en présence et sous les auspices de l'Etre suprême, les droits suivans de l'homme et du citoyen.

Art. 1er. Les hommes naissent et demeurent libres et égaux en droits. Les distinctions sociales ne peuvent être fondées que sur l'utilite commune.

2. Le but de toute association politique est la conservation des droits naturels et imprescriptibles de l'homme. Ces droits sont la liberté, la propriété, la sûreté et la résistance à l'oppression.

3. Le principe de toute souveraineté réside essentiellement dans la nation ; nul corps, nul individu ne peut exercer d'au-

tempt of human rights, are the sole causes of public misfortunes and corruptions of Government, have resolved to set forth in a solemn declaration, these natural, imprescriptible, and inalienable rights : that this declaration being constantly present to the minds of the members of the body social, they may be for ever kept attentive to their rights and their duties ; that the acts of the legislative and executive powers of government, being capable of being every moment compared with the end of political institutions, may be more respected ; and also, that the future claims of the citizens, being directed by simple and incontestible principles, may always tend to the maintenance of the Constitution, and the general happiness.

For these reasons, the National Assembly doth recognise and declare, in the presence of the Supreme Being, and with the hope of his blessing and favour, the following *sacred* rights of men and of citizens :

I. Men are born, and always continue, free and equal in respect of their rights. Civil distinctions, therefore, can be founded only on public utility.

II. The end of all political associations, is the preservation of the natural and imprescriptible rights of man ; and these rights are liberty, property, security, and resistance of oppression.

III. The nation is essentially the source of all sovereignty : nor can any individual, or any body of men, be entitled to any

torité qui n'en émane expressément.

4. La liberté consiste à pouvoir faire tout ce qui ne nuit pas à autrui : ainsi l'exercice des droits naturels de chaque homme n'a de bornes que celles qui assurent aux autres membres de la société la jouissance de ces mêmes droits. Ces bornes ne peuvent être déterminées que par la loi.

5. La loi n'a le droit de défendre que les actions nuisibles à la société. Tout ce qui n'est pas défendu par la loi ne peut être empêché, et nul ne peut être contraint à faire ce qu'elle n'ordonne pas.

6. La loi est l'expression de la volonté générale. Tous les citoyens ont droit de concourir personnellement, ou par leurs représentans, à sa formation. Elle doit être la même pour tous, soit qu'elle protége, soit qu'elle punisse. Tous les citoyens étant égaux à ses yeux, sont également admissibles à toutes dignités, places et emplois publics, selon leur capacité, et sans autre distinction que celle de leurs vertus et de leurs talens.

7. Nul homme ne peut être accusé, arrêté ni détenu que dans les cas déterminés par la loi, et selon les formes qu'elle a prescrites. Ceux qui sollicitent, expédient, exécutent ou font exécuter des ordres arbitraires, doivent être punis : mais tout citoyen appellé ou saisi en vertu de la loi, doit obéir à l'instant ; il se rend coupable par la résistance.

authority which is not expressly derived from it.

IV. Political liberty consists in the power of doing whatever does not injure another. The exercise of the natural rights of every man, has no other limits than those which are necessary to secure to every *other* man the free exercise of the same rights ; and these limits are determinable only by the law.

V. The law ought to prohibit only actions hurtful to society. What is not prohibited by the law, should not be hindered ; nor should any one be compelled to that which the law does not require.

VI. The law is an expression of the will of the community. All citizens have a right to concur, either personally, or by their representatives, in its formation. It should be the same to all, whether it protects or punishes : and all being equal in its sight, are equally eligible to all honours, places, and employments, according to their different abilities, without any other distinction than that created by their virtues and talents.

VII. No man should be accused, arrested, or held in confinement, except in cases determined by the law, and according to the forms which it has prescribed. All who promote, solicit, execute, or cause to be executed, arbitrary orders, ought to be punished, and every citizen called upon, or apprehended by virtue of the law, ought immediately to obey, and renders himself culpable by resistance.

8. La loi ne doit établir que des peines strictement et évidemment nécessaires, et nul ne peut être puni qu'en vertu d'une loi établie et promulguée antérieurement au délit et légalement appliquée.

9. Tout homme étant présumé innocent jusqu'à ce qu'il ait été déclaré coupable, s'il est jugé indispensable de l'arrêter, toute rigueur qui ne serait pas nécessaire pour s'assurer de sa personne, doit être sévèrement réprimée par la loi.

10. Nul ne doit être inquiété pour ses opinions, mêmes religieuses, pourvu que leur manifestation ne trouble pas l'ordre public établi par la loi.

11. La libre communication des pensées et des opinions est un des droits les plus précieux de l'homme ; tout citoyen peut donc parler, écrire, imprimer librement, sauf à répondre de l'abus de cette liberté dans les cas déterminés par la loi.

12. La garantie des droits de l'homme et du citoyen nécessite une force publique : cette force est donc instituée pour l'avantage de tous, et non pour l'utilité particulière de ceux auxquels elle est confiée.

13. Pour l'entretien de la force publique, et pour les dépenses d'administration, une contribution commune est indispensable, elle doit être également répartie entre tous les citoyens en raison de leurs facultés.

VIII. The law ought to impose no other penalties but such as are absolutely and evidently necessary; and no one ought to be punished, but in virtue of a law promulgated before the offence, and legally applied.

IX. Every man being presumed innocent till he has been convicted, whenever his detention becomes indispensable, all rigour to him, more than is necessary to secure his person, ought to be provided against by the law.

X. No man ought to be molested on account of his opinions, not even on account of his *religious* opinions, provided his avowal of them does not disturb the public order established by the law.

XI. The unrestrained communication of thoughts and opinions being one of the most precious rights of man, every citizen may speak, write, and publish freely, provided he is responsible for the abuse of this liberty, in cases determined by the law.

XII. A public force being necessary to give security to the rights of men and of citizens, that force is instituted for the benefit of the community and not for the particular benefit of the persons to whom it is intrusted.

XIII. A common contribution being necessary for the support of the public force, and for defraying the other expenses of government, it ought to be divided equally among the members of the community, according to their abilities.

14. Tous les citoyens ont le droit de constater, par eux-mêmes ou par leurs représentans, la nécessité de la contribution publique, de la consentir librement, d'en suivre l'emploi, et d'en déterminer la quotité, l'assiette, le recouvrement et la durée.

15. La société a le droit de demander compte à tout agent public de son administration.

16. Toute société dans laquelle la garantie des droits n'est pas assurée, ni la séparation des pouvoirs déterminée, n'a point de constitution.

17. La propriété étant un droit inviolable et sacré, nul ne peut en être privé, si ce n'est lorsque la nécessité publique, légalement constatée, l'exige évidemment, et sous la condition d'une juste et préalable indemnité.

XIV. Every citizen has a right, either by himself or his representative, to a free voice in determining the necessity of public contributions, the appropriation of them, and their amount, mode of assessment, and duration.

XV. Every community has had a right to demand of all its agents an account of their conduct.

XVI Every community in which a separation of powers and a security of rights is not provided for, wants a constitution.

XVII. The right to property being inviolable and sacred, no one ought to be deprived of it, except in cases of evident public necessity, legally ascertained, and on condition of a previous just indemnity.

DECLARATION PREFIXED TO CONSTITUTION OF JUNE 24, 1793.

Le Peuple français, convaincu que l'oubli et le mépris des droits naturels de l'homme sont les seules causes des malheurs du monde, a résolu d'exposer, dans une déclaration solennelle, ces droits sacrés et inaliénables, afin que tous les citoyens, pouvant comparer sans cesse les actes du gouvernement avec le but de toute institution sociale, ne se laissent jamais opprimer et avilir par la tyrannie; afin que le peuple ait toujours devant les yeux les bases de sa liberté et de son bonheur, le magistrat la règle de ses devoirs, le législateur l'objet de sa mission.

En conséquence il proclame, en présence de l'Être suprême, la déclaration suivante des droits de l'homme et du citoyen.

Art. 1er. Le but de la société est le bonheur commun. Le gouvernement est institué pour garantir à l'homme la jouissance de ces droits naturels et imprescriptibles.

2. Ces droits sont l'égalité, la liberté, la sûreté, la propriété.

3. Tous les hommes sont égaux par la nature et devant la loi.

4. La loi est l'expression libre et solennelle de la volonté générale;

elle est la même pour tous, soit qu'elle protége, soit qu'elle punisse : elle ne peut ordonner que ce qui est juste et utile à la société ; elle ne peut défendre que ce qui lui est nuisible.

5. Tous les citoyens sont également admissibles aux emplois publics. Les peuples libres ne connaissent d'autres motifs de préférence dans leurs élections que les vertus et les talens.

6. La liberté est le pouvoir qui appartient à l'homme de faire tout ce qui ne nuit pas aux droits d'autrui : elle a pour principe la nature, pour règle la justice, pour sauve-garde la loi ; sa limite morale est dans cette maxime : *Ne fais pas à un autre ce que tu ne veux pas qui te soit fait.*

7. Le droit de manifester sa pensée et ses opinions, soit par la voie de la presse, soit de toute autre manière, le droit de s'assembler paisiblement, le libre exercice des cultes, ne peuvent être interdits. La nécessité d'énoncer ses droits suppose ou la présence ou le souvenir récent du despotisme.

8. La sûreté consiste dans la protection accordée par la société à chacun des ses membres pour la conservation de sa personne, de ses droits et de ses propriétés.

9. La loi doit protéger la liberté publique et individuelle contre l'oppression de ceux qui gouvernent.

10. Nul ne doit être accusé, arrêté ni détenu, que dans les cas déterminés par la loi et selon les formes qu'elle a prescrites. Tout citoyen appelé ou saisi par l'autorité de la loi, doit obéir à l'instant ; il se rend coupable par la résistance.

11. Toute acte exercé contre un homme hors des cas et sans les formes que le loi détermine, est arbitraire et tyrannique ; celui contre lequel on voudrait l'exécuter par la violence, a le droit de la repousser par la force.

12. Ceux qui solliciteraient, expédieraient, signeraient, exécuteraient ou feraient exécuter des actes arbitraires, sont coupables, et doivent être punis.

13. Tout homme étant présumé innocent jusqu'à ce qu'il ait été déclaré coupable, s'il est jugé indispensable de l'arrêter, toute rigueur qui ne serait pas nécessaire pour s'assurer de sa personne, doit être sévèrement réprimée par la loi.

14. Nul ne doit être jugé ou puni qu'après avoir été entendu ou légalement appelé, et qu'en vertu d'une loi promulgée antérieurement au délit. La loi qui punirait des délits commis avant qu'elle existât serait une tyrannie ; l'effet rétroactif donné à la loi serait un crime.

15. La loi ne doit décerner que des peines strictement et évidemment nécessaires : les peines doivent être proportionnées au délit et utiles à la société.

16. Le droit de propriété est celui qui appartient à tout citoyen de jouir et de disposer à son gré de ses biens, de ses revenus, du fruit de son travail et de son industrie.

17. Nul genre de travail, de culture, de commerce, ne peut être interdit à l'industrie des citoyens.

18. Tout homme peut engager ses services, son tems ; mais il ne peut se vendre ni être vendu ; sa personne n'est pas une propriété aliénable. La loi ne connait point de domesticité ; il ne peut exister qu'un engagement de soins et de reconnaissance entre l'homme qui travaille et celui qui l'emploie.

19. Nul ne peut être privé de la moindre portion de sa propriété, sans son consentement, si ce n'est lorsque la nécessité publique légalement constatée l'exige, et sous la condition d'une juste et préalable indemnité.

20. Nulle contribution ne peut être établie que pour l'utilité générale. Tous les citoyens ont droit de concourir à l'établissement des contributions, d'en surveiller l'emploi et de s'en faire rendre compte.

21. Les secours publics sont une dette sacrée. La société doit la subsistance aux citoyens malheureux, soit en leur procurant du travail, soit en assurant les moyens d'exister à ceux qui sont hors d'état de travailler.

22. L'instruction est le besoin de tous. La société doit favoriser de tout son pouvoir les progrès de la raison publique, et mettre l'instruction à la portée de tous les citoyens.

23. La garantie sociale consiste dans l'action de tous pour assurer à chacun la jouissance et la conservation de ses droits : cette garantie repose sur la souveraineté nationale.

24. Elle ne peut exister, si les limites des fonctions publiques ne sont pas clairement déterminées par la loi, et si la responsabilité de tous les fonctionnaires n'est pas assurée.

25. La souveraineté réside dans le peuple ; elle est une et indivisible, imprescriptible et inaliénable.

26. Aucune portion du peuple ne peut exercer la puissance du peuple entier ; mais chaque section du souverain assemblée doit jouir du droit d'exprimer sa volonté avec une entière liberté.

27. Que tout individu qui usurperait la souveraineté soit à l'instant mis à mort par les hommes libres.

28. Un peuple a toujours le droit de revoir, de réformer et de changer sa constitution. Une génération ne peut assujétir à ses lois les générations futures.

29. Chaque citoyen a un droit égal de concourir à la formation de la loi et à la nomination de ses mandataires ou de ses agens.

30. Les fonctions publiques sont essentiellement temporaires ; elles ne peuvent être considerées comme des distinctions ni comme des récompenses, mais comme des devoirs.

31. Les délits des mandataires du peuple et de ses agens ne doivent jamais être impunis. Nul n'a le droit de se prétendre plus inviolable que les autres citoyens.

32. Le droit de présenter des pétitions aux dépositaires de l'autorité publique ne peut, en aucun cas, être interdit, suspendu ni limité.

33. La résistance à l'oppression est la conséquence des autres droits de l'homme.

34. Il y a oppression contre le corps social, lorsqu'un seul de ses membres est opprimé : il y a oppression contre chaque membre, lorsque le corps social est opprimé.

35. Quand le gouvernement viole les droits du peuple, l'insurrection est pour le peuple et pour chaque portion du peuple, le plus sacré des droits et le plus indispensable des devoirs.

DECLARATION PREFIXED TO THE FRENCH CONSTITUTION OF 5 FRUCTIDOR, AN III. (=AUG. 22, 1795): ACCEPTED BY THE PEOPLE AND PROCLAIMED LOI FONDAMENTALE 1ʳᵉ VENDEMIAIRE, AN IV. (SEPT. 23, 1795).

Déclaration des Droits et des Devoirs de l'Homme et du Citoyen.

Le peuple français proclame, en présence de l'Être suprême la déclaration suivante des droits et des devoirs de l'homme et du citoyen.

DROITS.

Art. 1ᵉʳ. Les droits de l'homme en société sont la liberté, l'égalité, la sûreté, la propriété.

2. La liberté consiste à pouvoir faire ce qui ne nuit pas aux droits d'autrui.

3. L'égalité consiste, en ce que la loi est la même pour tous, soit qu'elle protège, soit qu'elle punisse.

L'égalité n'admet aucune distinction de naissance, aucune hérédité de pouvoir.

4. La sûreté résulte du concours de tous pour assurer les droits de chacun.

5. La propriété est le droit de jouir et de disposer de ses biens, de ses revenus, du fruit de son travail et de son industrie.

6. La loi est la volonté générale, exprimée par la majorité générale des citoyens ou de leurs réprésentans.

7. Ce qui n'est pas défendu par la loi ne peut être empêché. Nul ne peut être contraint à faire ce qu'elle n'ordonne pas.

8. Nul ne peut être appelé en justice, accusé, arrêté, ni détenu, que dans les cas déterminés par la loi, et selon les formes qu'elle a prescrites.

9. Ceux qui sollicitent, expédient, signent, exécutent ou font exécuter des actes arbitraires, sont coupables et doivent être punis.

10. Toute rigueur qui ne serait pas nécessaire pour s'assurer de la personne d'un prévenu, doit être sévèrement réprimée par la loi.

11. Nul ne peut être jugé qu'après avoir été entendu ou légalement appelé.

12. La loi ne doit décerner que des peines strictement nécessaires et proportionnées au délit.

13. Tout traitement qui aggrave la peine déterminée par la loi est un crime.

14. Aucune loi, ni criminelle, ni civile, ne peut avoir d'effet rétroactif.

15. Tout homme peut engager son tems et ses services, mais il ne peut se vendre ni être vendu; sa personne n'est pas une propriété aliénable.

16. Toute contribution est établie pour l'utilité générale; elle doit être répartie entre les contribuables en raison de leurs facultés.

17. La souveraineté réside essentiellement dans l'universalité des citoyens.

18. Nul individu, nulle réunion partielle de citoyens ne peut s'attribuer la souveraineté.

19. Nul ne peut, sans une délégation légale, exercer aucune autorité, ni remplir aucune fonction publique.

20. Chaque citoyen a un droit égal de concourir, immédiatement ou médiatement à la formation de la loi, à la nomination des représentans du peuple et des fonctionnaires publics.

21. Les fonctions publiques ne peuvent devenir la propriété de ceux qui les exercent.

22. La garantie sociale ne peut exister si la division des pouvoirs n'est pas établie, si leurs limites ne sont pas fixées, et si la responsabilité des fonctionnaires publics n'est pas assurée.

DEVOIRS.

Art. 1er. La déclaration des droits contient les obligations des législateurs: le maintien de la société demande que ceux qui la composent connaissent et remplissent également leurs devoirs.

2. Tous les devoirs de l'homme et du citoyen dérivent de ces deux principes, gravés par la nature dans tous les cœurs:

Ne faites pas à autrui ce que vous ne voudriez pas qu'on vous fît.

Faites constamment aux autres le bien que vous voudriez en recevoir.

3. Les obligations de chacun envers la société consistent à la défendre, à la servir, à vivre soumis aux lois, et à respecter ceux qui en sont les organes.

4. Nul n'est bon citoyen s'il n'est bon fils, bon frère, bon ami, bon époux.

5. Nul n'est homme de bien, s'il n'est franchement et religieusement observateur des lois.

6. Celui qui viole ouvertement les lois, se déclare en état de guerre avec la société.

7. Celui qui, sans enfreindre les lois, les élude par ruse ou par adresse, blesse les intérêts de tous ; il se rend indigne de leur bienveillance et de leur estime.

8. C'est sur le maintien des propriétés que reposent la culture des terres, toutes les productions, tout moyen de travail et tout l'ordre social.

9. Tout citoyen doit ses services à la patrie et au maintien de la liberté, de l'égalité et de la propriété, toutes les fois que la loi l'appelle à les défendre.

CONSTITUTION DE LA RÉPUBLIQUE FRANÇAISE DU 4 NOV., 1848.

PRÉAMBULE.

En présence de Dieu et au nom du peuple français, l'Assemblée nationale proclame :—

1. La France s'est constituée en République. En adoptant cette forme définitive de gouvernement, elle s'est proposé pour but de marcher plus librement dans la voie du progrès et de la civilisation, d'assurer une répartition de plus en plus équitable des charges et des avantages de la société, d'augmenter l'aisance de chacun par la réduction graduée des dépenses publiques et des impôts, et de faire parvenir tous les citoyens, sans nouvelle commotion, par l'action successive et constante des institutions et des lois, à un degré toujours plus élevé de la moralité, de lumières et de bien-être.

2. La République française est démocratique, une et indivisible.

3. Elle reconnaît des droits et des devoirs antérieurs et supérieurs aux lois positives.

4. Elle a pour principe la Liberté, l'Égalité et la Fraternité. Elle a pour base la Famille, le Travail, la Propriété, l'Ordre public.

5. Elle respecte les nationalités étrangères, comme elle entend faire respecter la sienne ; n'entreprend aucune guerre dans les vues de conquête, et n'emploie jamais ses forces contre la liberté d'aucun peuple.

6. Des devoirs réciproques obligent les citoyens envers la République, et la République envers les citoyens.

7. Les citoyens doivent aimer la patrie, servir la République, la défendre au prix de leur vie, participer aux charges de l'État en

proportion de leur fortune ; ils doivent s'assurer, par le travail, des moyens d'existence, et par la prévoyance, des ressources pour l'avenir ; ils doivent concourir au bien-être commun en s'entr'aidant fraternellement les uns les autres, et à l'ordre général en observant les lois morales et les lois écrites qui régissent la société, la famille et l'individu.

8. La République doit protéger le citoyen dans sa personne, sa famille, sa religion, sa propriété, son travail, et mettre à la portée de chacun l'instruction indispensable à tous les hommes ; elle doit, par une assistance fraternelle, assurer l'existence des citoyens nécessiteux, soit en leur procurant du travail dans les limites de ses ressources, soit en donnant, à défaut de la famille, des secours à ceux qui sont hors d'état de travailler.

En vue de l'accomplissement de tous ces devoirs, et pour la garantie de tous ces droits, l'Assemblée nationale, fidèle aux traditions des grandes assemblées qui ont inauguré la révolution française, décrète, ainsi qu'il suit, la Constitution de la République.

INDEX

This index is only intended to supplement the analytical table of contents. *n* after the number of a page indicates that the reference is to a footnote.

www.ingramcontent.com/pod-product-compliance
Lightning Source LLC
Chambersburg PA
CBHW060527030726
47498CB00004B/1102